New Media, Old News

New Media, Old News

••••• ••••• ••••• ••••• ••••• ••••• ••••• ••••• ••••• ••••• ••••• •••••

Journalism & Democracy in the Digital Age

Edited by
Natalie Fenton

SAGE

Los Angeles | London | New Delhi
Singapore | Washington DC

First published 2010

SAGE Publications Ltd
1 Oliver's Yard
55 City Road
London EC1Y 1SP

SAGE Publications Inc.
2455 Teller Road
Thousand Oaks, California 91320

SAGE Publications India Pvt Ltd
B 1/I 1 Mohan Cooperative Industrial Area
Mathura Road, Post Bag 7
New Delhi 110 044

SAGE Publications Asia-Pacific Pte Ltd
33 Pekin Street #02-01
Far East Square
Singapore 048763

Library of Congress Control Number 2009923294

British Library Cataloguing in Publication data
A catalogue record for this book is available from the British Library

ISBN 978-1-84787-573-0
ISBN 978-1-84787-574-7 (pbk)

Typeset by Printed in C&M Digitals (P) Ltd, Chennai, India
Printed by CPI Antony Rowe, Chippenham, Wiltshire
Printed on paper from sustainable resources

Mixed Sources
Product group from well-managed
forests and other controlled sources
www.fsc.org Cert no. SGS-COC-2953
© 1996 Forest Stewardship Council
FSC

Contents

Acknowledgements vii
Notes on Contributors ix

Part I   Introduction: New Media and Democracy 1

Drowning or Waving? New Media, Journalism and Democracy 3
Natalie Fenton

Part II   New Media and News In Context 17

1 Technology Foretold 19
   James Curran

2 The Political Economy of the 'New' News Environment 35
   Des Freedman

3 An Ethical Deficit? Accountability, Norms, and the Material 51
   Conditions of Contemporary Journalism
   Angela Phillips, Nick Couldry, Des Freedman

Part III   New Media and News in Practice 69

4 Culture Shock: New Media and Organizational Change 71
   in the BBC
   Peter Lee-Wright

5 Old Sources: New Bottles 87
   Angela Phillips

6 Liberal Dreams and the Internet 102
   James Curran and Tamara Witschge

Part IV   New Media, News Sources, New Journalism? 119

7 Politics, Journalism and New Media: Virtual Iron Cages 121
   in the New Culture of Capitalism
   Aeron Davis

8   New Online News Sources and Writer-Gatherers   138
    Nick Couldry

9   NGOs, New Media and the Mainstream News: News from
    Everywhere   153
    Natalie Fenton

Part V   New Media, News Content and International Context   169

10 A New News Order? Online News Content Examined   171
    Joanna Redden and Tamara Witschge

11 Futures of the News: International Considerations and
    Further Reflections   187
    Rodney Benson

References   201
Index   219

Acknowledgements

This book is the culmination of a team research project including myself and including James Curran, Nick Couldry, Aeron Davis, Des Freedman, Angela Phillips, Joanna Redden, Tamara Witschge and Peter Lee-Wright, who make up most of the authors in this book. And it is the research team to whom I would first like to pay homage. We all came to the project with divergent perspectives, interests and ideas. We spent many pleasurable hours debating, critiquing, analyzing and then debating some more. The process was sometimes frustrating and often exhausting, but always fascinating and carried out in a spirit of intellectual ardour, academic passion and good humour. Indeed it was as all good research projects should be but so rarely are. These meetings, dinners, journeys, conferences, emails, phonecalls and parties have all contributed to this book. I have learnt a great deal from this genuine team endeavour, but I have also cemented firm friendships. A better experience of a research project and a better research team, one could not hope for.

Particular thanks must go to Tamara Witschge as the Research Associate on the project for all her research skills, support and good nature throughout. I would also like to thank the occasional guests to our research meetings, Jonathan Hardy, Michael Bailey and Colin Leys, who offered their own insights willingly and openly; and the many speakers who came and shared their own research with us including Michael Schudson, Dan Hallin, Robert Picard, Greg Elmer, Lesley Henderson and Julian Petley and Jane Singer. The data collection and analysis for the project also drew on the skills of a team of research assistants – Veronica Barassi, Su-Anne Yeo, Mireya Marquez, Paulo Gerbaudo, Hatty Oliver and Emily Seymour – thank you all for your time and commitment.

To Rodney Benson who contributed the final chapter – my gratitude for your professionalism, sound critique and useful comments throughout.

This project is one of five under the auspices of the Goldsmiths Leverhulme Media Research Centre: Spaces, Connections and Control. Sincere thanks are due to the funders, the Leverhulme Trust for the award that enabled this project to come to fruition and to all the other staff at Goldsmiths who are part of the Centre – in particular Elisabeth Baumann-Meurer as the research administrator (and previously Guinevere Narraway) without whom things would quite simply have fallen apart; Chris Berry, Janet Harbord, Kay Dickinson, Rachel Moore, Kevin Robins and Monika Metykova from within Media and Communications but also Scott Lash and Goetz Bachmann from Cultural Studies and Terry Rosenberg and Mike

Waller from Design. Their comments and all of the debate within the centre have helped form this book.

The Goldsmiths Leverhulme Media Research Centre runs with the help of the wisdom and guidance of an excellent Advisory Committee. Two people on this committee, Anne Spackman of *The Times* and Georgina Henry of the *Guardian*, deserve special mention for their support of this research. I am constantly amazed and endlessly appreciative that in their unbelievably hectic schedules they still found the time and energy to contribute so enthusiastically to this research programme. Anne Spackman encouraged us to release the initial draft of this book for discussion at a seminar of news industry professionals which she then chaired. The event was a great success and helped further crystallize our analysis and shape the book itself. To all those who turned up to the seminar and the numerous people who contributed good ideas, critical insights and reflections – this book is all the better for it.

This project was also conducted at a time of resurgence of academic interest in journalists and their practice. At times it was hard to imagine a single journalist who had escaped being interviewed by some wily researcher. So to all of those interviewees who gave up their time when often they had none to give, I am deeply grateful. Thanks also to the BBC, the *Guardian* and *Manchester Evening News* for opening their doors and allowing us to observe them at work – a difficult and sometimes awkward ethnographic endeavour that they consented to with good grace and a spirit of openness.

A large project such as this, involving so many staff, inevitably puts other strains on a busy department. Sincere thanks must go to the Head of Department, Gareth Stanton, the Departmental Administrator Jim Rowland and Sarah Jackson for their assistance and cooperation with all things official; but also, importantly, to all the other staff in the department who gave encouragement and goodwill.

Aside from the research team itself, many other friends and colleagues have supported me, often unknowingly, throughout the gestation of this project; Mariam Fraser, Angela McRobbie, Peter Golding, Milly Williamson, David Hesmondhalgh, Gholam Khiabhany, Clare Wardle, Bob Franklin, Steve Barnett, Ben Levitas, Ivor Gabor and many more – your encouragement and wisdom is endlessly motivating. And to Sage, of course, but particularly Mila Steele for making the whole process of putting the book together so straightforward and surprisingly, so much fun.

And finally heartfelt thanks to Justin, Isaac and Jude, who forced me to forget about the book as often as they could.

Notes on Contributors

RODNEY BENSON is Associate Professor of Media, Culture, and Communication and Affiliated Faculty Member in Sociology at New York University. He has published numerous articles on comparative media systems and the sociology of news, focusing on the U.S. and French press, in such leading journals as *The American Sociological Review, Political Communication*, and the *European Journal of Communication*. He is the co-editor, with Erik Neveu, of *Bourdieu and the Journalistic Field* (Polity, 2005).

NICK COULDRY is Professor of Media and Communications at Goldsmiths, University of London where he is founding Director of the Centre for the Study of Global Media and Democracy. He is the author or editor of seven books, including most recently *Listening Beyond the Echoes: Media, Ethics and Agency in an Uncertain World* (Paradigm Books, 2006) and (with Sonia Livingstone and Tim Markham) *Media Consumption and Public Engagement: Beyond the Presumption of Attention* (Palgrave Macmillan, 2007).

JAMES CURRAN is Director of the Goldsmiths Leverhulme Media Research Centre and Professor of Communications at Goldsmiths, University of London. He is the author or editor of 18 books about the media, some in conjunction with others. These include *Media and Power* (Routledge, 2002), *Power Without Responsibility*, 7th edn (Routledge, 2009), *Mass Media and Society*, 4th edn (Hodder Arnold, 2005) and *Culture Wars* (Edinburgh University Press, 2005). He has been a Visiting Professor at Penn, Stanford, Stockholm and Oslo Universities.

AERON DAVIS is a Senior Lecturer and Director of the MA in Political Communications in the Department of Media and Communications, Goldsmiths College. He has conducted research on communications at Parliament at Westminster, the London Stock Exchange, amongst the major political parties and across the trade union movement. He is the author of *Public Relations Democracy* (MUP, 2002), *The Mediation of Power* (Routledge, 2007) and *Politics, Communication and Social Theory* (Routledge, forthcoming). He is currently working on a book on the rise of promotional culture for Polity Press.

NATALIE FENTON is a Reader in Media and Communications in the Department of Media and Communications, Goldsmiths, University of

London where she is also Co-Director of the Goldsmiths Leverhulme Media Research Centre: Spaces, Connections, Control, and Co-Director of Goldsmiths Centre for the Study of Global Media and Democracy. She has published widely on issues relating to media, politics and new media and is particularly interested in rethinking understandings of public culture, the public sphere and democracy.

DES FREEDMAN   is the author of *The Politics of Media Policy* (Polity, 2008), *The Television Policies of the Labour Party 1951–2001* (Frank Cass, 2003) and co-editor of *War and the Media: Reporting Conflict 24/7* (Sage, 2003). He was one of the UK representatives on the management committee of the COST A20 project examining the impact of the internet on the mass media and he has taught in the Department of Media and Communications at Goldsmiths, University of London since 2001.

PETER LEE-WRIGHT   is a Senior Lecturer at Goldsmiths, University of London where he leads the MA in Television Journalism and directs undergraduate television practice courses. A former BBC Television executive producer, he has been a broadcast journalist and documentary film-maker, filming in some 40 countries around the world and working for all the terrestrial television channels in the UK. His work on subjects from international child labour to religion and politics have led to him being invited to speak at international conferences from Amsterdam to Tehran; and he has taught documentary film-making at various establishments from the National Film and Television School to New Delhi.

ANGELA PHILLIPS   has over thirty years of experience in newspaper and magazine journalism and convenes the MA in Journalism at Goldsmiths, University of London. Her research looks at journalism across the divide between theory and practice. She is co-editor, with Risto Kunelius and Elizabeth Eide, of: *Transnational Media Events: The Mohammed Cartoons and the Imagined Clash of Civilisations* (Nordicom, forthcoming) and is also the author of *Good Writing for Journalists* (Sage, 2007). Recent research on the role of agony aunts in newspapers appeared in Bob Franklin (ed.) *Pulling Newspapers Apart*, (Routledge, 2008).

JOANNA REDDEN   is a PhD student in the Department of Media and Communications at Goldsmiths, University of London. Her research considers news coverage of poverty in Canada and the UK and how such coverage both shapes and is shaped by politics, policy and advocacy. She holds a masters degree in Communication and Culture from Ryerson University (Toronto, Canada) and in History from Dalhousie University (Halifax, Canada). Joanna has worked in the field of politics as a legislative and policy researcher for the New Democratic Party in

Canada, and in the field of journalism as a print reporter and researcher for a television documentary series.

TAMARA WITSCHGE was a research associate in the Media and Communications Department, Goldsmiths, University of London and is now a lecturer at Cardiff University. Tamara obtained her PhD degree from the Amsterdam School of Communications Research, University of Amsterdam in May 2007. Her thesis, '(In)difference Online', focused on online discussions of immigration in the Netherlands. Tamara is the General Secretary of the European Communication Research and Education Association (ECREA) and a member of the editorial board of the international journal *New Media and Society*.

Part I

....

Introduction: New Media and Democracy

Drowning or Waving? New Media, Journalism and Democracy

Natalie Fenton

News is often claimed to be the life-blood of a democracy – news journalism as contributing vital resources for processes of information gathering, deliberation and action. The ethos and vocation of journalism is embedded in a relationship with democracy and its practice. It is also embedded in a history of commercial practice, regulatory control and technological innovation – it is the tensions between these aspects that underpin this book.

Journalism comes in many forms – from the entertainment-driven and celebrity-laden to the more serious and politically focused; it is many things to many people. Here, we are concerned to address news and current affairs journalism that purports to be for the public good and in the public interest, even if this is experienced as no more than an ideal ethical horizon both by those who produce it and those who consume it. In a world of communicative abundance this ethical horizon is still pertinent: there remains a sense that there are many things that news journalism *ought* to be doing – to monitor, to hold to account and to facilitate and maintain deliberation – that forms a line in the sand against which contemporary practice can be critiqued. It would be wrong, however, to see such an approach as peddling a 'golden age' thesis that harks back to a time that never was. We are more concerned with a time that is yet to come but is nonetheless worth aiming for. In a world of information overload and one-click communication, news matters (maybe more than it ever has) and interrogating the nature of news journalism is one of the most urgent challenges we face in defining the public interest in the contemporary media age.

News is also what journalists make it. How journalists make news depends on their working environment. Their working environment is shaped by economic, social, political and technological factors, all of which form a dense inter-meshing of commercial, ethical, regulatory and cultural components. If we are to understand the nature of news in contemporary societies then we must interrogate news in all of its contextual complexity. This book attempts to do just that: it is a book about journalism, news and new media in the digital age.[1] It explores how technological, economic and social changes have reconfigured news journalism and the consequences of these transformations for a vibrant democracy.

The discussion is rooted in empirical enquiry from one of the first large-scale studies in the UK into new media and journalism.[2] Using interviews, ethnography and qualitative content analysis to investigate news production processes in a representative sample of news media, the research combines macro-social critique with micro-organizational analysis to gain a complex, critical understanding of the nature of news and news journalism in the digital age. Our central concern in this endeavour is to subject to empirical scrutiny the ways in which new media, news and journalism contribute to democratic political practice and feed public interest. This book is not, therefore, an edited collection of loosely connected chapters. It has been written by the entire research team engaged in this investigation. Although each chapter considers a different dimension of the research, all are closely inter-related.

Many commentators have claimed that journalism is undergoing a fundamental transformation. One of the key reasons cited for this transformation is the changing nature of technology, which is claimed to impact directly upon the practice of journalism and access to the profession. The nature of this transformation is considered variably as a negative and a positive development. The judgments made are usually based upon the perceived contribution of news media to fully functioning modern democratic systems and hence upon journalism's role in contributing to the public sphere (Habermas, 1989). In all approaches what is described, in one way or another, is the dismantling of the structures of news media as we know them. Certainly, on the face of it there has been a step change in the nature of news productivity. Ofcom (2007b: 34) reports that the

> *Daily Telegraph* launched the first UK online national news operation – Electronic Telegraph – in 1994, followed three years later by the BBC's news website. The last major UK national newspaper to launch its website was the *Daily Mail*, in 2004. Within the last decade, web-based operations have come to be viewed as essential for newspapers – national, regional and local – and for all major broadcasters and news agencies.

These debates raise critical questions that run throughout this book: Has new technology revitalized the public sphere or become a tool of commerce for an increasingly un-public, undemocratic news media? In what ways have economic and social change contributed to this process? Has technological, economic and social change reconfigured the job of the journalist and the production of news in terms of enquiry (including media-source interactions), observation, research, editing, and writing? Who are the journalists and how do they exert influence on one another? Does this influence support or challenge economic and/or regulatory constraints within the newsroom? In what way is technological, economic and social change influencing the prospects for and nature of online news and participatory journalism as well as increasing the role of citizen journalists and NGOs as news sources?

The chapters that follow present insights from across a range of perspectives employed to interrogate these questions. From an *historical* perspective – through a critique of past (mis)conceptions of the power of technology to transform perceived inadequacies in public culture and democracy; an *economic* perspective – through an investigation into the market dynamics, pressures and technological responses of the news industry; a *regulatory* perspective – through a consideration of the opportunities for and threats to the practice of ethical journalism; a *socio-political* perspective that seeks to understand journalism and politics from within a critique of the cultures of new capitalism; an *organizational* perspective – through analysis of journalistic practice in different news production contexts; a *socio-cultural* perspective that examines how old news sources are adapting to the new news environment and how new news sources are emerging and the consequent impact this may have on news content – we explore the nature and context of new media and journalism and its contribution to democratic practice.

In adopting a holistic, multi-dimensional approach we have sought to challenge traditional divides in media and communication studies that tend to prioritize either structure (mostly from within political economy) or agency (largely situated in cultural studies) (Fenton, 2007), to reach a position that understands the place of both and seeks to uncover the dynamics of power therein. Although the political economy and cultural studies have often been seen as entirely contrasting with irreconcilable differences (Garnham, 1995; Grossberg, 1995) this research reveals that in practice such distinctions are less clear-cut and there is much to be gained from embracing a dialogic inter-disciplinarity. To understand new media and the news requires a consideration of the role of structural factors such as commerce and finance along with the cultural complexities of journalism and, with it, journalistic subjectivities.

It should be clear from this introduction that we do not attribute the nature of change to technology alone but rather the convergence of many forces that may be contingent upon local circumstance at any one time. In his study of American online newspapers, Boczkowski (2004) stresses that 'new media emerge by merging existing socio-material infrastructures with novel technical capabilities [...] this evolution is influenced by a combination of historical conditions, local contingencies and process dynamics' (2004: 12). In other words online newspapers merge print's old ways with the web's new potentials in an ongoing process in which different local conditions may lead to different outcomes. In this manner, we foreground technical novelty rather than technological determinism and place the research within a media landscape structured by a contemporary history of globalization, deregulation and marketization.

Our approach is particularly mindful of the fact that there has always been 'new' technology in one form or another and it has usually been accompanied by eulogizing on its democratic potential, its ability to become a tool of the people wresting power from the elite structures of society (explored here in Chapter 2). These debates echo the celebrations of plurality, accessibility and participation. Likewise, journalism and journalists have faced a long history of criticism. The (supposed) decline of journalistic integrity and the professional standards of journalism have been attributed variously to journalists' egomania, their being parasitic, exploitative of human tragedy and generally squalid and untrustworthy. Hargreaves (2003: 12), a former journalist, writes:

> Journalism stands accused of sacrificing accuracy for speed, purposeful investigation for cheap intrusion and reliability for entertainment. 'Dumbed down' news media are charged with privileging sensation over significance and celebrity over achievement.

It is no surprise that new media has offered a fresh means of anxiety and an extension of these concerns but the hopes and fears of new media are not new. Importantly, we acknowledge from the outset that these concerns do not arise because of the technology per se or indeed because of the diminishing ethical behaviour of journalists. Rather, they are part of a more complex socio-economic, political and cultural history.

Since the mid 1990s a number of studies have explored the implications of the internet for journalistic practice (for example, Reddick and King, 1997; Miller, 1998; Singer, 1998; Deuze, 1999; Garrison, 2000, 2001, 2003; Rivas-Rodriguez, 2003; Gillmor, 2004). They have looked at the nature of news content, the way journalists do their job, the structure of the newsroom and the shifting relationships between journalists, news organizations and their publics (Pavlik, 2001). In their quest to make sense of the impact of new media on the news they have considered the interactive nature of the internet; the complexity of its content in volume and variety as well as its accessibility and its convergence across previously distinct media. The majority of these studies report that the internet brings new ways of collecting and reporting information into the newsrooms. This new journalism is open to novices, lacks editorial control, can stem from anywhere (not just the newsroom), involves new writing techniques, functions in a network with fragmented audiences, is delivered at great speed, and is open and iterative. In this manner the technology of the internet is said to have reinvigorated democracy.

In stark contrast, others (see below) denounce the impact of new media on the news environment largely from a position of criticism of neo-liberalism more generally. Often these are the same voices as those that take a dim view of the present concentration of ownership and dominance of commercial imperatives. Whatever their take, all studies coalesce at some point around three paired, central characteristics of the internet in news production: speed and space; multiplicity and polycentrality; interactivity and participation – which taken together, are argued to have created a new brand of journalism (Deuze, 1999). It is these debates that have informed this study and it is to these that we now turn.

New Media and the News: Reinvigorated Democracy or Throttling Good Journalism?

Speed and Space

The argument begins simply enough: more space equals more news. The sheer space available online is said to open up new possibilities for news presentation that cannot be found in hard copy form. Through archiving facilities the ability to provide more depth of coverage is increased exponentially. Similarly the ability to update regularly is vastly enhanced. The space for multimedia formats also allows news to be presented in innovative and interesting ways (Gunter, 2003).

Space is also linked to geographical reach. Some theorists believe that the web is capable of linking communities of interest across the globe, thereby creating greater political participation. Reach is further enhanced by speed. The speed of the internet enables journalists to get to data without having to leave the newsroom (Quinn, 2002). Reports can be downloaded in seconds, public databases interrogated in a fraction of the time it would have previously taken. These changes signal potential improvements in the relevance and timeliness of news and journalism.

But there are also negative assessments where speed and space translate into 'speed it up and spread it thin'. Researchers describe how established news organizations are encouraged by the speed of the internet to release and update stories before the usual checks for journalistic integrity have taken place (Gunter, 2003; Silvia, 2001); how the increasing emphasis on immediacy in news coverage is frequently satisfied by reporters working for news agencies (Ofcom, 2007) to the detriment of original reportage (Scott, 2005; Davies, 2008), turning journalists into 'robohacks' (Hargreaves, 2003) practising 'churnalism' (Davies, 2008), rather than reporters and editors.

An intensification of pressure in the newsroom to produce more articles in less time is claimed to have led to fewer journalists gathering information outside of the newsroom. In these accounts, often the entire production process is a desktop activity with journalists not only writing but also composing a complete presentation package onscreen. This form of multi-skilling has been argued to lead to a reduction in levels of professionalism associated with standards as individuals are expected to do everything from acquiring the pictures, to writing the copy and designing the page (Gunter, 2003). As newsrooms have become increasingly decentralized and flexible, employing staff with a different range of skills from those traditionally associated with journalism, so working conditions are also reported to have become more flexible and workforces more transient (Pavlik, 2001), bringing with them less journalistic autonomy as job security becomes paramount.

Multiplicity and Polycentrality

The space available also gives rise to the potential for a plurality of news providers that threatens the monopoly of provision from major transnational corporations, opening up news production to all citizens able to get access to a computer and the right software. The internet is claimed to provide a many-to-many model of information dissemination, putting the smaller and the smallest news providers on an equal footing with the transnational conglomerates (Rheingold, 1993). This in turn, unlocks the possibility for smaller online news providers providing spaces for minority views and news that do not make it into the dominant news media because of their apparent lack of appeal to a mass audience (Rivas-Rodriguez, 2003).

McNair (1999: 213) states that a proliferation of news platforms calls into question the notion of the public as a single, monolithic construct 'defined and serviced by a metropolitan elite', and encourages its replacement with a vision of 'multiple publics, connected in key ways'. As a result, online journalism is claimed to offer audiences a view of the world that is more contextualized, textured, and multidimensional than traditional news media.

In this space it is more difficult for journalists to claim privilege and for anyone fully to control its flows. The internet provides a space where interested readers can check the validity of one news report against another and even access the news sources referred to. The nature of news gathering is exposed like never before, placing notions of journalistic objectivity and impartiality, the holy grail of professional journalism, under scrutiny. In online journalism these normative anchors become dislodged in favour of the acknowledgement of the impossibility of objectivity and an increased awareness of subjectivity. The multiplicity of views and voices from a diversity of cultures and viewpoints is claimed to keep the mainstream news 'on its toes' and render its construction more transparent. The omnipotent voice of the journalist is diluted and journalist–audience distinctions blurred (McCoy, 2001).

However, multiplicity does not always translate into diversity. Content analyses of online news have found that mainstream newspapers with online versions use a fraction of their print stories in the online edition (Singer, 1997); use mostly the same news stories with similar news judgments (Redden and Witschge, this volume) and operate under similar financial constraints. In other words it is more of the same only in a less extensive manner.

In an online world multiplicity does, however, add up to increased quantity. There are now more news platforms available to more citizens than ever before. Quantity, of course, has never been a predictor of quality. Finding information can be an ever more difficult task as people attempt to navigate their way through a morass of search engines and news sites. Many have argued that the sheer abundance of news across a range of different media is nothing more than sophisticated marketing and the ever-increasing commodification of the news product. This, it is argued, leads us irredeemably down the path of tabloidization and infotainment. More simply means more opportunities for the news market to sell its wares – in a manner that maximizes audiences (and hopefully profit) rather than public interest. Issues of political discourse become assimilated into and absorbed by the modes and contents of entertainment. The idea that in a fragmented news environment with the most popular online interfaces being situated in social networking sites (such as Facebook and MySpace) personalization is on the increase is argued to have a negative impact on the processes of rational, democratic thought processes. Sunstein (2001: 192) writes that 'a market dominated by countless versions of "Daily Me" would make self government less workable [and] create a high degree of social fragmentation.' News, we are warned, will be transformed further into a discourse of personalization, dramatization, simplification and polarization.

In this argument more translates into more of the same. The major news sites online are said to provide little by way of original material and have a heavy reliance on the limited news spread of the major news agencies. Paterson (2003) discovered that major news organizations simply provided almost verbatim foreign news reports from Associated Press (AP) and Reuters 43 per cent of the time. The major internet portals like Yahoo and AOL provided unaltered Reuters and AP material 85 per cent of the time. Similarly, Ofcom (2007: 3) reports that despite the proliferation of news sources, 'news outlets of all kinds often tell the same stories, from the same perspective, using much the same material.' Our own research (Chapter 5) found that journalists frequently use rival news organizations as news sources. Hoge (1997) puts a different slant on this, arguing that the internet provides information aplenty on the news agendas as fixed by the dominant news players but little on subjects of which we may know hardly anything. Far from providing a diversity of views we are left with a public discourse that is largely homogenous (see Chapter 10).

Interactivity and Participation

These negative consequences are rebutted by those who proclaim that the interactive and participative nature of the web means that everyone or anyone can be a journalist with the right tools. Civic journalism is increasing and access to public information and government services is expanding (Pavlik, 2001). Citizen journalism is said to bleed into mainstream journalism and vice versa. The blogosphere has been credited with taking on the major news corporations through instant feedback that is often lively, openly subjective and highly critical. In the more renowned cases bloggers have been attributed with helping to topple Senator Trent Lott and the *New York Times* editor, Howell Raines from their offices; helping to organize and co-ordinate protests over the Iraq war; boosting the presidential hopes of Howard Dean and Barack Obama by gaining them followers and cash contributions (Hachten, 2005). In the online environment, it is argued readers can have a greater impact on the news through an increase in the intensity of their exchanges with journalists and for example the presentation of their own views in online papers. News online is thus open to a higher degree of contestation than is typical of traditional news media. This demystification of journalism is claimed to break down the barriers between audience and producer facilitating a greater deconstruction of the normative values embedded in the news genre and a re-imagining of what journalism could and/or should be.

But for many, the open and iterative world of online commentary is not seen to be taking journalism to new heights. Rather the limitless opportunities for anyone to have their say on anything, is decreed to result in opinion and vitriol replacing the hard-won gains of investigative journalism. One-off fragmentary commentaries are the norm rather than sustained analysis. 'Old news' values are argued to be replaced by populist ranting or those more interested in self-publicity than the ethics of public value. Spaces for online discussion blur into the wider provision of news. The lack of accountability and anonymity of those responding online also introduces concerns of verification, accountability and accuracy. There are criticisms of the blogosphere as doing nothing more than opening the floodgates to unverified, de-professionalized gossip (Silvia, 2001). Similar concerns are voiced regarding consumer-generated video and audio material. Worse, it is feared that this new interactive multiplicity threatens to economically undermine traditional professional journalism with grave consequences for politics and public life (Singer, 2003).

The arguments are multi-faceted and contradictory because the terrain of their discussion – new media, journalism, news and democracy – is uneven (across many different types of news industry and news platforms), and often in uncharted territory (what do people do when they are given the ability to challenge the 'facts'?). In this volume we hope to provide the first steps towards a detailed examination of these issues in all their complexity.

A Note on Methodology

Analyzing the practices that enact apparent technological and social/ political transformation helps us to understand them and contemplate their potential consequences. Social histories of the news media have demonstrated how institutional and technological factors have shaped the news over the last 200 years (Schudson, 1978; Blondheim, 1994), establishing that news is a culturally constructed category. Ethnographic accounts have revealed how local contingencies impact upon the reporting therein. Carey (1986: 180) summarizes this body of work, writing that news is not 'some transparent glimpse at the world. News registers, on the one hand, the organizational constraints under which journalists labor [and] on the other hand, the literary forms and narrative devices journalists regularly use to manage the overwhelming flow of events'. The understanding of these 'organizational constraints' and 'narrative devices' was key to our study; so not surprisingly, journalists and their tools were central subjects of analysis.

But we also needed a research design that could reflect the massive changes in the nature of news and news production over the last two decades. We have seen the globalization of news (Boyd-Barrett, 1998) take hold; the concentration of ownership increase; and technology transform. A non-technologically deterministic and anti-essentialist approach suggests that studying new media and news still purports that news is what those contributing to its production make it. And this is precisely the point – those who contribute to its production are changing. The social actors involved in the construction of news have expanded and extended outside of the newsroom resulting in the expansion of the locus of news production.

These new voices form a crucial part of this research. They include the news users who, by voicing opinions in chat rooms, forums and interactive news pages, may seek to shape what is seen as newsworthy and how it is reported. But these voices are not the only ones increasing in relevance. In an era of electronic news media marked by economic liberalism, globalization and the potential of the internet, other crucial voices, often forgotten, enter the fray with ever more importance. For example, advertising and marketing personnel influence what gets covered via topic selection and budget allocation to a greater extent than in traditional media as online news sites strive to be profitable. Technical and design personnel also have a greater contribution to play in how news gets reported from the use of multimedia and interactive tools to the visual interface (Boczkowski, 2004). News is as much about these actors as it is about journalists and we were at pains to include these voices in the research.

To reflect the changing dynamics of news production the research was based on three methodological strands. The first was based on 160 semi-structured interviews[3] with a range of professionals from a cross-section of news media, stratified by type of media, geographic reach and professional roles (generalists, specialist correspondents, dedicated new media staff, production and editorial staff, managerial and business personnel), and from commercial and public sector broadcasting relating to news. These included interviews conducted with a range of personnel in local and national (UK-based) print newspapers and local, national and international (UK-based) television news (both public service in the form of the BBC and commercial) with particular emphasis on their online services. We also interviewed representatives of news agencies and freelance journalists.

We did not presuppose control or dominance of the news agenda by news professionals and we were conscious to include a range of news sources. This part of the sample comprised of traditionally privileged and authoritative voices such as Members of Parliament (MPs) and those with traditionally less news authority such as NGOs. New news sources were clearly important and a range of bloggers, 'citizen-journalists' and producers within alternative news platforms were also interviewed.

In order to flesh-out the interviews and add contextual depth the second strand of research included mini ethnographies in three places of news production: the BBC, *Manchester Evening News* and the *Guardian*. Although the time spent in each place was not long in ethnographic terms (up to two weeks), it did allow for a greater sense of the organizational texture and better insight into the daily realities of working life in contemporary newsrooms.

To further critique emergent findings a third research strand, a qualitative analysis of online news content, was undertaken.[4] This analysis tracked a range of story types across online mainstream news media, online alternative media, social networking sites and YouTube.

The research team of nine (all represented in this volume) included two journalists. Each member of the team took part in data collection and analysis. Interview data was analyzed with NVIVO software and a central databank maintained allowing all team members access to all data. Each author(s) explains in more detail the precise nature of the data under discussion in each chapter.[5] However, all of the data collected informs, at some level, each of the chapters since a critical part of the research process was the regular research team meetings where we discussed at length each aspect of the research practice. All data collection and analysis was cross-checked and critiqued by members of the research team, often leading to further data collection or re-appraisal of analysis. This form of team interrogation and critique enabled ever deeper mining and explication of the empirical data.

Conclusion: Drowning or Waving?

What follows is a critique of an industry and a practice in flux. There have been massive changes to the way in which news is produced and journalism performed. We should remember that the history of communications technology shows us that if innovative content and forms of production appear in the early stages of a new technology and offer potential for radical change this is more often than not cancelled out or appropriated by the most powerful institutions operating within dominant technological and socio-political paradigms (Curran, Chapter 1). 'Newness' of form and content is quickly smothered by predominance, size and wealth (Winston, 1995). But history does not always repeat itself.

The argument that in a digital age, the relations of power remain on the whole the same to the increasing advantage of global media conglomerates is difficult to dispute yet similarly simplistic. It is true that analyses rooted in models of media ownership and control show nothing more than a deeper entrenchment of power and neo-liberal consensus. Undoubtedly, as our interviewees remind us, news media are (mostly) businesses and the news is a product. The economics of news remains stacked against newcomers on the national news stage be it in traditional or new media. Concentration of ownership is likely to filter ever outwards to the internet – and how to make online news profitable is still a puzzle waiting to be solved (see Chapter 2). As mainstream news providers plough more resources into online operations that are generally lossmakers, this research explores how further commercial pressures are likely to increase the temptation to rely on cheaper forms of newsgathering to the detriment of original in-depth journalism (Chapters 2, 5 and 10). It seems ever likely that the voices on the web will be dominated by the larger, more established news providers that will duplicate the same commercial interests according to the same understanding of how news fits those commercial concerns, leading to anything but increased diversity.

But we should equally be wary of economic reductionism. The frameworks of news on offer in the digital age are articulated by the nexus of interests producing them. This is neither a straightforward nor direct relationship between wealth and power. The codes and conventions of professional journalism are being challenged as they are being reinstated. The cultural dynamics of capitalism and markets are concerned not only with economics but also with questions of representation, identity and meaning. A straight political economic analysis misses, or cannot account for, the possibility that under certain conditions 'journalism or journalists' (whoever these may be) may transform power relations both within their own domain and in others. The increasing presence of non-professional or 'citizen' journalists is suggestive of a type of journalistic autonomy that may be able to disrupt and change institutionalized journalism in particular ways in certain circumstances (although currently these instances are rare).

So where does this leave us? This book argues that the two prominent views outlined in this introduction are wrong. The techno-optimists who see the internet as reinvigorating democracy, enabling active citizenship and forging new connections across old frontiers within news remain firmly wedged in the starting blocks of potential. The techno-pessimists who see new media as commodified by corporations and the market as any 'old media' have also missed the point. The Luddite pessimism that subscribes to the socio-economic logic of capitalism in which any change operates inevitably in favour of a business model and against the public good is misleading. The internet has modified things, sometimes in positive and productive ways. New voices have found expression – from soldiers' online complaints (Couldry, Chapter 8) to alternative e-zines in civil society (Curran and Witschge, Chapter 6); new means of brokering intelligent dialogue across nations have emerged. It has enabled established communities of interest to be more efficient in their circulation of communication and sharing of information with one another (Fenton, Chapter 9). Alternative interpretations of news and current affairs have found space and voice online (Redden and Witschge, Chapter 10). And as a repository of information and knowledge the internet is unparalleled.

But this book is also at pains to point out that the utopian vision of a brave new world with everyone connected to everyone else, a non-hierarchical network of voices with equal, open and global access, is also far from true. Curran's chapter notes that many of the forecasts of new media visionaries have been risibly inaccurate, though they have often been taken seriously at the time and promoted a media deregulation agenda. Rather, this study is testimony to enduring forces that cultivate continuity and limit change. This latest 'new' world of 'new' media has not yet destabilized the ascendancy of dominant news brands; it has not transformed news values and traditional news formats sustained by tenacious journalistic cultures – news is, what news always was; and it has not connected a legion of bloggers to a mass audience (Couldry, Chapter 8), or NGOs with limited resources to spheres of influence (Fenton, Chapter 9).

One of the unexpected conclusions of this book is that the internet can in many ways be seen as contributing to the stifling of journalism for the public good and in the public interest. Davis (Chapter 7) describes journalistic iron cages wherein technology is enshrined in news practice that foregrounds rationalization and marketization at the expense of ideal democratic objectives. Phillips (Chapter 5) details how some journalists, subject to the need to fill more space and to work at greater speed while also having improved access to stories and sources online, are thrust into news production more akin to creative cannibalization than the craft of original journalism. As news production becomes more expansive so engagement with the public and news sources diminishes, becomes more symbolic and increasingly 'virtualized' (Davis, Chapter 7). Redden and Witschge (Chapter 10) reveal how, far from breeding a diversity of views, online news content is largely homogenous.

New technologies of production operate within the systemic constraints of media institutions. They do not liberate these constraints but are seen more as a technical fix to the increasing problems of cutting costs and increasing efficiency (Lee-Wright, Chapter 4). For newspapers in particular, a decline in advertising revenues and reader figures since the 1970s has forced them to increase output while cutting back on staff and diminishing conditions of employment (Freedman, Chapter 2; Davis, Chapter 7). The material conditions of contemporary journalism do not offer optimum space and resources to practise independent journalism in the public interest. On the contrary, job insecurity and commercial priorities place increasing limitations on journalists' ability to function ethically (Phillips, Couldry and Freedman, Chapter 3). Indeed, we found little evidence of new media being deployed to allow journalists to do more journalism or to engage the public more effectively (although there were notable exceptions); rather new technology both facilitated and was dependent upon cuts in funding (Lee-Wright, Chapter 4).

But the social and political context of technology is a contested domain. The contemporary mediation of news is complex and contradictory – ranging from traditional bulletins on the BBC to discussions on MySpace to user-generated documentaries on YouTube; the future of journalism is being carried on a tide of uncertainty. Is it drowning or waving? Sometimes it is difficult to tell but one thing is for sure, it is far too important to ignore. Read on.

Endnotes

1. Though this is a book that is ostensibly engaged with 'new media', the discussion frequently focuses on the internet because our empirical investigation consistently revealed the internet as having the most ramifications for journalism and news. Other new media – such as mobile telephones and digital cameras – figure less prominently because they were not perceived by the various actors in this study to be as important; but also because in an increasingly converged mediascape, most forms of digital media have an online configuration at some point.

2. This research has taken place under the auspices of the Goldsmiths Media Research Centre: Spaces, Connections, Control and funded by the Leverhulme Trust.

3. This is not the final sample. The research is ongoing and data is being collected up to and beyond the submission date of this book. The number of interviews stated here refers to particular sub-sections of our sample. Data excluded from this discussion includes related personnel on national and local radio news, Yahoo! and AOL news and a complete sample of national tabloid newspapers.

4. The research does not extend to an audience study in the traditional sense as our intention was primarily to explore news production. We do not take the view, however, that the audience is absent from this investigation. Our analysis is informed by audience data generated by others while in the interviews, news sources from bloggers to MPs to NGOS were considered both as news source, news audience and news producer; and in the content analysis postings on YouTube, Facebook and MySpace were analyzed in relation to particular news stories.

5. As interviews covered a range of different types of people the conventions employed for attributing quotations differs from chapter to chapter. Some public figures in high profile positions were more comfortable with being named whereas others, either reflecting insecurity about their position, or as in the case of bloggers, protection of their off-line identity, requested anonymity.

Part II

New Media and News
in Context

Chapter One

· ·

Technology Foretold

James Curran

Introduction

There is a long tradition of millenarian prophecy in relation to new media.[1] It was predicted that the 'facsimile newspaper', dropping 'automatically folded from the home radio receiver', would rejuvenate the monopolistic American press (Hutchins Commission, 1947: 34–35); citizen's band radio, said to be 'taking the US by storm' in 1975, would recreate a sense of community;[2] computer-assisted print technology was destined to subvert the established press;[3] the camcorder would democratize television, and empower the people (*New York Times*, 26 June, 1989); the CD-Rom would transform publishing and 'replace books in classrooms entirely'.[4] All these predictions, mostly American, proved to be wrong.[5]

The case studies that follow look at what was predicted, and what actually happened, in relation to four 'new media' developments during the last quarter of a century in Britain. While they are British in terms of their specificity, they have more general implications. They underline the need for sceptical caution when assessing the impact of new communications technology. They offer an explanation of why techno-fantasies are constructed, and circulated, that probably has parallels elsewhere. This study suggests also that spurious projections about the future of the media were sometimes used to justify media deregulation, something that clearly happened in other countries, though in complex and variable ways (Horwitz, 1989; Galperin, 2004; Mosco, 2005; Hart, 2007). Thus, while this study is UK-centred, it has a wider resonance for our times.

Cable Television

In 1982, few people were better placed to discern the future of the media in Britain than Kenneth Baker, the newly appointed Information

Technology Minister. A rising star destined to become a long serving member of the Cabinet,[6] he had been briefed by civil servants and leading industry experts. His considered judgement, delivered in a Commons speech, was that the advent of cable television 'will have more far-reaching effects on our society than the Industrial Revolution 200 years ago'.[7] Not one member of the opposition benches rose to contradict this confident pronouncement. It was based on the apparently secure premise that 'wide band' cable television would deliver a popular 'film-on-request' service; a multiplicity of minority channels including some for the deaf, elderly and adults seeking education; and, above all, a range of new *consumer* services that would be delivered through 'off-air television sets'. These last, according to Kenneth Baker, 'could literally change the fabric of society in which we shall be living in the course of the next few years'.[8]

Speaking on another occasion, Baker promised that 'by the end of the decade [1980s], multi-channel cable television will be commonplace countrywide'. By then, cable TV 'will be used for armchair shopping, banking, calling emergency and many other services' (cited in Goodwin, 1998: 62).

In fact, we now know that cable television did not even eclipse the industrial revolution in terms of its impact. It did not even become commonplace during the 1980s: cable TV was adopted in just 1 per cent of homes by 1989,[9] and by only 13 per cent in 2008 (Office of Communications (Ofcom), 2008b: 211). Many of cable TV's much vaunted new services, such as facilitating utility meter-reading, opinion polling, home security services, home banking, and home visits by the doctor, either never materialized or were short-lived.

Yet, Kenneth Baker was not alone in misreading the runes. Much of the national British press, during the period 1992–4, gave prominence to confident forecasts that cable TV would usher in an entertainment-led revolution, accompanied by information channels and exciting new services that would boost economic growth. Publications differed primarily in terms of what they stressed (with the partial exception of the sometimes sceptical *Financial Times*). Thus, the *Times Educational Supplement* (4 November, 1983) likened the advent of cable TV to the arrival of public libraries, and excitedly predicted that its educational programmes would be consumed by the home-bound, the very young, and adults who shunned evening classes. The *Financial Times* (13 October, 1982) in an upbeat moment foresaw cable television as enabling 'direct buying and selling from the home', while the *Times* (11 January, 1982) conjectured that cable television might usher in a more decentralized, leisured society. The *Sunday Telegraph* (26 March, 1982) reported the expert claim that cable TV would destroy the postal service, apart from 'one postal delivery a week'. Yet, despite all these differences of emphasis, the underlying message was the same: cable television was going to have a profound impact. Even the normally sober *Economist* (6 March, 1982) declared the cable TV initiative to be 'the most important industrial decision' of the Thatcher administration.

Interactive Digital Television

However, there were some early cable TV sceptics, and their number grew significantly by the mid 1980s. But if neophytes did not have it all their own way to begin with, they carried all before them in the 1990s. Essentially, the same story that had been told in relation to 'two-way' cable television was re-told about 'interactive' digital TV. But this time, the story was repeated at regular intervals from 1994 onwards, and encountered little criticism. The technological messiah had at last risen, and the good news was spread to the four corners of Britain, and unto all those who would believe.

Thus, it was claimed that interactive digital TV (now sometimes called iTV) would be endowed with the same 'killer application' that had been promised for early cable TV. However, 'film-on-request' – now named 'video-on-demand' – was to be even better than anything promised before. According to the *Independent* (12 January, 1996):

> Video-on-demand, once fully operational, will allow us to call up almost any film in the world, to watch any TV programmes, and to compile 'dream schedules' – our own perfect evenings' viewing.

A heart-warming vision was again invoked of a caring technology: interactive TV, according to the *Sunday Times* (4 October, 1998), would offer a 'glut of new services for the sick, elderly and infirm.' A futuristic fantasy, this time pitched at a new level of extravagance, was projected on to the interactive consumer experience that digital TV would provide. Viewers would shortly be able to have 'elaborate conversations' through their TV sets with travel companies about the kind of holidays they wanted (*Independent*, 24 October, 1994); women would be able to try out new clothes on a virtual catwalk (*Times*, 27 November, 1994); and viewers would soon be sauntering down a shopping mall, walking into virtual shops, and buying whatever they liked, without ever moving from their sofas (*Independent*, 6 October, 1994).

As before, it was anticipated that the new technology would have far-reaching effects on society. 'This futuristic device,' proclaimed the *Sunday Times* (30 April, 1995), 'is an "interactive TV", poised to revolutionize the way information, education, media, commerce and entertainment are channelled into the twenty-first century home'. But in one important respect, the good news message of interactive, digital TV had a different rhetorical register from before. It laid much greater emphasis on empowerment. 'Within a year', according to the *Guardian* (21 June, 1994), viewers would be able to 'vote on key issues'. They would also 'be able to choose the storyline for a drama and [specify] whether they want a sad or happy ending' (*Independent*, 16 August, 1997). Viewers would soon order their TV sets to scan and select from hundreds of channels of information overnight, 'to report whatever news you are interested in' (*Sunday Times*, 20 November, 1994). In short, interactive digital TV meant the kiss of death for the couch potato, and would lead to a 'fundamental shift in power from the TV director to the consumer in the home' (*Sunday Times*, 30 April, 1995).

In fact, the iTV that was developed in the late 1990s and early 2000s was neither very interactive nor empowering. Shopping on TV meant choosing between a limited number of heavily promoted products; video-on-demand offered a restricted number of often not very good films; home visits by the doctor amounted in the end to NHS Direct, in effect the accessing of a glorified medical dictionary; NatWest pioneered an interactive TV banking service in 1995, only to close it down in 2003;[10] there was a restricted choice of camera angles for some football games on certain subscription channels; and iTV provided an alternative way of placing a bet.

Yet, despite the fanfare of press publicity, viewers were mostly unimpressed. A mere 20 per cent, in a 2003 Ofcom survey, indicated a willingness to pay in principle for interactive television services (Ofcom 2004: 4). Indeed, interactive services accounted for only 36 per cent of British television's non-broadcast revenue in 2006 (Ofcom 2007a: 120)[11] and most of this was attributable to premium rate phone calls.[12] The most important form of commercial TV interaction was probably mass voting in the *Big Brother* show. However, *Big Brother* discontinued the option of red button voting in 2004, and SMS voting in 2006, but retained voting by telephone,[13] a technology first developed in the late nineteenth century. This was not what the transformation of 'dumb' television sets into 'intelligent machines' had been intended to achieve.

According to a number of market research studies, only a minority with red button facilities actually used these (*New Media Age*, 27 April, 2006). The number of interactive users even decreased between 2003 and 2006 (*Precision Marketing*, 9 March, 2007; cf. *New Media Age*, 6 April, 2006). The epiphany that iTV disciples had been expecting for a quarter of a century never materialized.

Local Community Television

The rise of local community television was another hardy perennial of fallible forecasting. It was predicted in the early 1980s that cable TV would give rise to local community TV services which would strengthen local communities, and improve the flow of communication within them (Information Technology Advisory Panel (ITAP) Report, 1982). This conception of a new tier of local television stations, comparable to the local newspapers, captured the imagination of politicians, journalists and activists alike in the 1980s and 1990s. Thus, the television journalist, Richard Gregory, wrote in 1990 that 'new cable operators have tremendous opportunities' to create through community channels 'a television equivalent of the best of the weekly newspapers', achieving 'a closeness with the community that not even local radio can match' (*Guardian*, 6 August, 1990). Some like Graham Allen, Labour Opposition media minister, went further, hoping that local television would regenerate a sense of local community, democratize programme-making and ensure that a plurality of social experiences 'found life on the screen' (*Times*, 24 May, 1995).

This mixture of prediction and advocacy was repeatedly confounded. The leaden growth of cable TV in the 1980s 'delayed' the anticipated growth of local community television. It was not until the mid 1990s that ambitious local television *news* channels were launched in major urban centres like London, Birmingham, and Liverpool. Most of these failed disastrously, dampening hopes that new technology would give rise to a renaissance of local journalism.

A different strategy was then embraced, based on the issue of short-term, localized (RSL) licences for new local TV stations authorized by the 1996 Broadcasting Act. This gave rise to renewed expectations that grassroots television journalism was about to take off (even though it was actually employing 'old' technology). For example, the *Sunday Times* (27 September, 1998) reported lyrically that 'a quiet revolution is taking place in British television', based on the plans of '50 new local companies' to launch new local community channels. The same, arresting image was invoked by the *Independent* (14 February, 1998) when it reported that 'in a backroom in Oxford this week a small revolution was under way...'. The Oxford Channel, was being launched with 30 professional staff, numerous local volunteers and an appealing schedule of local programmes. According to its joint managing director, the new channel aimed to 'get the community involved in programming'.

As it turned out, most of these newly licensed local channels did not have a viable economic model to sustain them. They gained only small audiences, and therefore limited advertising, and had no significant public funding. Fatality among local TV channels was consequently high. Out of 23 local TV channels licensed after 1996, only 13 were still in operation in early 2006 (Ofcom, 2006a). Many of the survivors had only a vestigial connection to the dream of grassroots, locally produced programming that had so excited sympathetic journalists. Thus, Oxford Channel's employees were all sacked in 2000, and replaced with a skeletal crew by its new owners, the chain-owning Milestone Group. Under the new regime, the Oxford Channel transmitted Sky News, pop videos, 'advertisement features', and 'up to' three hours of new local factual programming each week (Ofcom, 2006b).

Apart from a few hopeful exceptions, local community television proved to be a failure. In 2007, all local community TV channels combined accounted at most for a mere 0.5 per cent of viewing time in Britain.[14] The 'quiet revolution' had been postponed for another day.

The Dotcom Bubble

Panglossian predictions about the impact of new communications technology reached their apotheosis in the dotcom bubble. Extravagant forecasts of the *immediately* transformative impact of the internet on the economy were reported in the business sections of the press, supported by a large volume of news stories recording the enormous fortunes that were being made by dotcom entrepreneurs. Thus, the *Independent on Sunday* (25 July, 1999) recorded, under the headline, 'Web Whiz-Kids Count Their Cool Millions', that 'the precocious and proliferating breed of "dot com" millionaires are fabulously rich and ludicrously young. Their fortunes reduce national Lottery jackpots to peanuts ... '. Similarly, a *Times* (31 December, 1999) article commented that 'it should be impossible for 14 men to make £1.1 billion in twelve months out of nothing but a few second-hand ideas, a handful of computers, and some petty cash. Yet that is exactly what happened ... .'

The implication was that readers could also share in this market jackpot. The *Sunday Times* (26 December, 1999) reported that 'the mania for investing, to hitch a ride on the road to wealth, is reflected in the cover of the current *Forbes* magazine, which proclaims that: "Everyone Ought to Be Rich"'. The *Sunday Mirror's* (17 October, 1999) advice was characteristically more direct: 'Your Wealth: Get on the Net to Get Ahead'. The *Independent* (14 July, 1999) concluded that the good times were still rolling due to the 'Billion Dollar Brains behind the Net'. Financial analyst, Roger McNamee, was reported as saying: 'logic would suggest that this market [cycle] would have ended four or five years ago. But anyone following logic would look foolish today. The fools are dancing, but the greater fools are just watching'. Silicon Valley venture capitalist, Joel Schoendorf, echoed this view: 'I wouldn't be surprised if we saw a 5 per cent increase in investment next year, and every year for the next five to 10 years.'

In fact, the dotcom boom came to an end less than twelve months later. Yet, very few British publications – with the notable exceptions of the *Financial Times* and *The Economist* – clearly foresaw the bust before it happened (resembling in this respect the American press that was no less gullible (see Cassidy, 2003)). For the most part, British newspapers were content to chronicle the accumulation of wealth during the dotcom boom without properly investigating whether it was based on a secure foundation. There was little informed discussion about the extent of cost reductions secured through net retailing (which varied widely between different market sectors), or analysis of which consumer groups were most accessible to net retailing. Indeed, there was very little awareness of just how low home internet penetration then was in Britain – still only accounting for 3.23 million households in the first quarter of 1999 (Curran and Seaton, 2003: 279).[15]

While the internet is potentially a transforming technology, its impact is contingent on the wider societal context (Livingstone, 2005, among others). In this instance, a large number of dotcom companies in the UK went bankrupt during 2000–2 without ever making a profit. Pension funds were seriously depleted, and Britain only narrowly missed following the US into recession.

Influence of News Sources

British journalists are not a naturally trusting group of people, untouched by scepticism. Yet, the mistakes they made in reporting the dotcom boom were not an isolated event, but part of a recurring pattern in which they responded uncritically to the hyping of new communications technology. What, then, explains this blind spot?

The mistakes that journalists made in reporting the advent of new media were also mistakes that authoritative people – seemingly well briefed politicians, entrepreneurs primed with the latest market information, financial analysts, and academic experts – also made. This goes a long way towards explaining journalists' lapses: they were exposed to mutually reinforcing misjudgement.

This conclusion is consistent with a large body of literature which argues that how journalists report the news is strongly influenced by their news sources.[16] It is also corroborated by differences in the way in which new media were reported. There were more cable TV sceptics in the early 1980s than there were interactive television sceptics in the 1990s, and this resulted in more doubts being registered – at least *sotto voce* – in the earlier period.

Those questioning, in the early 1980s, whether cable TV had an assured future came mainly from two quarters: terrestrial television executives who argued that cheap entertainment programmes, vital for cable TV's success, were not easy to find, and some city analysts who doubted whether cable TV would be profitable in the short run. The former tended to be discounted on the grounds that they were self-interested rivals with obvious axes to grind. Their scepticism was seemingly refuted by the optimistic report produced by industry experts (ITAP, 1982), in which the government placed so much faith. But senior terrestrial broadcasters were nonetheless an 'accredited' voice, and their doubts about cable TV's future, were reported occasionally (e.g. *The Times*, 9 December, 1982). Sceptical city analysts of cable TV's prospects had the ear only of the *Financial Times* during 1982–3, but contributed to its more critical coverage.

Another potential source of scepticism was insider knowledge. An advanced cable TV experiment (QUBE) had been pioneered by Warner Cable Corporation in Columbus, Ohio in 1977. It offered multiple channels, pay-per-view films, computer games, interactive services, and offline services like domestic security and energy conservation systems. A similar, though more civic-oriented, interactive cable television experiment had been developed in Nara, Japan in 1978. Both experiments had yielded disappointing results, because interactive services had proved to be very costly, and consumer responses to them had been less than enthusiastic. This information had already leaked out, and been documented for instance in an academic study in Italian (Richieri, 1982). However, most British journalists reporting cable TV in the early 1980s were not experts, and had seemingly little connection with the American and Japanese TV industries. An exception was Brenda Maddox, an American journalist with extensive US media contacts and author of a good book about the media (Maddox, 1972). She broke free from the journalist pack by attacking the ITAP report. 'Based on wishful and selective reading of American experience by a panel composed of vested interests in computing and cable television,' she wrote, 'it made optimistic and unfounded calculations about the likely popularity of cable services in Britain' (*Time*, 10 June, 1982). Her specialist knowledge had enabled her to be critically independent.[17]

By contrast, there was no significant group of sceptics in relation to interactive TV during the mid 1990s. Broadcasters – in the terrestrial, cable and satellite sectors alike – were all committed to developing interactive services, as were major players like the telecommunications giant, British Telecom. City analysts were also more convinced of the case for iTV than they had been for early cable TV. Governments, led by John Major and Tony Blair, provided third party endorsement of the iTV hype during the 1990s. Overseas specialist expertise among British journalists was again sparse. Time Warner launched in 1995–7 a second experimental interactive television service (this time deploying more advanced technology and a wider range of services), called Full Service Network, in Orlando, Florida, only for it to flop (Richieri, 2004). Yet, it was some time before this was reported in the British press. The Brenda Maddox equivalent in the mid 1990s was sceptic Azeem Azhar, who did something unconventional: instead of relying on accredited briefing, he actually interviewed people who had taken part in a local BT interactive television experiment. His respondents complained about 'totally naff content', and technology that sometimes did not work and delivered little (*Guardian*, 18 January, 1996).

There was also a difference in the duration of the cable and iTV hype. The cable TV spell broke by the mid 1980s when it became clear that the cable TV industry was having difficulty in attracting both investors and customers. Kenneth Baker was pointedly asked why there were no homes with 30 TV channels in 1985 when he had predicted in September 1982 that 'over half the country' could have these within two years. His uncomfortable reply was that 'we have shown a capacity bordering upon genius to institutionalize torpor' (*Guardian*, 19 February, 1985).

By contrast, interactive TV's hype lasted for much longer because it was sustained from 1994 through to the 2000s with new interactive initiatives often supported by impressive endorsements. When the *Guardian*'s current Director of Digital Content, Emily Bell, concluded that it was impossible to ignore evidence of some iTV failures, she none the less insisted that 'iTV is threatening to be the hot platform of tomorrow' (*Guardian*, 7 May, 2001). Seven years later, she was still writing enthusiastically about the power of 'red button interactivism' (*Guardian*, 24 November, 2008).

The early doubts that were entertained about cable TV's prospects were thus the exception. There was far greater agreement that the internet would be an immediate money-spinner (at least until 1999) and that interactive digital television would make a major impact. Journalists in effect reproduced the 'informed' consensus of the time. This, then, raises the larger question of why this consensus was wrong.

Dynamics of Misjudgement

The principal source of misinformation about new media was, in every instance, the business interests promoting these new media. Thus, the hyping of cable television in the early 1980s came primarily from electronic consumer, computer and cable television interests (Howkins, 1982; Dutton and Blumler, 1988; Goodwin, 1998). They deliberately presented an industrial case for cable television partly in order to outflank the prevailing consensus in favour of public service broadcasting. Their extravagantly optimistic projections for cable TV growth, and the way in which it would generate new services and economic growth, were also intended to promote deregulation. Their promise was that cable TV would succeed providing it was allowed to develop unfettered by bureaucratic controls (ITAP, 1982; Hunt 1982).

The main source of iTV hype was interactive TV developers, most notably BSkyB, British Telecom (BT), and Videotron, and was intended to drum up consumer interest in new interactive services. To take one specific example, numerous articles were published in 1999 in the national press about the start-up of the Open Channel on Sky digital (a project jointly owned by BSkyB and BT, among others). The central themes of these articles were that television shopping was finally coming of age; it would profoundly change social habits; and (in the business sections) that the Open Channel would make large profits. This hype was especially prominent in Murdoch-owned newspapers, sister companies of the new venture. For instance, *The Times* (15 April, 1999) reported city analysts as valuing the Open Channel at £1.4 billion before it had even started trading. This fanfare of publicity bore little relationship to Open Channel's real importance: it was an ignominious failure, and closed in 2001.

Similarly, the main source of the dotcom hype in Britain was a coalition of dotcom entrepreneurs, venture capitalists and investment analysts, who reinforced each other. Senior executives in local community TV start-ups were the principal source for stories about the 'quiet revolution'.

The second influential group contributing to the new media 'informed consensus' was senior politicians, both Conservative and Labour. Ever since the early 1980s, successive governments supported the development of the 'new information economy' as a way of offsetting the decline of Britain's manufacturing sector. They also sought to foster the acquisition of information technology skills as a way of assisting the British workforce to compete effectively in the global economy. Conversion from analogue to digital broadcasting became a bipartisan objective partly in order to boost public revenue through the sale of spare spectrum. More generally, new communications technology was hymned as a tool of education and citizenship.

This official championship provided background mood music conducive to new media hype. For example, the Labour government proclaimed during the height of the dotcom bubble: '... the explosion of information has fuelled a democratic revolution of knowledge and active citizenship. If information is power, power can now be within the grasp of everyone' (HMSO, 2000: 8). Endorsement could also go much further than this generalized cheerleading. Kenneth Baker, Minister for Information Technology in the first Thatcher government, became the cable TV industry's most eloquent spokesman because he believed – like the Prime Minister – that its success would contribute to the modernization of the British economy. Tony Blair became a similarly committed and outspoken ambassador for interactive TV. As Opposition leader in the mid 1990s, he urged people to have 'your television connected through your phone line to a world of almost limitless opportunities'. He continued, in the style of a salesman: 'You would be able to choose what shops to visit and what items to buy simply by sitting in front of your TV. Because the system is interactive, you will even be able to decide what estate agent or travel shop brochures you want to view' (*Daily Mirror*, 4 October, 1995). He continued in this vein in his early days as Prime Minister. 'The day is not far off,' he declared, 'when interactive TV will give us the convenience of home visits [by the doctor] that can be done through technology' (the *Guardian*, 3 July, 1998). This resurrected a false prediction that Kenneth Baker had made sixteen years earlier.

The third major source of endorsement was technology experts in industry and universities. Here, a very idiosyncratic selection was made by the press that included academics outlining implausible new technological applications that never happened. For example, Steven Gray, professor of communications and computer graphics at Nottingham Trent University, featured in *The Times* (27 November, 1994) because he had developed a way of enabling viewers to 'try on a new dress on your TV screen'. This facilitated, the professor explained, a 'personalized home fashion show, allowing shoppers to see what they will look like in the clothes before buying them'. Nothing more was heard subsequently of this breakthrough. This points to the fact that journalists were not simply 'victims' passively reproducing a source consensus, but were also making editorial judgements about what was newsworthy, and orchestrating stories in ways that made for good 'copy'. A stress on novelty accorded with traditional news values. Articles about how new media would change how people live (with headlines like 'Are You Ready for the Future?' (*Sunday Times*, 20 November, 1994)) were well suited to filling the expanding space devoted to consumer and lifestyle content. The more extravagant the claim about the impact of new communications technology, the more interesting – or at least attention-seeking – was the article that reported it.

The United States was another source of seemingly disinterested endorsement. It featured as a country where new media were blazing a pioneering trail: in the early 1980s as a place where cable TV was creating a 'wired society', and in the later 1990s where dotcom companies were generating great wealth, and advanced interactive television systems were being developed. The United States was also the home of revered prophets. The ITAP Report (1982), widely reported in the British prestige press, drew heavily on two popular American books on cable television that proved to be misleading (Martin, 1978 and Smith, 1972). Press reports quoted on a number of occasions the MIT guru, Nicholas Negroponte (for example, *The Economist* 19 August, 2000), many of whose euphoric predictions (Negroponte, 1996) about interactive digital television were never realized. The recurring tenets of this tradition of US futurology – that new media would create wealth, rejuvenate local communities, and empower the citizen – connected to central themes of the American Dream.

Cultural Framing

British reporting was influenced not only by seemingly authoritative sources but also by ways of viewing the world that were embedded in British culture. One central organizing framework for narrating new media was a story of progress. In particular cable and interactive digital TV were repeatedly hailed as new technologies that would create a better world in which people would be better connected, have more choice, greater power, increased opportunities for self-expression, and enhanced prosperity. In narrating new media in this way, British journalists were drawing upon the foundational theory of modernity: the belief that science and technology is the midwife of social and economic advance that was central to the Victorian vision of progress. Claims that belief in all 'master narratives' has been undermined as a condition of postmodernity (for instance McRobbie, 1994) are not borne out by the way in which the advent of new media were reported in the later twentieth and early twenty-first centuries.

But while there was an underlying continuity in the narrating of new communications technology as a story of progress, there was also a shift of emphasis between the reporting of cable in the early 1980s and interactive digital TV in the 1990s. Cable television in the early 1980s sometimes excited millenarian prophecy about a transformed world. This is typified by a *Times* editorial (11 January, 1982) that ruminated about the coming of 'the new industrial revolution' as a consequence of cable. The first revolution 'saw a total change in the means of manufacture', whereas 'this one is envisaged as seeing a total change in the means of organizing society and its knowledge, overthrowing the old need for centralized units and repetitive labour and substituting a new decentralized society with infinite leisure'. One great advance, the editorial hoped, would be followed by another.

By the 1990s, the millenarian language remained, and the theme of advance remained important. But what was actually envisaged in relation to iTV was often more modest than before. This led to a recurring combination of utopian rhetoric and mundane prophecy, typified by this opening to a *Sunday Times* feature (4 October, 1998), entitled 'Your Gateway to the World':

> Television has been the 20th century's window on the world. The dawn of the 21st century will mark the first time we will open it. The interactive television which digital broadcasting will make possible will elevate the status of the box in the corner from household icon to a home multiplex cinema, a sports grandstand with an editing suite and a shopping centre to put Oxford Street to shame.

Despite its rhetoric of 'opening the window on the world' through interactive TV, the article in fact makes no mention of the wider world outside Britain, still less advances claims about increased interaction between nations. Its core message is more limited: switch on, go shopping, you get to choose. However, it still invokes an image that connects to a Victorian conception of technology and enlightenment, and begins with the opening narrative device of telling a story of progress.

The second key way in which the culture of British society influenced reporting was to supply a tacit framework of interpretation. The social sciences have had a weak (and now declining) influence in the United Kingdom. Their characteristic way of making sense of innovation in terms of the wider social and economic processes of society has not been widely disseminated, and is therefore not readily available to journalists. Instead, the press tended to adopt a more 'common sense' approach which reported the superior capabilities of new technology, and assumed that these would be fully realized in transforming ways. The taken-for-granted belief was that new technology would prevail, and determine outcomes.

The shortcoming of this approach is that it ignores the way in which the wider context of society influences the new technology's development, content and use. This can be illustrated best by considering a prominent feature of newspaper coverage of both cable and interactive digital TV. It was reported, at periodic intervals, for a quarter of a century that new, advanced TV sets would enable viewers to have an almost infinite choice of films from an electronic 'library' or digital 'store'. Two-way technology, it was explained, would enable TV viewers to summon up almost any film they wanted.

But while this advance became technologically possible, it did not happen because it was contrary to the interests of major holders of American film rights. The US-based 'sexopoly', which dominated ownership of back as well as current film 'catalogues', had developed a profitable business model that was based on the careful sequencing of the same product on different platforms – through film exhibition, merchandizing, the rental of transmission rights to television companies around the world, and the marketing of videos/DVDs – in a way that maximized revenue. The rise of video rental stores had temporarily threatened this business model, prompting Hollywood majors to take effective control of the dominant Blockbuster video chain. In this way, they shared in its profits, and ensured that rented videos supplemented rather than undermined their business (Epstein, 2005). However, the Hollywood majors concluded that video-on-demand represented a more serious threat to their business, and declined to collectively back – and adequately stock – its development. This explains why video-on-demand was a relative failure: many of the films that could be viewed on two-way TV were not very good. Thus the near infinite choice of film that, potentially, new technology could provide was blocked by the economic power of the film oligopoly, protected by international copyright law. Unless circumstances change (arising from the mass piracy of films online), this obstruction is likely to persist. Yet, this point was repeatedly overlooked in the press because it meant examining not what new technology could do, but what economic power would permit.

Brief reference should also be made to the politics of the press. British national dailies were very much more right-wing than their readers in terms of party preference in every general election between 1979 and 1992 (Curran and Seaton, 2003). While there was a realignment behind New Labour in 1997, most national newspapers continued to favour market-friendly policies. This general editorial orientation accorded with the assumption that technological innovation, in a free market, would engender social advance that underpinned some reporting of media 'breakthroughs'.

Retrospect

The British press was caught up in the hype of early cable TV, local community TV, the dotcom bubble and interactive digital television. On each occasion, the press failed to see through the emptiness of the promises that were made.

This failure can be attributed to two main explanations. The press reflected the mistaken consensus of the time mediated through 'authoritative' sources. It also drew upon pervasive cultural scripts, in particular a belief in the power of technology to engender progress, and a techno-determinist perspective little influenced by economics and sociology.

But what should not be lost sight of is that the hyping of new technology sometimes took a form that served a neo-liberal political agenda, and originated from sources that favoured media deregulation. Vested business interests dominated the Information Technology Advisory Panel (1982),[18] whose report provided the blueprint and justification for the largely deregulated development of cable TV. The Conservative government led by Margaret Thatcher was strongly predisposed to accept its advice because it offered the promise of releasing private capital and energy to 'modernize' the economy. 'Margaret Thatcher – very unpopular at the time – immediately saw the potential of this,' recalls Lord Baker, 'because it provided a way of tackling unemployment'.[19] The compliant press promotion of cable TV facilitated the rupturing of the cross-party consensus in favour of public service broadcasting that had prevailed for over half a century. Cable TV (unlike ITV) was developed broadly outside a public service framework.

Similarly, the no less misleading prospectus that accompanied the development of interactive digital television came primarily from self-serving corporate interests (prominent among them, Murdoch's News Corporation, which controlled BSkyB). By responding often uncritically to this hype, the press rendered more acceptable the partial deregulation of television during the 1990s and early 2000s, and the prospect of more far-reaching deregulation in the future.

Of course, new technology did change television, most importantly by enabling an increase in the number of channels.[20] Yet, what was promised in relation to cable TV and interactive digital TV did not, by and large, happen. During the 1980s, cable TV did not inaugurate an economic and social revolution: on the contrary cable TV suffered from underinvestment, lost money and was a consumer flop. And during the 1990s and early 2000s, iTV did not place the user in control, and reconfigure the television experience: instead, it introduced new facilities that were a welcome but modest improvement. However, a cumulative impression was cultivated that television was being so transformed that legislative safeguards protecting programme quality and diversity were less needed. In brief, change was interpreted in ways partly intended to influence the future.

Endnotes

1. My thanks to Joanna Redden for her valuable assistance.
2. *US News and World Report*, 29 September, 1975; *Washington Post*, 5 June, 1978.
3. This view was championed by a number of senior British journalists in the mid 1980s (see Curran and Seaton, 2003: 98).
4. Industry expert, Tom Laster, reported in *Boston Globe*, 7 November, 1993.
5. For other false, 'new media' predictions in the US, see Mosco (2005).
6. Kenneth Baker (now Lord Baker) entered the Cabinet as Environment Minister (1985–6), and held a succession of Cabinet posts as Education Minister (1986–9), Chancellor of the Duchy of Lancaster (1989–90) and Home Secretary (1990–2).
7. Kenneth Baker, *Parliamentary Debates*, Satellite and Cable Broadcasting, 20 April, 1982: London: Hansard, 6th series, vol. 22, p. 230.
8. *Idem.*
9. As recorded by Goldberg et al. (1998: 10). This figure is so low that it was double-checked, and found to be correct, on the basis of the number of cable TV homes in 1989 reported by the Cable Authority (1990: 283) and the total number of TV homes in 1989, as recorded by BARB, http://www.barb.co.uk/tvfacts.cfm?fullstory=true&includepage=ownership&flag=tvfacts (accessed on 10 Nov, 2008).
10. Information derived from the *Daily Telegraph*, 6 September, 1995: and NatWest Customer Services.

11. Revenue from TV shopping has been added to that for 'interactive services', as recorded in figure 2.16 (Ofcom, 2007a: 120).

12. Information derived from an interview with a senior research executive, Office of Communications, 2008.

13. Information provided by Nikki O'Shea, Factual Entertainment, Channel 4.

14. This estimate is derived from an Ofcom survey conducted in 2007, and is based on an internal extrapolation by its research team. Local community TV audiences are too small to be measured reliably with standard national samples.

15. Ironically the personal computer and home internet 'boom' only took off in the summer of 1999, and persisted long *after* the dotcom bubble had burst.

16. There is a very extensive literature documenting the importance of news sources in shaping the news, and also academic debate about its implications. For examples, see two classic studies (Hallin, 1989 and Schlesinger, 1990), an overview (Manning, 2001), a recent case study (Curran, Gaber and Petley, 2005) and good insider account (Davies, 2008).

17. Brenda Maddox subsequently left full-time journalism, and wrote a number of acclaimed biographies (including a perceptive study of the scientist, Rosalind Franklin).

18. They made up its entire membership apart from one computer services academic.

19. Lord Baker: conversation with the author, June 2008.

20. In retrospect, many experts' key mistake was to assume that the change would take place through the television set rather than the computer. Thus, interactive television's most important manifestation so far has been the BBC's computer-based replay facility (iPlayer).

Chapter Two

....

The Political Economy of the 'New' News Environment

Des Freedman

The End of News (As We Know It)?

The traditional business model for delivering news is in crisis. This is a story that would probably not make the headlines of your evening news bulletin but it relates to a series of developments that is set to have a massive impact not simply on the future of the news business but on the ability of ordinary citizens to secure information that allows them more effectively to participate in public life. As the established news organizations see their audiences decline in the face of increasing competition from new types of suppliers and observe the spectacular growth of online advertising, some commentators are predicting the near collapse of the existing news environment. According to the *Vanity Fair* columnist Michael Wolff (2007), 'news – as a habituating, slightly fetishistic, more or less entertaining experience that defines a broad common interest – is ending. Newspapers, the network evening news, news magazines, even 24-hour cable news channels, these providers and packagers of the news, are imperiled media.'

They are in danger because younger audiences are deserting them for the immediacy and interactivity of the internet, because advertisers are increasingly attracted by the possibilities of more accurately targeting audiences online, because traditional news organizations have lost their privileged position in delivering the world to their audiences, and because in a world dominated – at least until the global financial crisis that started in 2008 – by a fierce commitment to the efficacy of market forces, governments and regulators are reluctant to step in and help prevent the haemorrhaging of readers, viewers and revenue. News, as we have known it for many years, has no natural right to exist if it cannot pay its way in a capitalist economy. Now, as Wolff (2007) concludes, '[t]he news business – our crowd of overexcited people narrating events as they happen – is going out of business.'

This seems to be especially true for the print press. Who will be there to write its obituary when the final newspaper dies out, as Philip Meyer (2004) argues, some time in 2043? In the meantime, a series of financial analysts and private investors are keen to certify the decline of print news. 'There is absolutely no question that the next 10 years are going to be really bad for the newspaper business' argues Barry Parr of Jupiter Research. 'The format, the business model, the organization of newspapers have outlived their usefulness' (quoted in Seelye, 2007). For Warren Buffett, celebrated investor and print publisher, the newspaper is an inferior technology: 'Simply put, if cable and satellite broadcasting, as well as the internet, had come along first, newspapers as we know them probably would never have existed' (Buffett, 2007: 12).

But this is also a complex story irreducible to fatalistic and singular explanations based on 'economic realities' of profit and loss, political apathy or, above all, technological innovation. The internet features in many accounts (for example, Beckett, 2008) as the decisive driver of change in the news environment and is marked out for its transformative potential. Yet this is not the first crisis to affect the gathering and circulation of news and it can only be fully evaluated by placing the challenges to existing business models in a wider political and economic context and by confronting the assumptions of those who foresee an inexorable decline in the value of traditional news suppliers given the challenge of the internet. News has never been an 'ordinary' commodity in the sense that it has always had a special status in facilitating a public sphere by providing elites with a powerful channel of influence and publics with at least some of the information necessary to participate in democratic life. Its future, therefore, cannot be predicted in relation to exclusively economic or technological factors.

Based on financial data and interviews with a number of finance directors and media strategists, this chapter firstly identifies the scale of the economic problems faced by traditional news providers and then discusses some of the strategies adopted by organizations to cope with an insecure environment. In particular, it assesses the viability and implications of an online business model before attempting to puncture some of the myths concerning the internet's challenge to incumbent news organizations and the resulting 'inevitable' transformation of the news business. The internet is most certainly disrupting existing news business models but it is likely that, if organizations continue to invest in journalism, the priorities and personalities that shape today's news will also play a prominent role in the news of the future.

Decline in Readers and Viewers

National newspaper readership is declining steadily in the UK. The House of Lords Select Committee investigating media ownership and the news commissioned research that indicated a 19 per cent fall in the number of British adults reading a national daily paper between 1992 and 2006 (House of Lords (HoL), 2008a: 11). As a proportion of the total population, this involved a 24 per cent decline, from 59 per cent of the population reading a daily paper in 1992 to only 45 per cent reading one 14 years later. Circulation of national titles fell by a similar amount: from nearly 13.2 million in 1995 to just over 11.1 million in 2007, a reduction of 22 per cent (ibid.: 12) while local newspaper circulation declined from nearly 48 million in 1989 to 41 million in 2004, a fall of 15 per cent (Williams and Franklin, 2007: 11).

There has also been a significant decrease in the number of hours of national news watched on the main UK terrestrial television channels. Viewers consumed 108.5m hours of national news in 1994, a figure that declined – even with the introduction of a fifth terrestrial network in 1997 – to 90.8m in 2006, a fall of 16.3 per cent (Ofcom, 2007b: 19). This reflects a more general shift in audience share away from the terrestrial channels, from a 78 per cent share in 2003 to a 64 per cent share in 2007 (Ofcom, 2008b: 40). This poses particular problems for ITV's regional news bulletins where, according to the media regulator Ofcom (2007b: 53) costs are six times greater than advertising revenue. In the face of such economic 'logic', Ofcom has sanctioned cutbacks in ITV's regional news and current affairs provision.

More Competition; Less Advertising

This decline in readers and viewers is intimately related to the tremendous growth in the number of news outlets available. Competition, according to Andrew Griffith, director of group finance at BSkyB, 'has gone exponential. It's about the rate of change. It's not that there was no competition and now there is, it's that the competition is now more numerous and the playing field changes and reinvents itself at a much faster velocity' (interview with the author). The rapid increase in free papers, the emergence of 24-hour television news and the popularization of online and mobile platforms have all contributed to a far more volatile and unstable environment for news organizations.

The problems for newspapers and network news bulletins are accentuated by their declining share of advertising revenue. From playing an insignificant role at the end of the 1990s, internet adspend surpassed that of national newspapers in 2006 and regional newspapers

	1998	1999	2000	2001	2002	2003	2004	2005	2006	2007
National newspapers	13.9	14.2	14.7	13.7	12.7	12.0	11.7	11.1	11.0	10.7
Regional newspapers	18.2	17.7	18.0	18.9	18.9	18.8	18.6	17.4	16.0	15.2
Television	26.2	26.2	25.7	23.5	24.2	23.6	23.5	23.8	22.5	22.1
Direct Mail	12.7	13.4	13.3	14.8	15.6	15.6	14.7	13.8	13.4	12.0
Outdoor	4.3	4.3	4.5	4.5	4.6	5.0	5.0	5.2	5.4	5.4
Radio	3.2	3.3	3.5	3.2	3.2	3.3	3.2	3.0	2.8	2.8
Cinema	0.7	0.9	0.8	1.1	1.2	1.1	1.1	1.1	1.1	1.1
Internet	0.1	0.4	1.0	1.1	1.3	2.9	4.9	7.9	11.6	15.6

Figure 2.1   Advertising expenditure by media (UK), percentage of total

Source: The Advertising Association's *Advertising Statistics Yearbook 2008*, researched and compiled by the World Advertising Research Center (www.warc.com), pp. 13–14.

in 2007 and is, according to Zenith Optimedia, set to be the dominant source of advertising in the UK by 2010 (Sweeney, 2008: 10). Figure 2.1 shows how the internet's share of advertising has climbed spectacularly since the sector's recovery from the dotcom crash earlier this decade.

The internet's ability to target niche groups at low cost has especially affected newspapers' revenue from classified advertising. *Guardian* editor Alan Rusbridger claims that classified revenues for his title are declining by 10 per cent a year and that, in his opinion, 'the overwhelming majority of classified advertising is going to go on to the Internet and may well therefore be lost to newspapers' (quoted in HoL, 2008b: 43). Even Associated Newspapers, publishers of the highly successful *Mail* and *Mail on Sunday* titles, saw its classified advertising revenue decline by 7 per cent in 2007 despite an overall increase in advertising of 3 per cent (DMGT, 2008: 18). As classified advertising migrates online, those who depend on it the most, like regional newspapers, are expected to fare the worst. Advertising researchers Group M forecast that media spending on the regional press was likely to decline by 4 and 5 per cent in 2008 and 2009 respectively and argued that '[w]ith costs rising and revenues falling, we would expect closures of titles, if not whole publishers, this year or next' (quoted in Fenton, 2008).

Newspapers have even more reason to be worried in the US where an 18.8 per cent increase in online news advertising failed to make up for the 9.4 per cent drop in 2007 in newspaper advertising revenue. This was the steepest fall in advertising since the Newspaper Association of America started measuring advertising expenditure in 1950 (NAA, 2008). As in the UK, classified advertising suffered the greatest decline, down 16.5 per cent on 2006, a highly significant 28 per cent decline since 2000. The gloomy figures around circulation and advertising led to a 10 per cent drop in profits in the first nine months of 2007 and a 42 per cent drop in newspaper company stocks from 2005 to the end of 2007 (PEJ, 2008: 9).

This apocalyptic scenario regarding declining audiences and revenues is not simply of concern to media owners, corporate shareholders and news workers but to the wider viewing and reading public. This public has, over the years, benefited from an arrangement whereby advertisers have been happy to pour money into bulletins and titles that provide them with desirable audiences while these audiences are, in turn, provided with public affairs-oriented material that contributes to their ability to make the informed choices that are the hallmark of democratic political life. This arrangement has been bolstered by the willingness both of regulators to insist on minimum levels of television news and of press proprietors to subsidize loss-making titles in pursuit of political influence (and eventual profitability). The internet's attractiveness as an increasingly important destination for advertisers seeking to target niche demographics now threatens to undermine what Sparks has powerfully argued was an 'extraordinary set of circumstances' (Sparks, 2000: 276) that supported journalism's democratic role. The internet's ability to connect advertisers directly to consumers without the mediation of a newspaper (or, to a lesser extent, a television channel) raises the possibility that the historic link between advertising and editorial will be broken and, with it, the model that underpinned the delivery of news for many years.

In this context, the major problem affecting traditional news providers is not the decline of audiences in and of itself but the degeneration of the existing news business model that tied together news and advertising. The central question therefore for news organizations is how to bring about the radical changes needed, as Max Alexander, former managing director of new ventures and strategy at Trinity Mirror, argues, to 'recreate the business' (interview with the author) in the light of the challenge of the internet. Whether you accept that the situation for newspapers and television news is one of inexorable structural decline precipitated by the immediacy, flexibility and interactivity of the internet or, rather, the fragmentation of a business model that has, up till now, made an important contribution to public knowledge and debate, it is clear that the news business will have to rethink its approach if it is to remain relevant and prosperous in a digital future.

Coping Strategies in An Online Age

This section identifies some of the strategies adopted by 'traditional' news organizations in response to the challenges posed and opportunities offered by the internet and other digital platforms. These strategies have been developed in the context of a high degree of uncertainty about what changes need to be made. 'Anybody who tells you that they have the answer to that question,' argues Phil Bronstein, former editor of the *San Francisco Chronicle* and now an editor at Hearst Newspapers, 'or the answer to the question, "what's the successful business model for journalism", is lying to you. Because no one has it' (quoted in MacMillan, 2008). The state of the news media, admits Rupert Murdoch, is 'fairly chaotic' (quoted in HoL, 2008a: 118).

This combination of uncertainty and chaos has contributed to a relatively cautious approach by many news organizations in terms of their investment in the online world. There are, of course, exceptions like the BBC and the *Guardian*, both of whom were anxious to secure first-mover advantage in a digital news environment and were able to use their unusual ownership status – the BBC is publicly funded and the *Guardian* is answerable to trustees and not shareholders – to make bold, long-term investment decisions. More generally, however, there was an initial reluctance on the part of news organizations to commit substantial resources to the internet, partly because of lessons learned and fingers burnt during the 'dotcom crash' of 2000–2, partly because of institutional conservatism, and partly because for some, despite earlier predictions, their worlds were not falling apart. For Peter Williams, finance director of the Daily Mail and General Trust (DMGT), '[t]he decision not to invest too much nationally on the internet was a definite decision because we just thought everybody was putting too much money in too early and, touch wood, I hope we've got our timing roughly right' (interview with the author).

One long-term research project evaluating the impact of the internet on the mass media has highlighted the 'incremental and adaptive nature' of media organizations' recent strategic responses to the online world (Kung et al., 2008: 171). Even the $580 million spent by Rupert Murdoch in acquiring the social network site MySpace in 2005 to take advantage of its targeted advertising potential was far from a panic measure, at least according to Andrew Griffith at BSkyB:

> The chairman was talking about putting capital to work. Every existing business, whatever it does frankly, needs an internet strategy and we have one. These will broadly be incremental because the fundamental business hasn't changed and you could lose a hell of a lot of money saying that we think the world is all going to be online when it just is not. (Interview with the author)

For most news organizations, 'future-proofing' strategies are, therefore, tentative, experimental, defensive and evolutionary, rather than revolutionary.

Cost-cutting

Having said that, those sections of the news business most preoccupied with their survival in the face of competition from the internet, have resorted to a more tried-and-tested response to uncertain conditions: saving money through cutting costs and increasing productivity. The internet has provided newspaper groups, in particular, with the opportunity to demand more 'efficient' ways of working through multi-skilling – requiring an individual journalist to produce copy for both print and online editions. The National Union of Journalists' Commission on multi-media working found that 75 per cent of respondents felt that cross-media integration led to increased workloads with 37 per cent claiming that, as a result of integration, journalists were now working longer hours (NUJ, 2007: 14). Furthermore, less than one quarter of NUJ branches responded that their members had received additional pay for integrated working (NUJ, 2007: 12). The consequence of journalists working with more deadlines, across more media, for often no increase in pay is what Davies refers to as 'churnalism,' the 'rapid repackaging of largely unchecked second-hand material', gathered overwhelmingly from public relations and news agency sources (Davies, 2008: 60).

The internet's siphoning off of advertising revenue has also led news organizations to cut back on expensive editorial commitments like investigative reporting and specialist and foreign correspondents. 'The first thing that newspapers do when they are in financial trouble is close foreign bureaux' argues *Times* editor Robert Thomson (quoted in HoL, 2008b: 52). The situation is worse in the local and regional press where *Guardian* editor Alan Rusbridger claims that 'Google is killing off classified advertising. The property, cars and jobs ads are all going, so your two main sources of revenue are disappearing and the response of virtually all the newspapers' owners is to then cut back on the editorial costs' (quoted in HoL, 2008b: 46).

Of course, it is impossible to link these cuts directly to the presence of the internet in the news environment. For example, while the NUJ's commission found that there had been editorial job cuts at 45 per cent of titles since online operations were introduced, 'most respondents felt that the redundancies would have happened with or without online working as part of general cost saving measures' (NUJ, 2007: 16). Some titles, like the *Guardian*, have actually now employed additional staff to cope with the extra demands of online news. The point is, however, that the internet features as an increasingly significant factor in the 'restructuring' that is occurring throughout the news industry. According to NUJ general secretary Jeremy Dear, the internet is the big bogeyman that's held up every now and again against us in negotiations. Before that it was always general problems with circulation, before that it was recession. It has now become much more the reason given for both circulation falls in traditional print media and advertising revenue declining because it's going elsewhere. (Interview)

Diversifying

A more forward-looking response by traditional news organizations to the internet's disruption of their territory is to diversify operations in order to expand both audience and revenue streams. After a slow start, news businesses have now begun to invest in, above all, online classified advertising sites in an attempt to win back some of the revenue they have lost to the internet. KPMG's Richard Bawden (2008) emphasizes the need for news organizations to diversify: to 'replicate the sources of income they had before' and to leverage their 'skill set' into the online world (interview). He singles out the Daily Mail group for the way it has embraced the potential of the internet, an assessment shared by investment bank Merrill Lynch in November 2007 in an unusually positive recommendation – at least for the publishing sector – to buy shares in the company. The report argues that 'DMGT has transformed itself in the last decade from an essentially pure play newspaper business to a diversified group' (Merrill Lynch, 2007: 3) and praises the company for recognizing the opportunities that the internet presents to well-placed media brands. Indeed, since 2004, DMGT has spent some £203 million acquiring a series of high-profile online recruitment, holiday, property and auto classified sites (Merrill Lynch, 2007: 12).

Acquisitions are not the only method of expanding operations and revenue. Organizations are also exploring joint ventures and partnerships in order to distribute 'branded content' more widely. BSkyB, for example, is working with mobile phone companies to extend the reach of Sky News but, according to group finance director Andrew Griffith, 'short of buying a mobile phone company and just setting it [the phone] to autotune into news constantly and make people hold it to their ear, there's not a lot more we can do' (interview with the author). Instead, the company's strategy is to 'seed' new platforms, to invest small amounts so that 'if it's really big we haven't missed an opportunity – we've got in at the ground floor – but if it doesn't fly, then we haven't tied up a lot of capital.' We are still in, he claims, the 'very early days' of the relationship between broadcast and mobile or online platforms.

The most significant example of diversification, however, has not involved acquisitions and partnerships but the attempt by traditional news providers to re-create themselves as fully integrated news

	Unique users (m)	Unique users – UK only (m)
Sun Online	27.3	8.3
Telegraph.co.uk	26.2	9.2
Guardian.co.uk	25.3	10.2
Times Online	22.0	7.7
Mail Online	21.8	6.9
Independent.co.uk	9.4	4.0
FT.com	7.1 (March 2008)	N/A
Mirror Group Digital	7.0	3.6

Figure 2.2   National newspaper website traffic (February 2009)

Source: ABCe

businesses by providing online, as well as offline, news. All news organizations now have a web presence (see Sparks, 2000 for an analysis of the original business rationale for turning to the internet) and an online audience that is generally much higher than their offline audience. In the case of national newspapers, this has particularly benefited the 'quality' press who largely dominate online news traffic (see figure 2.2). While the BBC continues to be by far the most popular online news source – with more than 13 million unique UK users visiting BBC News Online each *week* at the end of 2007 – even Sky News is able to punch above its offline weight with for example some 4.7 million users per month in March 2008 (*New Media Age*, 2008).

The internet therefore provides news organizations with a wonderful opportunity to engage new audiences in the hope that they may somehow compensate for declining ratings and advertising. The key, of course, is how, and indeed whether it is possible, to extract revenue from these new audiences – the topic of the next section. In any case, building and sustaining popular news websites requires both additional investment and some imagination. KPMG's Richard Bawden argues that companies cannot just use the web as an extension of their existing practices: 'They need to think about how their core service will be consumed in the future and not just replicate the production of their newspaper online and some got that completely wrong when they first started as online is a different product' (interview with the author). The *Guardian*'s hiring of 60 new journalists in 2007–8 to enhance its digital output recognizes the distinctiveness of online news and, judging by its huge online audience, appears to have been a highly successful strategy.

For some, this has led to re-thinking the focus of the brand itself: should they be a newspaper group or a news channel or a converged information and services provider? According to Peter Williams, building up DMGT's online profile required a whole new business strategy. In terms of his group's regional titles, his view is that 'we no longer own regional newspapers, we own regional media businesses, and their objective is to deliver the news, the information, the advertising, to their audience in whatever form both the advertiser and the consumer want to receive it' (interview with the author). The danger is that more short-sighted news organizations start to prioritize the development of new non-news services and new revenue streams at the expense of their core commitment to 'hard' news. This is a familiar characteristic of convergence where previously distinct media forms are 'integrated' in such a way as to maximize popular appeal and audience numbers with a resulting emphasis, in the case of news, on human interest stories, dramatic narratives, celebrity gossip and 'infotainment'. 'It expresses,' according to Schiller (2007: 115), 'the universalizing market ambition that has always suffused the corporate drive for convergence.'

There is a further problem in that this kind of restructuring has been forced on companies in the face of external pressure and, for many, in the context of the prospect of declining revenues. It is not, by and large, a strategy that they have willingly embraced and they are undertaking it in a climate which, as we have seen, is increasingly competitive and uncertain. The building of these cross-platform, 'integrated' news businesses presents, therefore, a fundamental challenge to many news organizations: 'somehow they must reinvent their professional and their business model at the same time they are cutting back on their reporting and resources' (PEJ, 2008: 1). This is the troubling context in which a new business model is being developed.

Features of an Online News Business Model

The central economic fact about online news is that users have shown a marked reluctance to pay for news content, partly because of a residual belief that all generalist online content should be free. The vast majority of online news is now freely available with only the *Financial Times'* FT.com able to retain a 100,000-strong subscription base because of its ability to provide targeted financial information from a trusted brand. This has not stopped online news sites from charging for more specialist content, for example, digital editions of newspapers, crosswords and games, and leading columnists. Herbert and Thurman (2007: 223) found that online newspapers 'are more likely to charge for content that is closely identified with the newspaper brand, rather than what is most popular' although they recognize that this is never likely to be a major source of revenue.

If news providers are not able meaningfully to charge for content, then they are even more keen to maximize the number of (especially domestic) users in order to extract increased revenue from their internet advertising. Much has been made of the huge growth in online advertising in recent years with a 38 per cent increase in the UK and a 26 per cent increase in the US in 2007 alone. Yet these figures are nowhere near enough to compensate for the decline in newspaper advertising revenue. According to Gavin O'Reilly, president of the World Association of Newspapers, online readers are far less valuable than print readers as they use online news in a 'haphazard and fragmented way' (quoted in *The Economist*, 2006), generally reading fewer pages and spending less time than they would with the print edition. As the *Financial Times* put it, 'the loss of a single print reader in terms of subscription and advertising has to be compensated with tens of online readers' (van Duyn, 2007). In the relatively mature US internet environment, online still only represented 7.5 per cent of total newspaper advertising revenue by the end of 2007 (NAA, 2008) while a web-savvy news organization like DMGT in the UK generated a similar proportion, of around 6 to 7 per cent, of its total advertising from online operations by mid-2008 (Williams, 2008). As Mort Zuckerman, chairman of the New York *Daily News* concluded to the House of Lords inquiry on news and ownership, the balance between online advertising and print advertising revenue is one of 'substituting pennies for dollars' (quoted in HoL, 2008a: 17).

A further reason why online advertising is an unreliable source of additional funds is that, for traditional news organizations, it is largely the wrong type of advertising. Display advertising, in which news incumbents generally have an advantage, amounts to only 21 per cent of the online share; classified, where incumbents are investing heavily to challenge pure-play internet sites, accounts for 20.8 per cent of the market; while search, 84 per cent of which is monopolized by Google in the UK (Efficient Frontier, 2008), dominates online advertising with 57.6 per cent of the total share (IAB, 2008). In other words, traditional news groups are strongest in one of the smallest sectors of the market and weakest in the main sector of online advertising. This is not a sound basis on which to compensate for declining revenues nor to seek additional funds for future investment in core services.

There is the added danger that by focusing on either acquiring or developing their own online classified sites, news groups run the risk of accelerating the decline of their own print classifieds and therefore cannibalizing existing (and precious) revenues. Herbert and Thurman report that the online newspaper managers they interviewed believed that their products were distinctive from their offline cousins and that, in general, cannibalization was not a major concern (2007: 213), a position countered by Gentzkow (2007) and Ala-Fossi (2008) who argue that print and online are substitutes, that the growth of the latter negatively impacts the former. Either way, there are dangers in over-emphasizing the value of online advertising for news operations. First, there is no evidence that online advertising will be immune from the economic cycles that afflict traditional advertising. This appears to be particularly true for the online classified and display ad sectors – where news organizations are well placed – that are more vulnerable to an economic downturn and less so for search advertising which, as we have seen, is an area dominated by Google and which, thus far, has 'proved more robust' (Waters, 2008). Second, despite claims by *Guardian* editor Alan Rusbridger that internet advertising is increasing by 50 per cent a year (quoted in HoL, 2008b: 43), its rate of growth in the UK is now *slowing*: from 66 per cent in 2005, 42 per cent in 2006, 38 per cent in 2007 to what was a predicted 27 per cent in 2008 and 20 per cent in 2009 (GroupM, 2008). The impact of recession is likely to see growth slowing even more than these figures suggest. Of course, these are still by far the highest growth rates in the sector (albeit starting from a very low base) but, as we have seen, the majority of this revenue will go not to existing news producers but to 'pure-play' internet advertisers and search engines.

The internet's great advantages – its low entry costs, interactivity and abundant capacity, all of which make possible a greater range and interaction of voices – are, in many ways, a problem for traditional news organizations. According to News Corporation's Peter Chernin, there is simply too much 'inventory' on the internet to justify high advertising rates. In order to be profitable, content companies will 'have to create category scarcity' (quoted in Olsen, 2008), precisely the opposite of what is held up as the democratic potential of the internet. The situation for existing news content providers is made worse by the fact that the online news environment is increasingly dominated by aggregators like Google News and Yahoo! News who use the openness of the internet to repurpose original content from a very restricted number of sources (see Paterson, 2005) without paying a penny. While the aggregators argue that, by linking to news content websites, they help to drive up traffic and increase revenues, others, like Paul Myners, former chair of the Guardian Media Group, feel 'that the current situation does not fairly represent the value the content providers bring to the search engines and the aggregators' (quoted in HoL, 2008b: 533). Moreover, the fact that one of the emblems of the 'new journalism', the influential US news aggregator, the Huffington Post, says that it has no plans to pay any of the thousands of bloggers who have made it the fifth-most linked-to blog on the internet, represents a real challenge to the professional livelihoods of journalists. Co-founder Ken Lerer insists that paying his contributors is simply 'not our financial model' (quoted in Graham, 2007).

For all the possibilities of vigorous debate and fresh perspectives, the business model of online journalism appears to be one in which audiences largely refuse to pay for content, advertising revenue is dominated by search engines and pure-play companies, cannibalization remains a concern (just as it does in the recorded music industry) and traffic goes more and more to internet portals and aggregators who invest virtually nothing in original news content and simultaneously fail to expand significantly the range of source material.

This is a very challenging environment for traditional news organizations so, perhaps not surprisingly, at the end of 2007 digital revenues for these businesses remained quite low: for example 3.7 per cent of Trinity Mirror's business (Trinity Mirror, 2008: 13) and 8.7 per cent of DMGT's national newspaper revenues (DMGT, 2008: 18). Of course these figures are set to rise over time – Merrill Lynch (2007: 12) estimates that this will rise to 20 per cent of DMGT's newspaper business by 2012 – but it is clear that the vast majority of the revenue of news incumbents will continue to flow from their 'traditional' businesses for some years yet. According to Peter Williams, DMGT's finance director:

> I think over the next three of four years, the online side will definitely still be in growth mode so we'll still be investing in it to find the best business model. You know, at the moment with the *Mail* sites, we are spending more than we are generating in revenue. We're losing money on them to generate audience and we have to generate revenue off the back of our [existing] audiences. It's chicken and egg: you've got to have the audience before you can get the revenue online. (Interview with the author)

The business model for online news, therefore, remains very much at an experimental stage (Ala-Fossi, 2008: 151; Herbert and Thurman, 2007: 223).

Conclusion: Apocalypse Postponed

Predictions about the 'end' of newspapers and the 'collapse' of network news in the light of the dramatic shift online of audiences and advertisers miss out on a number of important points. Captured by the 'drumbeat narrative' (Siklos, 2007) of the internet's triumphant rise to power, such predictions are ahistorical and partial and underplay some of the complexities of the environment in which news has long operated.

First, as Robert Picard points out (2002: 31), there is no single, fixed business model for newspapers but one that evolved from serving relatively small, elite audiences in the eighteenth and second half of the nineteenth centuries to a mass market model in the twentieth century. Under the pressure of competition and changing consumption patterns, it may well change again (and indeed return to something like its initial position) but there is no reason to think that the industry is not flexible enough to evolve and meet the demands of a changing society. Clearly, this is not the first 'crisis' confronting newspapers as they have had to deal, in previous years, with competition from newsreels, radio broadcasts and television bulletins. Indeed, faced with a constant series of challenges, newspapers, according to *Times* editor Robert Thomson, 'have been forced to adapt and evolve not only in the last three or four years but over the last 30 years' (quoted in HoL, 2008b: 50).

Moreover, the decline in circulation, so often attributed to competition from the internet, obviously predates the digital age. Circulation of national dailies peaked in 1951 – many years before the first web browser – with total sales of 16.62 million (Seymour-Ure, 1991: 16) while in 1950, just before the popularization of television, newspaper circulation per 1000 people stood at 573 before dropping to 332 in 1996 and to 289.75 in 2004 (Norris 2000: 77; UNESCO n.d.). By this measure, consumption of daily papers dropped by 42 per cent in the 'television age' (from 1950 to 1996) and by 12.7 per cent in the 'internet age' (from 1996 to 2004). The closure of local and regional titles that we have heard predicted as classified advertising moves online also pre-dates the internet age. The number of provincial morning papers in the UK declined by one-third between 1945 and 1990, mostly under the influence of chain ownership (Seymour-Ure, 1991: 43) while, according to Davies, 24 per cent of all local titles were killed off between 1986 and 1996 not because of the power of the internet but because 'the logic of pure commerce' (Davies, 2008: 65) dictated that they were not profitable enough. The point here is not to underestimate the rapid pace of decline in recent years but to emphasize that the decline itself is not new and cannot be explained by sole reference to the internet.

A more profound reason for declining advertising revenues at the time of writing may well be the experience of an economic downturn which has already cut into the crucial advertising sectors of property, auto sales and recruitment. Of course, this is not the first time that advertising revenue has slumped: in both 1991 and 2001, news organizations were badly affected by a substantial decline in advertising only for revenues to pick up in the following years. The question this time concerns the extent to which news organizations are facing a cyclical or a structural challenge to their position as valuable carriers of advertising: whether revenues will return after the 'credit crunch' or whether a proportion of advertising will be lost forever to online competitors.

Some of the signs are favourable. There is still a very healthy appetite for news and while much is made of the internet's transformation of the news environment, only 6 per cent of the UK population identify the internet as their main source of news in contrast to 65 per cent who opt for television and 15 per cent for newspapers (Ofcom, 2007b: 17). This is a figure that Ofcom's chief executive Ed Richards does not expect to rise significantly: 'I am sure that it will change a little more over time, but I think that the finding about the significance of television news compared to the supplementary role ... that the internet is playing, we may see as a resilient finding in the years to come' (quoted in HoL, 2008b: 192). More up-to-date research amongst 16 to 24-year-olds, the demographic of most concern to existing news providers, confirms this supplementary role: only 3 per cent turn to the internet as their main source of news about the UK in contrast to 14 per cent who said newspapers and 45 per cent television (and 17 per cent who declared no interest in the question) (Ofcom, 2008b: 30).

News organizations are not therefore about to lose entire swathes of readers and viewers as long as they continue to invest in original journalism and look for ways to make themselves relevant to audiences. This is certainly true for television which remains a crucial medium for delivering mass audiences to advertisers and where news consumption is less likely to be cannibalized by online news. It also remains true for newspapers, described by KPMG's Richard Bawden as 'still generally profitable cash generators' (interview with the author) – a claim supported by the profit margins in 2007 of, for example, 19.3 per cent for Trinity Mirror's national titles, 15.9 per cent for the Guardian Media Group's regional titles and 21 per cent for DMGT's regional titles. According to the NUJ's general secretary Jeremy Dear, 'overall the industry is still hugely profitable ... If you took almost any other industry and said, "well, you're only going to be able to make a 20 per cent profit return next year", most industries would snap your hand off at the prospect of making 10 per cent' (interview with the author).

However, the news industry is, by and large, not a normal industry. True: it is just as keen as any other on making profits, reducing costs, and operating as 'efficiently' as possible. But it is also the case that the UK's most popular news website and television bulletin is backed by a public service mandate and paid for out of the BBC licence fee; that Sky News has long been supported by the profits made by sports subscriptions at BSkyB; that the *Guardian's* far-sighted investments in digital have been made possible by its unusual ownership status; and that many other print titles have been supported through loss-making times by wealthy proprietors eager for political influence. *Guardian* editor Alan Rusbridger touched on something significant when he testified before the House of Lords Communications Committee that the 'truth about our market is that, with the exception of the *Daily Telegraph*, we all exist on some form of subsidy, so you are not talking economic businesses' (quoted in HoL, 2008b: 43). Those who argue that, in an increasingly competitive climate, there is no economic rationale for regional television news or money for investigative reporting or resources to justify a particular foreign bureau, forget – or choose to ignore the fact – that the news industry has always been subject to multiple forms of financial, political and regulatory intervention. It is, then, especially important to confront arguments for cost-cutting based on the 'economic realities' and 'business imperatives' of such an imperfect market.

This is all the more vital because the internet does present a genuine, if over-hyped, challenge to the business operations of traditional news organizations. It *has* siphoned off significant amounts of advertising revenue, facilitated the emergence of competitors who do not have to worry about actually paying anyone to produce original news content, and forced news incumbents to think about their relationship with their audiences. The danger is, however, that by uncritically accepting arguments about the 'irrepressible' rise of the internet, existing news providers may feel justified in making editorial cuts, shifting their investments into more commercial and non-news areas and diluting their prime source of value: their ability to act as 'the trusted advisor to which people turn to gain orientation, reflection and, direction' (Picard, 2006: 135).

The internet has the potential to expand the diversity of news sources, to improve the quality and breadth of news coverage, and to deepen the interaction between news providers and their audiences. Yet, given today's harsh economic circumstances, the internet has instead contributed to a possibility that the news of the future is going to be sustained by a declining number of specialist news organizations, a growing band of generalist news and information businesses, and a handful of parasitical aggregators supplemented by an army of contributors working for free. Market logic, in this scenario, is set to prevail over news logic. However, the problem, as the NUJ's Jeremy Dear rightly points out, 'is not the technology, it's not the platform, it's not even citizen journalism or blogging or any of these things that are supposedly the threat to journalism. The threat to journalism is under-investment and that's the same across all platforms' (interview with the author). There are no short cuts: the future of news, as other chapters in this volume will show, depends on imagination and independence but, above all, on investment – in technology, in resources and, especially, in journalists themselves.

Chapter Three

······································

An Ethical Deficit? Accountability, Norms, and the Material Conditions of Contemporary Journalism

Angela Phillips, Nick Couldry, Des Freedman

Introduction

Whether we debate them or not, news media raise ethical questions. Since an important claim made for journalism is that it contributes, in an essential way, to the working of democracy, its ethics connect to questions of democratic functioning. But what if the conditions, analysed in this book, under which journalism is now practised, are inimical to ethical action? What are the wider implications for journalism, democracy, and for attempts to regulate journalism within the democratic process?

This chapter is in three parts. The first part offers, as a reference point for what follows, one version of the basic principles of media ethics, drawing in particular on the neo-Aristotelian ethical tradition. The second part reviews evidence from journalists working on newspapers for what it tells us about the conditions of ethical action among journalists in the UK. The third and concluding part considers the implications of the earlier discussion for the responsibilities and limitations of current processes of media regulation.

Some Ethical Reference Points

Media ethics is a large and growing area going beyond the detailed, 'technical' literature on journalistic codes of ethics regularly taught on journalism practice courses. By considering the wider philosophical options for grounding an account of how we might expect media to act, we aim to consider the potential *gap* between one relatively uncontroversial set of ethical expectations which could be made of journalists and their actual conditions of practice.

The literature offers various options for formulating principles of such a broader media ethics (Kantian, contractualist, Christian humanist, neo-Aristotelian).[1] We will take as our reference point a neo-Aristotelian approach, not because it is necessarily better, but because it is an approach with which we are familiar and which is distinguished by an emphasis on considering the values internal to particular practices, rather than abstract, universal obligations. Another important advantage of the neo-Aristotelian ethical tradition, generally and for our particular purpose, lies in the simplicity of the questions it asks. Two questions are fundamental:

1. How should I live?
2. How should each of us conduct our life so that it is a life any of us should live?

Question one is the question reputedly posed by Socrates in ancient Athens. From questions one and two a further question automatically follows:

3. How we should live *together* (since if we live, we have no choice but to attempt to live together drawing on shared resources)?

Note that in this further question no assumption is made about the 'community' (if any) to which questioner and respondent belong: they could be any two individuals anywhere. A specific media-related question can easily be developed:

4. How should any of us (whether media professionals or not) act in relation to media and available media resources, so that media processes contribute to lives that, both individually and together, we should live?

The wager of neo-Aristotelian approaches is that there are enough agreed-upon factual conditions – about human life in general and about particular practices such as medicine or journalism – to give substance to such general starting questions. A neo-Aristotelian approach also goes further and asks what type of a person would we need to be – and what type of dispositions, habits and capacities (that is, 'virtues') would we need to have – in order to act well in relation to media? One advantage claimed for the neo-Aristotelian approach is that, without claiming to prejudge what should be done in particular situations, it asks the broader and more manageable question: what type of dispositions do journalists need to have in order to act well (and make good decisions) in particular situations?

Let us start, apparently 'naively', by specifying what the virtues of someone working in the news media might be.[2] We suggest that the news media constitute a 'practice' in philosopher Alisdair MacIntyre's sense (1981: 175), that is, a coherent and complex form of cooperative human activity whose internal goods involve distinctive standards of excellence. Journalism is a practice with very general implications: it *matters* to how humans flourish overall in an era where we are dependent on the exchange of vast amounts of socially relevant information. Two aspects of journalism as a practice are crucial here. The first involves the circulation of information that contributes to the successful individual and collective life of a territory. The second aspect is more complex and raises the issue of plurality: we need news media that, by the circulation of facts but also by providing opportunities for the expression of opinion and voice, help us sustain a successful, indeed peaceful, life together – in spite of our conflicting values, interests and understandings. In other words, we need media that give us the information required to organize our lives and that, at the same time, allow us to feel we have a stake in the territory for which media speak. The latter point is of course particularly complex as media increasingly address, unwittingly or not, multiple territories, local, national and global.

From here, we can specify three journalism-related virtues. For the first two, we can turn to the philosopher Bernard Williams' book *Truth and Truthfulness* (Williams, 2002). In a complex argument, Williams suggests two basic 'virtues of truth' or truthfulness (2002: 44): *accuracy* and *sincerity*. The subtlety of Williams' argument lies in his insisting on the non-negotiable importance of these virtues for all human social life, while rejecting any assumption that particular embodiments and articulations of those virtues have an absolute and obligatory status for all historical periods. It has never, Williams argues, been enough for people to *pretend* to care about telling the truth, since if that was all they did, no one would ever have a stable basis for trusting them to tell the truth. It is only if truth-telling is stabilized *as a virtue* – a disposition that humans can rely upon – that truth-telling contributes to the good collective life. Since journalism is a practice which is directed towards the circulation of necessary information, it is plausible to see the two truth-related virtues (accuracy and sincerity) as applying to anyone practising journalism. Accuracy is the disposition to take the necessary care to ensure so far as possible that what one says is not false, sincerity is the disposition to make sure that what one says is what one actually believes.

Accuracy and sincerity would be plausible virtues whatever media we were discussing, and on whatever scale they acted. But there is a third possible virtue of particular relevance as media messages increasingly address multiple territories at once: *hospitality*.[3] Hospitality, first argued for in detail by Roger Silverstone – who calls it 'the first virtue of the mediapolis' (Silverstone, 2006: 136) – considers the role of media in sustaining a common space where diverse groups, who may differ radically in identity, religion, historical interests and values, can be recognised as social and moral agents. There are various ways of approaching this idea, for example through a theory of justice, a theory of rights, or through a theory of the disposition, or virtue, we need from the journalists who represent us and others in an unstable, intensely interconnected world. Once again, we are not concerned here with the philosophical debates to which the idea of media 'hospitality' gives rise.[4] Our point is merely that *the news media's need to take account of how what they do affects the conditions for dialogue between cultures and peoples is a necessary part of any media ethics.*

So to sum up this first stage of our argument, there are broad, relatively uncontroversial reasons for arguing that an 'ethical media practice' would be characterized by three virtues: accuracy, sincerity and hospitality. While most neo-Aristotelian approaches to ethics to date have concentrated on the virtues of individuals, this cannot be sufficient when thinking about a practice such as journalism that, while it involves individual initiative, is unthinkable without considerable institutional resources. The issue then arises: how well do the conditions under which individual journalists work match the conditions needed to enable them to acquire and sustain the disposition to act ethically? If the match is small, non-existent or unstable in today's digital age, what are the implications for media ethics and media's accountability within democracy?

The View from Contemporary News Practice

For Foucault, ethical behaviour as a 'practice of freedom' depends on power relationships:

> [O]ne sometimes encounters what may be called situations or states of domination in which the power relations, instead of being mobile, allowing the various participants to adopt strategies modifying them, remain blocked, frozen. [...] In such a state it is certain that practices of freedom do not exist or exist only

unilaterally or are extremely constrained and limited. (Foucault, 1984, cited in Rabinow, 1994: 285)

The question one must ask then is how power relationships operate within news media, the degree to which individuals are 'dominated' or free, whether the environment of the internet increases or decreases that freedom for individual journalists and the consequences of this for ethical behaviour. Here Bourdieu has some useful insights. He suggests that journalism is a 'weakly autonomous field' (Bourdieu, 2005: 41) in which freedom of action depends on where a journalist is located within a particular field. Bourdieu's concept of autonomy depends on an understanding of power held in tension between economic and cultural capital. In the field of journalism, the requirements of economic capital involve circulation, advertising revenue and marketing, whereas cultural capital is usually tied to the production of original stories, uncovering scandal or dishonesty, or influencing the social and political agenda. Sometimes these two forms of capital reinforce one another: an original story can push up circulation and therefore strengthen economic capital. However the imperative in mass circulation, popular news media to sell as many copies as possible, or to attract as many 'hits' as possible, tends to weaken the cultural in relation to the requirements of the economic.

The British Journalism Field

In the peculiarly hierarchical and chronically insecure atmosphere of a British national newspaper, nobody, from the editor down, has the kind of security of employment enjoyed, for example, by most academics. According to Andrew Marr, former editor of the *Independent* newspaper: 'The truth is that, except for editors who are highly influential in trusts or companies owning their titles, editors are hirelings. Proprietors regard their editors as talented and interesting servants ... The newspaper editor gets status and the apparent respect of the social elite of modern London, but the proprietor gets what he wants' (Marr, 2004: 235).

This insecurity is transferred down through the staff and, as Bourdieu observes, 'precarity of employment is a loss of liberty, through which censorship [...] can be more easily expressed' (Bourdieu, 2005: 43). Young reporters, even on the most liberal newspapers, are under the thumb of the news desk. Although they accrue cultural capital (status) through finding their own stories, their first loyalty must always be to 'the desk' (see Phillips, this volume). On the more serious newspapers this means prioritizing the stories you are told to report rather than your own leads. On 'popular' newspapers junior reporters are not just told what to report but how to report it. The editors come up with the storylines while the reporters merely colour them in. One young reporter on a highly commercial newspaper explained how she chose who to interview:

> They want attractive people in the paper, they want blondes, they want nice-looking girls: the younger the better. You know that's what they want so that's what you get because otherwise you'll either be in for a shouting at or you'll have to do it again. (Reporter, popular evening paper, 2003)

The practice of hiring young journalists on very short-term, often weekly, rolling contracts is like keeping a dog on a very short leash. Each time they move in the wrong direction they can be restrained so that, in the end, in order to gain a measure of employment protection, journalists are expected to 'internalize' the requirements of the newsroom and produce news according to the style and political inflection of the newspaper. On popular newspapers there is little or no space for independent ethical reflection.

Another reporter described a story he was asked to do shortly after joining a mass circulation national newspaper:

> I thought the story was appalling. I thought all along that it was a ludicrous exercise with no logic whatsoever and I felt very ashamed about it [...] I talked to a senior reporter and said that I wasn't very happy about it and he said to keep my head down and say nothing. [...] He said that I would lose my job if I raised it with anybody more senior than him. [...] I set about planning to leave. I'd just arrived so I knew I couldn't leave straight away [...] I kept my head down, I worked hard, I knew it would be at least a year before I could go. I was in a position the same as everybody who joins the [paper] from a local newspaper in that I was doing shifts on a daily basis. And it was up to them to decide whether to renew my job the next day. So if I lost my job I wouldn't be able to pay the rent or anything like that which probably isn't an excuse but there was still that thought there. (Reporter, mid-market popular daily, 2003)

A journalist working on the same newspaper, five years later, described a very similar crisis of conscience. He had been sent out to interview an allegedly 'feckless' family. Finding them charming and friendly, he tried to persuade the news editor that there simply wasn't a story. He failed. The story went in with his name on it and he spent the next few weeks avoiding phone calls from the family because he felt 'so bad'. He has only once been allowed to refuse to write a story, but only because he pointed out that it directly affected him and his family.

Of course, it would be wrong to suggest that the conditions for acting ethically are equally compromised in all news media and under all conditions. 'Cultural capital remains on the side of the "purest" journalists' (Bourdieu, 2005: 42) and even at the more commercial end of the field, over time, a reporter who stays the course or, alternatively, manages to move fairly frequently between news organizations, will build up a degree of respect, and therefore autonomy.

> I've got to the stage where I can bully desks a bit. I've been around a long time. It may not pertain forever, but I don't tend to worry about what the next job's going to be, I assume there will be one. (Reporter, popular evening paper, 2003)

As an imported 'star' reporter, with a string of 'exclusives' under his belt, he felt secure enough to refuse stories that seemed ethically dubious. However, job security is conditional. On most British newspapers changes of editor are frequent and often involve changes in specialist staff. One very experienced reporter explained that he knew he was on the way out when the news editor refused to publish a leaked, exclusive story which, when it did get released, hit the front page of every other paper. The editor was prepared to let the story go rather than allow a reporter who was out of favour get the credit for it.

When freedom is so heavily constrained, just how easy is it for journalists to act with 'accuracy, sincerity and hospitality'? It is to these three 'virtues' that we now turn with examples drawn from our research interviews.

Accuracy, Sincerity and Hospitality

All British newspapers are signed up to the Press Complaints Commission's (PCC) voluntary code of conduct whose first clause insists that: 'The Press must take care not to publish inaccurate, misleading or distorted information, including pictures' (PCC, 2008). A journalist explains how the sincerity of a story can be sacrificed while still retaining a fig leaf of 'truth':

> It isn't [that it's] untrue. It is giving prominence to a minor feature. There has to be some kernel of truth. It may be twisted or biased but there must be some truth. [The paper] works on the presumption that negative news sells – always go for the negative line even if it isn't typical. There is nothing untrue but

it isn't a balanced representation. It's been twisted to conform to an idea [...] if you leave ethics out, it's good professional journalism and it sells papers. (Reporter, mid-market popular daily, 2008)

Personally however, he recognizes that 'it's corrosive: people think crime is going up when it's going down. People think the NHS [National Health Service] is getting worse but in polls it's getting better.'

As we argued earlier, in an increasingly globalized and mediatized world, the question of how people live together is of overwhelming importance and the concept of 'hospitality' provides a useful ethical yardstick. Silverstone argued that the 'conditional hospitality' which allows space and a voice to the stranger in our midst, should be based upon '[i]ndividual responsibility which journalists everywhere have to take for their judgements and their actions' (2006: 141). But as we have already seen, individual journalists are not necessarily free to take responsibility for their actions. It is only when they band together that they are able to exercise influence, although this is often limited in comparison to the power of proprietors and editors. At the *Daily Express* (a British national tabloid newspaper) a string of anti-gypsy articles appeared in the paper in the run-up to the enlargement of the European Union. One day the newspaper ran a telephone poll asking: 'Should we let gypsies invade Britain?' Later that week it ran a story suggesting that a 'massive invasion' of gypsies would lead to 'economic disaster'. Journalists on the paper had, by now, had enough and called a well-attended union meeting that passed the following motion:

> This chapel [union branch] is concerned that *Express* journalists are coming under pressure to write anti-gypsy articles. We call for a letter to be sent to the Press Complaints Commission reminding it of the need to protect journalists who are unwilling to write racist articles which are contrary to the National Union of Journalists' code of conduct. (Ponsford, 2004)

The letter was duly sent to the PCC, the regulatory body established to offer protection to people who are abused by the press. It does not, however, offer similar protection to journalists who are put under pressure to be abusive. Robert Pinker, then acting chairman of the PCC, defending this position at the National Union of Journalists (NUJ) conference, said: 'It is not our job to be involved in disputes between employers and staff.' He also suggested that such a clause would affect sales by making newspapers 'so sanitised that people will not want to read them' (Pinker, 2004). If, however, a leading regulatory body, on the face of it responsible for upholding standards of truthfulness (a part of ethics), does not see it as its 'job' to defend the conditions under which ethical practice is possible, then its actual contribution to media ethics is rather tenuous. Consider, for example, if a medical ethics committee claimed that the instructions given to surgeons by hospital managers were outside its remit!

Ethics in the Internet Age

The examples above are all taken from mass market, popular newspapers. For those newspapers operating at the more commercial end of the field, the evidence from our own research suggests that the autonomy and authority of individual journalists has very little pull in comparison with the requirements of economic capital. These newspapers depend on a degree of sensationalism to attract readers in an intensely competitive environment. Serious newspapers also need to sell copies and advertising in order to survive but their object has always been also to accrue cultural and symbolic capital which in turn depends on serious and authoritative reporting. There is some evidence, from interviews carried out in the course of this research, that the commercial requirements of the internet, and the need to find new, younger and 'net savvy' readers, may be pulling the more serious newspapers towards the more commercial end of the field. This is a development that is likely further to undermine the autonomy of individual journalists and therefore their ability to act ethically.

As news goes online, journalists are encouraged to find ways of attracting readers via Google's search engine because advertising rates are, increasingly, being linked to the number of 'hits' received. *Private Eye*, the satirical magazine, explains how it works on the *Daily Telegraph*:

> News hacks are now sent a memo three or four times a day from the website boffins listing the top subjects being searched in the last few hours on Google. They are then expected to write stories accordingly and/or get as many of those key words into the first paragraph of their story. Hence, if the top stories being Googled are 'Britney Spears' and 'breast cancer', hey presto, the hack is duly expected to file a piece about young women 'such as Britney Spears' being at risk from breast cancer. (*Private Eye*, 11th July 2008: 4)

Newspapers cannot avoid the logic of Google but, depending on the place they occupy in the field, they have to balance the short-term commercial gains of 'hits', against the possible long-term loss of cultural capital if they are seen as too 'sensational' or too 'popular' for their core audience. As Anne Spackman of *The Times* explains: 'If I want to play the traffic tart game, there are certain things that we could write about all the time, like Britney Spears. But that's not really what *The Times* is for' (cited in Stabe, 2008). The concern for journalists working on these 'serious' titles is that managements trying to attract passing reader traffic via Google will start to lose sight of the audiences they already have and forget what they are really for.

The following example concerns an experienced, specialist correspondent and a newspaper which is generally considered to be a serious, national daily with a well-earned reputation for thorough and straightforward reporting. Reflecting on past working conditions, one reporter explained: 'Okay, they had a few issues which they were particularly interested in, which they always wanted you to write in certain ways [...] but apart from that, they just wanted you to write it the way you saw it'. Where previously specialists had been pretty much in charge of editorial decisions in their field of expertise, now, a new layer of management is pulling the newspaper in a more commercial direction, and the news desk takes the lead in deciding which stories should be covered and how.

> Well, when all this, when this pressure started happening, I just had daily fights with them. I'd stand at the news desk and go; 'but why do you want me to run it, it's not true' [...] You could actually see the veins in their neck kind of wobbling and they were going purple [...] But now, I just say 'yeah, fine, 600 words by 2 o'clock' and, you know, so what, I mean, you know. They don't care whether it's true or not. They literally do not. (Reporter, national daily, 2008)

This journalist was faced with a personal ethical dilemma. Should he collude with the popularizing agenda of the newspaper and publish stories that were amusing, or alarming, even if he considered them to be untrue? He had tried negotiating, then arguing, and now the only course left was either to do what they wanted, or walk out. Either way the management of that particular newspaper will have accrued greater power at the expense of individual journalists – not the ideal conditions in which to act ethically.

The stories the news desk demanded were not about individuals. No one was directly damaged, no one could sue, or could take a case to the Press Complaints Commission. Of course other experts in the field would know that the stories were not soundly based but the newspaper-reading public would probably be none the wiser and the stories were funny or sensational and attracted plenty of 'hits'. In the short term it is the journalist who has most to lose from this sort of ethical dilemma because he or she is faced with nothing short of the corruption of personal moral standards, but in the long term, news journalism as a whole suffers if lower standards of accuracy are normalized. The story told above was an individual case, on an individual newspaper, but it has implications for standards of behaviour elsewhere and implications for all news media. Journalists depend for their position in society on the trust of their readers/viewers/users and central to that trust must be the assumption that a serious and respected newspaper will attempt 'with sincerity' to be truthful.

Sincerity and Transparency

If sincerity means anything, it surely means openness. The prominent Kantian philosopher and 2002 BBC Reith Lecturer Onora O'Neill makes a related point about transparency (O'Neill, 2002: 95):

> If powerful institutions are allowed to publish, circulate and promote material without indicating what is known and what is rumour, what is derived from a reputable source and what is invented, what is standard analysis and what is speculation, which sources may be knowledgeable and which are probably not, they damage our public culture and all our lives.

Journalists do get things wrong. The test of sincerity is the effort aimed at achieving some fit between what one believes and what one says and making an effort to correct wrongs. Theoretically, the growing use of by-lines alongside email addresses and comment spaces online, should improve transparency and make journalists more careful about accuracy. This opening up of an exchange between writers and readers could be a positive and democratizing step but what does accountability mean in a world in which work that is produced under one name might have been written by three other people? A reporter explained how a randomly chosen story was put together:

Reporter: My story would have only been 250 words. They must have added to that, they must have then cut and paste with that.

Interviewer: So basically this story is pasted together: something that the newspaper had picked up from the *Sun* with bits from PA and then stitched together with yesterday's story?

Reporter: Yeah, I think so, that looks like what's happened, yeah.

Interviewer: And yet it's gone under your single by-line. I mean what is the by-line policy?

Reporter: They don't have policies. I think this is an old-fashioned view of the world.

Interviewer: So why do they bother to put names on at all?

Reporter: I don't know. I think because they just think that it looks
more authoritative with a name. I think they don't care,
that's the problem. They don't care so your name's
sometimes on it, someone else's name's sometimes on it.
(Reporter, national daily, 2008)

The production cycle of newspapers means that journalists rarely know
exactly how their work will look on the page. Sub-editors routinely rewrite copy, perhaps because a bigger story has broken and everything
has to be cut to accommodate it, or because several different people are
working on the same story, or because it doesn't read well or follow the
right style. What is new is that with the speed-up of work on the internet,
and the need for several daily deadlines, new material is routinely being
added to a story without any change of the original by-line (see Phillips,
this volume) and the 'cobbled together' results are ending up online and
in the newspaper. As one journalist put it:

I mean they add stuff in [...]. We'll get the paper the next day and
there's big chunks of stuff that have been shoved in from the
internet [...]; and they [other specialist reporters] are pulling their
hair out going 'well that's not true and it's got my name on it'.
(Reporter, national daily, 2008)

On the internet, where everything is accessible and checkable,
journalism could be moving towards a greater accountability. Kevin
Marsh, editor-in-chief of the BBC College of Journalism, looks to a future
in which journalism is all about '[g]athering data and helping each
individual in the audience mine it for a unique take' (Marsh, 2008: 33).
Alan Rusbridger, editor of the *Guardian*, appears to be moving his
newspaper in this direction: subject specialists will in future be allowed
to publish directly to the web without going through a news editor
(Smith, 2008), a move which will also make them directly responsible,
and therefore accountable, for their own ethical judgements.

However this view of the future of journalism does not quite square
with a present in which, according to research from Cardiff University
(Davies, 2008: 74) some 30 per cent of news stories in the five 'most
prestigious' national newspapers are unattributed rewrites of Press
Association stories in which there is little possibility of audiences being
able to 'mine' the original data because they have no idea where it comes
from. There is nothing necessarily wrong with the increased use of Press
Association copy, given the amount of space that newspapers now have
to fill each day. What is dubious, from an ethical point of view, is the
practice of using it without attribution. If individual journalists have no

ownership of what goes out under their name, and no obligation to attribute work taken directly from other journalists; if there are few practical means of ensuring a fit between what they individually believe and what they 'say' (or at least their institutions require them to say), it is hard to see how they can act with sincerity in their attempts to be accurate.

Conclusion: Ethics, Democracy and Regulation

In our introduction we asked what resources and working conditions journalists require if they are to have the opportunity to act with accuracy, sincerity and hospitality. It is clear from the evidence that, for many journalists those conditions do not exist. In the past, those who chose to work for 'serious' news organizations, could depend on regulation (in the broadcast sector) or the desire of their own proprietors to accrue cultural capital, as some form of protection for ethical action. On the basis of our research, as newspapers and broadcasters move online, and at a time when many of the old commercial certainties are being undermined, the already limited autonomy of journalists and their freedom to act ethically is in danger of being further eroded. If this happens then we can expect an accelerating loss of trust in the news media as a means by which people can inform themselves 'as citizens' (O'Neill, 2002) and a commensurate loss of cultural and symbolic capital for news organizations.

Clearly action is required but who should take the lead? Governments have been prepared to formulate policy on questions of media ownership and mergers, on intellectual property rights and freedom of information, but they have been extremely reluctant to press for formal regulation of media content, especially in relation to news:

> The Government strongly believes that a free press is vital to the health of our democracy. There should be no laws that specifically seek to restrict that freedom and Government should not seek to intervene in any way in what a newspaper or magazine chooses to publish. (DCMS, 2003: 1)

News content regulation has been limited to insisting that public service broadcasters carry prime-time news bulletins that should be free of the political partisanship that characterizes the British newspaper market. Other than that, the pursuit of accurate, sincere and hospitable reporting has been devolved to the voluntary code of the Press Complaints Commission and, above all, news organizations themselves.

The preferred mode of liberal democratic policy behaviour in relation to content issues is, therefore, not statutory control (with its implications of 'Big Brother' oversight) but *self*-regulation where industries work under the guidance of codes drawn up and monitored by members of those industries in a way that is designed to be less top-down and more 'flexible' than traditional governmental intervention. Self-regulation, according to its supporters, is the 'least worst' system of regulation in a democratic environment, as a senior official at the PCC explains:

> Self-regulation [has] got all kinds of rough edges, all kinds of ways it can be made to work better, but if you consider the alternatives which are either some kind of regulation by the state [...] or regulation through statute, politicians or judges, I think that all those outcomes would be worse than self-regulation. (Interview)

It is fairly obvious why the industries themselves should favour self-regulation. Voluntary compliance with the codes and the breaking of the rules often leads to negligible penalties. Consider the case of the PCC's regulation of the UK newspaper industry where the '[h]ounding of asylum seekers and trial by media [...] have shown how ugly the power of the press can be' (Riddell, 2003). One would expect in these circumstances frequent condemnations by the regulator of the excesses of the tabloid press in particular. However, a study of the first ten years of the PCC (Frost, 2004) showed that, out of more than 20,000 complaints it received between 1991 and 2001, it adjudicated on only 707 and upheld a mere 321, just over 1.5 per cent of the total. Although many complaints were made about the reporting of refugees and 'bogus asylum seekers', not a single one was upheld – indeed, just six discrimination complaints were upheld in those ten years (Frost, 2004: 113). Partly, this is because the PCC does not allow third-party complaints and partly it is because 'robust' language (even if offensive to some) is entirely acceptable; partly, however, it is because the PCC is a creature of the industry it seeks to regulate so that the chair of its code committee, for example, was for a long time the chairman of News International, publisher of the *Sun* and the *News of the World*, amongst other papers.

Even where it does uphold a complaint, the PCC has no power to fine newspapers for breaches of its code or to insist on a right to reply or a prominent correction or indeed to punish illegal or unethical behaviour on the part of journalists. When Clive Goodman, the royal correspondent for the *News of the World* was jailed in January 2007 for four months for illegally intercepting the voicemail of royal aides on nearly 500 occasions and for paying a private investigator more than £100,000 to unearth more material about the royal family, it was not the PCC but general laws on phone-tapping that undid him. Self-regulation is designed less to prevent press misdemeanours or to tackle the offenders than it is to deflect the threat of statutory controls. As John Whittingdale, the chairman of the Parliamentary Select Committee on the media, put it when reflecting on the case: 'I am a strong supporter of self-regulation but even I can only support it *if it is seen to be effective*' (quoted in Gibson, 2007: 1 – emphasis added). Self-regulation, then, is less effective in securing ethical and responsible media content than it is in protecting media industries from more formal systems of government intrusion.

The British government remains committed to a system of press self-regulation, accepting the liberal narrative that, as the current chairman of the PCC puts it (Meyer, 2006: 32), 'regulation by the State or Brussels [home of the European Commission] or some combination of the two would mark the beginning of the end of a freedom painfully acquired over the centuries.' The government rejected proposals in 2003 by the media Select Committee to introduce privacy legislation on the basis of the government's 'support for self-regulation as the best possible form for regulation of the press' (DCMS, 2003: 11) and the most effective way of balancing rights to privacy and freedom of expression. It could afford to do so because privacy legislation has effectively been brought in via European Law. Yet there is also a more pragmatic reason for a government's refusal to curb an industry that spends much of its time attacking the record of that government: it dares not alienate powerful newspaper proprietors whose support it will seek, particularly at election time. According to a former national newspaper editor, despite plenty of provocations, 'at every stage, confronted with cause for action, our masters [in government] have sidled away [from pressing for regulation]. They have looked at what could, in practice, be done. They have recoiled from doing it' (Preston, 2001: 16).

Indeed the government is determined to spread self-regulation into other areas of the media and to develop new instruments of 'co-regulation' whereby regulators and industries work in partnership to devise rules and supervise conduct. Ofcom, the regulator charged with monitoring commercial broadcast news, interprets the government's order to explore more self-regulation in a way that draws less on free speech principles than it does on giving more power to industry and identifies self-regulation quite explicitly with the possibility of rolling back state intervention:

> Ofcom's overarching principle to seek the least intrusive regulatory mechanisms to achieve its policy objectives, enables the regulator to step back from direct statutory control in some areas of its work,

placing greater reliance upon industry to take more responsibility for its actions. (Ofcom, 2004b)

This understanding of self-regulation dovetails quite neatly with the neo-liberal language of smaller government, market discipline and individual choice. Self-regulation can be seen as a form of policy conduct that embodies a more responsible and mature approach to governance but it can also be seen as a sub-contracting of power – and ethical responsibility – to private industries that are committed to putting their own narrowly commercial interests ahead of their responsibility to the public and are reluctant to provide any ethical protection to individual journalists. The evidence provided in the previous section demonstrates that individual journalists, far from being encouraged to act within both the letter and spirit of the PCC code, often find themselves under pressure from their employers to ignore it. If the employers really believed that self-regulation was workable and desirable, they would devolve the power to make choices about what is and is not responsible journalism to those on the 'front line' producing the news. The fact that they are unwilling to do this and, indeed, that the former chair of the PCC specifically ruled this out as a possibility, demonstrates a significant lack of faith in the concept of effective self-regulation.

Perhaps the most disturbing feature of the trend towards self-regulation is that once the principle of public supervision of the airwaves and print channels is undermined, it becomes harder to justify *any* system of regulation. Sir Christopher Meyer, chairman of the PCC, argues that statutory regulation is, by its very nature, incompatible with a modern democracy and predicts that 'one of these days the State will get out of the business of regulating content on television and radio; and that an expanded system of self-regulation will cover all forms of content delivery' (2006: 32). This assertion is given further impetus by the rapid development of the internet as a media platform whose content is exempt from many regulatory provisions. A clear distinction has now been made between material that is generally disseminated and that which is 'sought out', in other words between linear and non-linear, 'push' and 'pull' technologies. Representatives of the latter industries (ISPs, online content producers and advertisers) are calling for modest self-regulatory structures in order to stimulate innovation and creativity and to maintain the 'diversity' of the online world.

This perception of statutory regulation as 'stifling' and 'burdensome' and the equation of innovation with the freedom to manoeuvre in the market without regulatory impediments is becoming increasingly dominant in media policy debates. With the development of web TV, personal video recorders and online news, regulators are re-evaluating their approach to content regulation and shifting responsibility for content not just on to the industry but on to audiences themselves. According to a highly experienced regulator, formerly at Ofcom:

> A single regulatory body can't operate by *diktat* any more so there should be an emphasis on seeking self- and co-regulatory decisions because if we get a situation where there are many people viewing content that is falling completely out of Ofcom control, then you've got to try and look to the content providers to start shouldering some of the responsibility for the nature of that content. [...] [But] I actually think that the general public are going to have to become more savvy about the nature of content delivery and take more responsibility for themselves and their families, just as they do with choosing a nursery school and all the rest of it.

Self-regulation outsources ethical practice either to individual users who have little power to influence media content (except through their 'market power') or, overwhelmingly, to institutions who, because of competition and economic uncertainty, show little willingness to provide the space and resources to journalists to act ethically. The internet, far from expanding mechanisms of accountability and responsibility, is instead being used as a justification for minimizing regulation and for moving the burden to report ethically from a public duty to one of corporate self-interest and private reflection.

Endnotes

1. See for example Christians et al. (1993), Couldry (2006), Silverstone (2006), Ward (2005).
2. It is clear from the account of the changing dynamics of the media process given throughout this book that such ethical questions apply to *anyone* who now contributes to the media process, whether as source, as non-professional producer, as website poster, and so on. For more detailed accounts of these and related issues, see Couldry (2006) and Couldry (2008).
3. See Kant (1983), Ricoeur (2007), Silverstone (2006).
4. See Dayan (2007), but note that Dayan's concerns may be addressed by an account of 'hospitality' that builds less from Silverstone's territorial notion than from Ricoeur's idea of 'linguistic hospitality' (2007).

Part III

New Media and News in Practice

Chapter Four

· ·

Culture Shock: New Media and Organizational Change in the BBC

Peter Lee-Wright

Introduction

A culture that grew organically for the best part of a century is now undergoing a revolutionary transformation in response to changes in news consumption – facilitated by new technologies – and to accommodate the economic and political pressures bearing down on the BBC. Tracking this new dawn through the experience and opinion of many of those involved reveals divergent opinions on how radical, valuable and sustainable it all is, and exposes fault-lines within an organization keen to lay its old image of 'Auntie' to rest, while seeking a new relevance and appeal for the twenty-first century. New media has been a convenient Trojan Horse for importing a root and branch reorganization many thought long overdue at BBC News. This short account can only offer a few stanzas from that odyssey. It looks at how new technology meets changing patterns of consumption; how new platforms of delivery have pitted technology against creativity; and how the BBC has managed the change.

New Technology, Old Attitudes

'When they set up the BBC News website, just a few guys did a terrific job, but they wouldn't even allow links to any other BBC programmes,' recalled a senior BBC executive from that time.[1] All organizations tend to suffer from this sclerosis, where departmental imperia are fiercely defended as synonymous with job security and status, and change can only occur within established structures. There was a growing awareness among BBC management that cautious step-change was an inadequate response to exponential growth in multi-platform competition and recurrent attacks on the BBC's independence and licence fee. They needed a more radical approach to meet these multiple challenges. That would involve many minds and initiatives, but one key feature was the birth of Future Media and Technology (FM&T), an über-divisional body that was to claw back investment decisions from those traditionally warring departments and drive a more forward-looking approach to the future, predicated on a new media strategy. News, traditionally exempt from the organizational changes and strictures routinely visited on more ratings-driven departments, was not to escape the FM&T oversight. They too were to feel the white heat of new technologists breathing down their necks and demanding they up their game. In many respects, they responded positively.

Television is by definition a high tech game, but the senior journalists in News were used to being accompanied by producers and crews that looked after all the technology and left them to concentrate on the reporting. Today, correspondents often travel alone and unencumbered, enabling them to arrive unnoticed in a country closed to reporters. Both the BBC and ITN reported from Zimbabwe during the 2008 elections, when banned from doing so. As Robin Elias, Managing Editor of ITN says:

> We actually presented an evening news programme from the centre of Harare during the crackdown, during the election, when we weren't allowed in there let alone to broadcast out of it, and we broadcast live from a back garden over a BGAN mobile phone,[2] a satellite phone, and it sort of dawned on everybody [...] that there's virtually nowhere in the world that isn't accessible now.

Not only does this technology make stories easier to reach and report, but it can have a significant effect on cutting costs. While ITN claims to be spending roughly the same amount of money on foreign newsgathering as before, but spreading it further, BBC News has suffered severe budget cuts. Clearly the satellite phone does not deliver the world-class engineering standards for which British television was world-renowned, but a more visually sophisticated audience, used to home videos and low resolution internet pictures, is willing to wear that if the content justifies it. As the Head of Newsgathering Operations at BBC News, Martin Turner, says:

> There is no point every broadcaster doing the same because the audience now has access to the original sources of information. The successful news organization will be the one that supplies distinctive information and context.

Changing Patterns of Consumption

The process of news journalism has been profoundly affected by new media, not just in the technology available to its gatherers and to its editors and distributors, but to its consumers and their modes of consumption. The exploding multi-channel environment, the technology to manipulate it, and the internet with its endless options and direct sources all give the consumer the choice previously made by the news editor. These are the bigger drivers of change, because they challenge the very bedrock of the BBC's belief in its natural supremacy, and call into question its unique funding formula and the public service role it was devised to provide. The licence fee – a government-set, legally enforced levy on every television set in the land – was conceived when the BBC was without competition. Commercial terrestrial channels on both television and radio forced the BBC to become more competitive in most forms of programming, but News remained a fixed point largely above the fray. Before the arrival of BSkyB and the exploding number of digital channels, most viewers would encounter at least one full news bulletin during the course of an evening's viewing. The zapper, time shift technology and digital channels made news very avoidable, and the total audiences quickly began to slide. The BBC perceives this as not only a matter of audience fragmentation, but long-term cultural drift away from news. Responding to that threat has become a full-time concern for executives such as BBC News' Head of Development Simon Andrewes:

> We've got a long-term decline in our television news audiences [...] We have a particular decline among the more down-market audiences and particularly our younger audiences, and it's the younger audience in particular which you sense are leaving television altogether.

The television industry regulator Ofcom has commissioned two reports on the subject within five years, tracking the changing perception and demands of the audience:

> There are indications of greater levels of disconnect to the content of news. Some 55 per cent of people agreed that much of the news on TV was not relevant to them, up from 34 per cent in 2002. Indicatively, more people in 2006 than 2002 agreed that they only followed the news when something important or interesting was happening (26 per cent compared to 32 per cent). (Ofcom, 2007b: 8)

This drift presents a huge challenge to the very nature of broadcast news, namely news that is aimed at the whole population, reflective of communally held values and objectives. As historians of the BBC from Asa Briggs (1985) to David Hendy (2007) record, the Corporation has traditionally held the nation together but the verities that construct a central news agenda agreeable to all are under attack from social atomization and the technical alternatives. A 'pick and mix' culture has grown out of the plethora of sources, promoting a personalization of demand, the software for which is provided by many websites. RSS feeds and aggregation engines build a user profile and supply content that matches the individual's tastes and interests. Fuelled by a hostile right-wing press, a growing number of people not only see no need to buy into the shared platform of broadcast news, but actively oppose it for not suiting their particular interests. Thus the Ofcom report identified the young and immigrant groups as particular news refusers (Ofcom, 2007b: 61 and 66).[3] To add to News' woes, a recent BBC Trust review reported and endorsed widespread discontent within the national regions at a perceived metropolitan bias in BBC News.

> Audiences see the BBC as too preoccupied with the interests and experiences of London, and that those who live elsewhere in the UK do not see their lives adequately reflected on the BBC. It is not acceptable that a BBC funded by licence fee payers across the whole country should not address the interests of them all in fair measure. (BBC Trust 2008: 7)

BBC management have accepted the need to accede to these powerful voices from Scotland, Wales and Northern Ireland, but point out that they have neither the resources nor the share of the digital spectrum to deliver parallel news programmes in all these regions. But with the licence fee under constant review and frequent attack, they cannot afford to be complacent. Constantly buffeted by every special interest group, and accused of social, racial and political bias from all sides, BBC News has usually managed to remain aloof and retain an authority based upon the quality and certainty of its journalism. But the paradigm of telling people what they need to know to function in a democratic society appears to be giving way to a model that offers people what they want – when, where and how they want it. New media have not only facilitated this change, but expedited it. BBC Head of News Peter Horrocks sees the shift away from mass broadcasting to individualized news on demand as inevitable:

> People who've got an interest in [the news] through the web, through new devices, through mobiles and whatever, are going to have a plethora of information which they can assess for themselves, a range of opinions. But because of that kind of fragmentation of information, for people who are less interested in it, they're less

likely to come across it and they may just get quite an incomplete view of the world through the information sources that they will see.

The BBC cannot afford to move too far towards being merely a supply line for that incomplete view, not least because of the implications for democracy. A generation that elects to ignore all discourses of no immediate relevance to themselves worries politicians who fear their power base may wither with the audience. For some years the Government has pressurized the BBC to find new ways of re-engaging the young with the political process, warning them that their licence fee is dependent upon serving all sectors of the community, but news is necessarily immune to fad and fashion. New technology has been hailed as the Holy Grail that will help BBC News reconnect.

New Platforms of Delivery

With its reach down 4 per cent from 2001 to 2008,[4] BBC TV News is holding up better than ITN but is pledged to help the BBC stem their audience shrinkage as best it can, both by adopting the new devices and platforms attractive to the young and by adapting their current practices to better serve their audience's demands. The Future Media and Technology division has a range of strategies for, as they say at public presentations: 'keeping the BBC relevant in the digital world'. High hopes are invested in mobile telephony as the means for reclaiming the younger audience, because they use their mobiles as their main communication and information tool. FM&T see it as the '4th screen', after cinema, television and the internet. It is, as they say, 'personal, local and immediate', with the widest possible reach for keeping people connected, not least to the BBC, and to 'essential information', such as sports updates when entrapped in family weddings.

BBC Radio – whose news reach has remained stable at 50 per cent – is also exploring ways of aggregating content around the music and messages people want. Already radio is being consumed through digital TV sets (20 per cent), internet (15 per cent) and mobile phones (10 per cent),[5] and the inevitable move towards a single communications portal also offers the possibility of slipping personalized news services to people using ever more sophisticated metadata. You may not be interested in financial news but, for instance, if you listen to hip hop, the technology may well infer an interest in street culture. With the same sense of cultural positioning, the BBC runs content channels on the leading video-sharing site YouTube and has struck distribution deals with two of the biggest social networking sites, FaceBook and Bebo. By this means, not only are the more accessible stories made available to a wider, younger audience, but – it is hoped – the BBC News brand is made more desirable.

The internet remains the key platform in BBC FM&T thinking, and the BBC News website is infinitely more important to BBC News than the equivalent at ITN and Channel 4 News. Unlike the BBC, these do not run a 24-hour rolling news channel, so they do not enjoy the same close synchronicity of a 24–7 multimedia newsroom that the BBC has now become. The BBC News web team look upon the Sky News and the *Guardian* newspaper websites as their key competitors. Twelve per cent of BBC News uptake is through the website and it is growing. They talk of the progressively empowering process of 'Find–Play–Share', where the audience relationship with the news is transformed from passive to active, enabling them to contribute, challenge and correct the journalism. Some of the journalists are less excited by this new dawn, seeing a great deal of power vested in the hands of technical staff and feeling that their own worth has been downgraded. Some senior BBC News executives expressed confidential disquiet to me at the zealotry that puts so much belief and resources in the mechanics of delivery platforms, at cost to the core values of content creation:

> I think one of the big leaps for the BBC, which we haven't made yet, is to understand that we are content creators, we are not distributors. But of course the whole fibre of our being is about distributing it and we are spending an awful lot of money on doing that. I think that when history comes to be written, that will be seen as a mistake because, in fact, the people who will be really good at distributing content will be the people like Google, who can build server cities. We can't do that; we haven't the money to do that; we haven't the expertise to do it.

Technology versus Creativity

There has always been a tension between the production and broadcast sides of the BBC. This division finds cultural expression in the tension between 'creatives' and 'techies'. It has been observed that, during times of confidence and expansion, the BBC invest in programmes and people; at other times it favours the hardware that cannot argue back. The current emphasis on new media is the apotheosis of the techie ascendancy, with the FM&T newspeak its dominant argot. George Orwell got his inspiration for *Nineteen Eighty-Four* while working at the BBC: 'Newspeak was the official language [...] The purpose of Newspeak was not only to provide a medium of expression for the world-view and mental habits [...] but to make all other modes of thought impossible' (Orwell, 1949). Orwell will have encountered the sophisticated orthodoxy that determines journalistic standards within the BBC, an unspoken regimen that ensures the same stories are given roughly the same prominence and treatment across its many news platforms and exposes no editor to the charge of having a personal agenda, unlike that lauded in newspapers. Ethnographic studies of the BBC, such as those by Burns (1977) and Born (2005), have noted this corporate consensus that tends to stifle debate. But the FM&T newspeak has a different emphasis that challenges the old hierarchy of values, and unleashes a new set of tastes and standards, while demanding a corporate loyalty. 'Get web savvy, or we die...' raved former FM&T Director Ashley Highfield, dutifully headlined in the house newspaper *Ariel* (13/3/07: 1).

The BBC website was constructed early in the broadband cycle, and it has struggled to keep up with the exponential growth in demand for bandwidth, with more video and interactivity. The FM&T team are working to 'reconstruct the architecture of bbc.co.uk to increase findability and maximise routes to content' and 'harness the power of the audience to enhance journalism and help distribute the content more widely' (Kevin Hinde, BBC FM&T Head of Software Development, Journalism, 2008, interview with the author). But News has yet to find new ways of instant transmission, which distinguish it from the secondary uses being explored by other programme genres. Websites have the vital capacity to track usage instantly, and the BBC website announces its 'Most Popular Stories Now' in three separate lists: 'E-mailed, Read and Watched/Listened'. More pertinently, the multimedia Sky Newsroom is festooned with screens advising editorial staff of the most popular story on the website, and the one with the month's highest cumulative total of hits. Steve Bennedick, Sky News Head of Interactive, says it is not there to drive editorial decision-making, but to inform it:

> I think there's a lot to be said for a journalist being aware of what the clicks are going on, but following his own or her own instincts and judgement [...] It's a non-linear environment online but a broadcast is at the moment via the traditional linear running order, and the two are different.

A BBC online editor says that page hits 'influence' story priority, but admits that page leads may yield sufficient information, thereby evading clicks and skewing that assessment. Another problem is the marked disjuncture between these polls of audience predilection and the News editors' perception of news priority. On a day when the BBC News web page lead was 'Africa turns up heat on Zimbabwe', the most popular story was 'Foot mystery baffles Mounties' – the macabre mystery of five severed human feet washing up on the shores of British Columbia (BBC News website,

19 June 2008). As people vote with their feet to avoid the depressing, distant Zimbabwe elections, there is no sign that editors are yet moved to follow suit. But even before facing the audience and staff losses of the last two years, then Head of TV News Peter Horrocks raised the issue of stories more popular with the punters than with the editors. Speaking to the Reuters Institute of Journalism in Oxford in November 2006, he called for:

> ...an unembarrassed embrace of subject areas that have too often been looked down on as too pavement-level or parish-pump' and told through local accents and personalities. The days of the BBC talking down to them and trying to tell this audience what to think are over because they can simply switch off or ignore us if we don't speak to them in their voice. (http://reutersinstitute.politics.ac.uk)

This confronts the dichotomy at the heart of the BBC's current choices, maybe better defined as incipient schizophrenia. They have long balanced the cultural heights of arts and drama with the popular attractions of sports and entertainment. Now, shifting notions of reality and democracy challenge News' authority. Revered internationally as a beacon of truth and light, BBC News appears to believe it can only now survive if it does the people's bidding and adopts their modes of speech. BBC News now has an 'entertainment cluster'; and the biggest claim made for new media is that they democratize the process and allow other views to bloom than those of the man in the suit reading the news. Of course, he is only reading an autocue, and the extent to which viewers' e-mails or mobile phone footage influences what appears on screen remains firmly in the hands of the news editor.

The BBC makes much of the invitation to people to have their say and send in their shots, but there is little evidence of a transformed agenda. Former BBC producer Kevin Sutcliffe, now Deputy Head of News and Current Affairs at Channel 4, feels that the whole BBC News invitation to the audience is 'disingenuous, invented to look as if the licence payer has a say – they don't'. BBC News Channel anchor and former foreign correspondent Ben Brown takes a more pragmatic view of increased interactivity with the audience. 'What we broadcast is always subjective anyway and is informed by what we think the audience is interested in and I guess it just gives us a better idea of what they actually are interested in if we can hear from them not day by day, but minute by minute'. But he admits that UGC (User Generated Content) such as the pictures from people's mobile phones are only useful when they are a unique source from a particular event.

The pressure to involve the public has grown apace and has taken many different forms. In November 2006, the BBC News Channel launched the weekly half-hour *Your News*, 'the first news programme to be entirely based on emails and views sent in by you'. The re-launched nightly news on Britain's terrestrial channel Five also carries a final *Your News* item supplied with viewer stories about such local issues as cyclists and school campaigns. Neither initiative has yet broken a story to make the main news, and this remains the fault-line. The public has always been a potential source for stories, as have their pictures – like Abraham Zapruder's iconic 8mm film footage of the 1963 Kennedy assassination or mobile phone shots of the July 2005 London bombings – but these events are very rare. As the founding Director of the Institute of Ideas, Claire Fox suggested (at a combative BBC conference debating the relative merits of new media), academic researchers are 'obsessed with new media', while journalists are having 'a collective nervous breakdown':

> The BBC says the public are seen as important in creating news. But what do we think about reliability and trustworthiness? What happens if the news those users e-mail in is banal, local, parochial, not actually revealing at all? If objective truth-seeking – as aspirational classical journalism is – gives way, what does that mean for challenging the agenda of power?

What is the point of extending democracy in this way if the price is the atomization of voices and the destruction of investigative skills? Even the more determined fans of new media and its potential recognize the dangers of News primarily being delivered by associative choice rather than directed content. Tom Loosemore is one of the leading internet thinkers and was Project Director, BBC 2.0, before going to Ofcom in late 2007 to head up strategy on converging digital media and a planned Public Service Publisher. He rejects charges that the internet is a more isolated experience than television viewing, and feels it is the best thing that has happened to democracy. 'It's the most conversational medium that the world has yet invented, the internet. You can have conversations over time and space in a way you simply can't with television – and global conversations.'

Another guru, a former Silicon Valley dot.com entrepreneur, is an apostate who 'saw the light' over Web 2.0. Andrew Keen talks of the 'digital narcissism' that has delivered 'superficial observations rather than deep analysis, shrill opinions rather than considered judgement' (Keen, 2007: 10) and he says that 'the challenge for professional newspeople is to learn to emancipate yourselves from the mass humility and "noble amateurism"' that he sees throttling good journalism:

> The social network bubble is bursting. Web 3.0 will be where the smart people seize back control and get rid of this 'social' media, which fetishizes the innocent, the amateur, the child in us all. I am not against the internet, but I am for curating it by experts.

As both Keen and Loosemore agree, everyone needs some guidance, some authoritative aid in reading their world. That is BBC News' mission, but the argument continues to rage around whether this is, as Loosemore would contend, the painful self-reinvention of a democratized and diversified discourse that has thankfully replaced the old didacticism, or as Keen asserts, the time for those in the know to reassert control. Unlike print media, both the regulated impartiality and the editorial complexity of broadcast news make it more difficult for individuals to emerge who can define their respective worlds. Nonetheless, hammered by attacks on their integrity – from the government-ordered Hutton inquiry, following the BBC's exposure of the 'dodgy dossier' on which the UK went to war in Iraq, to a number of instances where programmes misled the public, which led to a crisis in public trust in 2007 – editors have looked for new ways to weld a relationship with their audience. New media have provided a kit of parts from which they can construct a new narrative.

New Ways of Working

On Sunday 15 June, 2008, the BBC News web team finally moved in alongside their television colleagues to complete the transformation of the BBC Multimedia newsroom. While considered for some time, the move was finally precipitated by economic necessity, with swingeing cuts visited on News as part of a corporation-wide cull to accommodate a reduced licence fee. Some 300 of the 3,400 journalist posts were being lost and the profligate duplication of resources in news cover was addressed by this refashioning of the culture as one machine, rather than a set of disparate factions. Newsgathering and the three output platforms – TV, Radio and Web – sit and work together now, served by a Mediawire service that aggregates all external video and sound sources. The BBC's main competitors have also gone through the multimedia process. Sky News had moved its online journalists alongside the television news teams the year before, and ITN and Channel 4 News have taken the same path. But none of these share the combined weight of a 24-hour news channel, a regional supply line and a radio network that the BBC has. As the Deputy Editor of Channel 4 News, Martin Fewell, says:

One of the BBC's big advantages when they moved online, apart from having oodles of cash, was the fact that it was already generating massive amounts of text. It had two radio newsrooms, a world service radio newsroom and a domestic radio newsroom. It already had a Ceefax operation as well and had forty local radio stations, all producing 24/7 or 18/7 radio bulletins [...] And it's a very sort of clever, ingenious way to make use of the copy they're already generating by re-versioning it slightly.

The digital hub at the heart of the multimedia newsroom allows all journalists and editors to access material from the moment of its logging in to use across all the BBC platforms. This works for the mass of facts and eyewitness accounts that make up some 80 per cent of news, but in some journalists' minds tends to reduce them to butchers supplying a sausage machine. Our limited ethnographic study among the BBC News web team found many frustrated journalists acting as no more than sub-editors reformatting copy. Elsewhere, news reporters are expected to cover a growing number of outlets, across multiple platforms and bulletins, which inevitably reduces the amount of time for the original newsgathering (see Davis, this volume). Meanwhile, senior correspondent appearances and live feeds overnight have also been cut to save money. At Channel 4 News, dot.com entrepreneur Ben Cohen was the first correspondent to be hired specifically to service the three daily television bulletins, their online site and their planned digital radio channels, relying largely on his expertise to comment on technology stories and leaving, as he points out, precious little time for original journalism. Peter Horrocks admits to the dangers of his journalists being spread too thin, but says that the balance has to be struck between coherence and diversity.

> There are some processes in terms of bringing the content from the field, from where the journalism is being originated to the platforms, which can be quite synthesized. You can have planning, and intake operations, which are shared but then the teams that choose the content for the different platforms, at the moment at least, are largely single platform. And especially in news areas which are very rapid response it makes sense to do that because if people have got to do more than one platform at a time that can slow things down. So yes, we're going in a multimedia direction but it doesn't mean that everyone is working in a multimedia way all the time.

Few of what ITN's Managing Editor Robin Elias calls 'the big beasts' are also expected to shoot and edit their own material as well, but 'some very old-established experienced reporters, producers, actually have taken to it very well. Because a lot of the systems are so intuitive, if you like, it's enabled even the old hands to get a grip of it very quickly.' He would not expect them to edit big rolling stories, but admitted that more were editing their own – and 30 of his editors were being laid off that very day. Broadcast journalist Vanessa Edwards is one of many who took voluntary redundancy from BBC News, because at 42 she felt new working patterns favour the young. She instances the replacement of graphic designers by software that she was expected to operate herself as one example of the technologization of her role, producing bulletins on the News Channel night shift.

> I loved my job, which I had been doing for 10 years, but they made me an offer I could not refuse. It was a time to move on: it is increasingly a young person's world. I would not say it is worse, but it is different.

Both Horrocks and Elias admit that the fast-moving technological demands do favour the young, for whom the skills are second nature, but even some of them complain at the workload and allege that it leads to many more mistakes being broadcast. The most far-reaching changes in work practices have occurred in regional newsrooms, where productivity has been kept up by a dwindling number of staff. Hemmingway (2008) spent 12 years as a BBC reporter, producer and news editor at BBC Nottingham. Her study, *Into the Newsroom*, uses Actor Network Theory to chart a reading of the advance of new technologies as a complicating factor in an already complex process. She takes various examples of the ways in which machinery such as the digital hub can become a narrow portal whose control is fought over by competing agencies, elevating the technically competent over the journalist:

> Those operators who consider themselves to be more technically adept, deliberately stress how their communication is between machines rather than human actors [...] the reporter is deliberately bypassed, perceived as a subsidiary actor whose presence is more often than not considered to be a hindrance. (Hemmingway, 2008: 153)

But digital technology has progressively conditioned content in ways that challenge the core values of news. The Electronic News Production System (ENPS) developed by Associated Press is the textual heart of the digital system, what former Head of BBC News Richard Sambrook called 'the spine of the BBC's daily news operation' and the Jupiter system is the video production system that Hemmingway calls 'the black box hub', one she reports journalists can be reluctant to use as it loses them control over their material, which can now be accessed by anyone on the system (2008: 148). Journalists prefer to preserve their own exclusives. One explanation Director-General Mark Thompson advances for the lack of national regional stories on the network news is that – if and when they occur – those regional newsrooms naturally hold them back for their own 6.30 regional bulletins, rather than have them poached for the national 6 o'clock bulletin.

Another key regional development in BBC News has been the training and deployment of video journalists, who do report, shoot and edit on their own. Since September 2001, Paul Myles has been responsible for putting 650 people through the 3-week video journalist training course. A former cameraman and picture editor, he feels that VJs have added new pictorial quality to regional news, where journalists too frequently 'wrote the story first' and did not let the pictures tell the story. 'You don't need to be a journalist to be a good video journalist' he says, although around 90 per cent of those he has trained are:

> Video journalism is very much the key to the BBC's plans for a new web-based service that it's constructing at this very moment. We can't make it happen if we're dependent on traditional ways of working. The only way we can make it happen is if we use VJs, because of cost essentially.

Some regional news editors have been less than enamoured by the quality of VJ work, and currently only use an average of two in a half-hour programme normally running eight items. They have been 'encouraged' to double this uptake to at least four in every ten reports, a fact retailed by Davies (2008), where he equates this imperative with the pressure on journalists across the print and broadcast spectrum to produce more at lower costs, with predictable effects on quality. Davies also quotes at length from memos and guides circulating in BBC News Interactive on beating the opposition by getting the story up first:

> Some of the results are worrying. Journalists on News Interactive say the pressure for speed is sometimes so great that they are required to write half of their story before it happens, a job which is made even more difficult by the fact that, in the same five minutes, they are expected to harmonise the story they write with the rest of the BBC's coverage. (Davies 2008: 7)

This pressure sits uneasily with the public rhetoric to include the 'user' more, the management of whom can take time. UGC is a much-sought source, particularly at times like the terrorist attacks in London and at Glasgow airport, where public images were the first to be broadcast until news crews made it through the security cordons. But, as we have seen, television has always grabbed the best pictures it can from any source. It may have recently discovered that its audience is composed of sentient beings with views of their own – and evolved means of tracking those views – but the running orders remain surprisingly unaffected, to the relief of many.

Change is noticed in local regions and local news, where resources have been run down at both the BBC and ITV. ITV, originally a federation of regional companies, is downsizing from 17 news regions to nine, albeit that 18 new 'sub-regions', including Tyne-Tees, will get their own six minutes of local news belted within the regional programmes at 6.00 p.m. On 21 November 2008, the BBC Trust overruled the BBC's proposals for a local TV news service delivered exclusively on broadband.[7] It decided that it did not meet the Public Value Test and would damage commercial competitors in that field, notably newspaper proprietors. With the digital switchover due in 2012, the BBC is not only fighting to retain audience share with a reduced income, but is also facing an encirclement of commercial interests keen to make inroads on its unique funding and its multiple fields of excellence, where those companies see their potential profits constrained by the BBC's free services. News is not under direct fire, but the BBC's economies of scale and the international pre-eminence that help sustain it are, so an overweening obsession with new media could be seen as threatening to divert attention from the democratic values at stake.

Former Channel 4 News Editor Charlie Beckett, now Director of Polis, the journalism and society think-tank, feels there is a false dichotomy about whether new media works for or against democracy. 'I don't think the e-mail us your view is that important [...] but I can't believe there are still people who argue citizens shouldn't be part of the [journalistic] process.' Patrick Barwise, who chaired the Department of Culture, Media and Sport's critical review of the BBC's new digital channels in 2004 and the BBC Governors' review of public attitudes to the licence fee, feels the BBC has protected its core business well, delivering great content and great value for money. 'All new technologies have been overhyped in terms of revenue and audience behaviour', he says, whereas all they do is enhance convenience. 'There is overwhelming evidence that in 2020 television will still be being watched the way it is now, mostly live as scheduled – none of it UGC'.

This is a variation on the observation that books were not killed off by modern media, any more than recording has replaced live music. Shirky argues that television – like the publishing and recording industries – is still stuck in a sixteenth century model of production, where its prohibitive economics allow centres of control (Shirky, 2008). The digital makes the means of production cheap and universal, shifting the filter to the consumer. The ubiquity of reception becomes the means of production. We may not have attained the future foretold in Brent MacGregor's study of the impact of new technologies on news in the 1990s (MacGregor, 1997), but many elements of his dystopian vision are here. The lone editor selecting feeds from a cornucopia of surveillance cameras for a wired society – augmented by live video journalist feeds from the stories serving the highest subscriber predilections – has not yet replaced the news machine, but these possibilities have shaken the corporation to the core, leaving journalists feeling in thrall to the machine.

Conclusion

As Curran says in Chapter 1, technological bandwagons come and go, few living up to their promise, and the danger in BBC News would be to jettison core journalistic content creation in favour of transient delivery platforms. While reporters risk their lives to retail the truth from China and Burma to Zimbabwe and Iraq, the values of a free, independent news media, robustly committed to informing us all on the affairs of the world, are constantly being reiterated. The technological tower of Babel that is the internet can add context and clarification to that critical role, but there is little evidence that it can transform it, let alone supplant it. Self-appointed citizen journalists can contribute novel insights, occasionally investigate issues the complacent ignore, but are no match for the citadels of power and their systems of control.

Morale at the BBC, as former Director of Programmes Bill Cotton once observed, is 'always at an all-time low'. Cuts and re-organization shake people's self-confidence, which is rarely as strong as their assured performances on screen may suggest. Budgetary pressures favour the young, biddable and cheap. As old dogs have difficulty learning new tricks, a naturally youthful industry says goodbye all the more quickly to the residue of talent and experience that it takes decades to build. Current Affairs, formerly a flagship department that has produced more BBC chiefs than any other, is now shrunk to a fraction of its former size and is merely a sub-division of News. None of this automatically presages bad programmes, but it is instructive that ITV Chairman Michael Grade jumped to the conclusion that the trust issues that paralyzed the British television industry in 2007 were a result of the inexperienced being over-promoted. In fact, the malaise was more systemic and ran into a senior management that had taken its eye off the moral compass.

Peter Horrocks says that public trust is now higher than it was before the debacle, and it is arguable that this and the licence fee cuts have forced a much greater, long overdue soul-searching than would otherwise have happened. Not all is rosy or settled in the multimedia newsroom, but there is a reborn sense of confidence in BBC News that is even willing to question some of the wilder claims of the new technologists. As Horrocks says:

We probably lowered the bar a bit too much and now we are elevating it a bit. I don't expect to see a huge amount of UGC on *Newsnight* in the future [...] But we will employ every trick in the book to bring people to content that is more illuminating and insightful than they will find elsewhere.

This is a relativist position that falls short of an endorsement of core values. Journalists who feel that those values are threatened by technologically-driven reductionism are dismissed as latterday 'Luddites'. They know that the Luddites were not thoughtless vandals opposing progress, but artisans concerned to preserve craft standards and appropriate rates of pay. Two hundred years on, their natural heirs may not face deportation or the gibbet, but they do face an uncertain future, with more illuminating tricks yet to be turned and more cuts to be found.

Endnotes

1. All quotations, unless otherwise stated, are from original interviews or meetings with the author.
2. BGAN is a mobile satellite data transfer system that offers internet access at more than twice the speed of GPRS in 99 countries around the world.
3. Ofcom report (2007b): '64 per cent of young people believe that much of the news is not relevant to them', p. 61 and 'Some 46 per cent of people from minority ethnic groups felt that ethnic minorities got too little airtime in mainstream news' (p. 66).
4. Data supplied by Kevin Hinde, BBC FMT Head of Software Development, Journalism, 26 March, 2008.
5. Source: Michael Gray, Interactive Platforms Producer, BBC Audio & Music, 26 March, 2008.
6. Ofcom's 'Second review of Public Service Broadcasting' closed its public consultation on 19 June, 2008.
7. 'BBC Trust rejects local video proposals', 21 November, 2008; http://www.bbc.co.uk/bbctrust/news/press_releases/2008/local_video_prov.html

Chapter Five

Old Sources: New Bottles

Angela Phillips

Journalists and Their Sources Online

The relationship between journalists and their sources is central to any claim that the news media may make to a role within a Habermasian 'public sphere'. Through each technological change, from the invention of the printing press, through radio, television and now the internet, news journalists have sought to play a mediating role between power and the people. Whether they see their role, in the American professionalized model, as merely a conduit for 'objective' information or in the Southern European model (Hallin and Mancini, 2004) as interpreter and power broker, or as Silverstone (1988) suggests, as story teller working to re-align cultural ties and allegiances through the establishment and re-enforcing of cultural myth, it is through their choice of relationships and prioritization of information that they seek to reflect, or indeed to determine, the political and cultural agenda of the moment.

So the question of who journalists speak to, how they obtain information, how they evaluate it and whose stories they choose to repeat is critical to any examination of the changing role of the news media. The purpose of this chapter is to consider whether the existence of the internet with its proliferation of sources and criss-crossing inter-connected networks, is changing the way in which information is gathered and assessed; whether it is changing the power relationships between those who have always had privileged access to journalists and members of less authoritative organizations, or indeed members of the public; and how it is impacting on journalists themselves and their sense of their own public place.

Broadly speaking, research in this field focuses on two aspects of this relationship. The first envisages an adversarial relationship in which, in the version preferred by journalists (for example, Bernstein and Woodward, 1974), the doughty reporter harries officialdom for the truth behind the official lies. Its mirror-image is suggested by media researchers. Here it is the official source (primary definer), who holds the power, defines the relationship and ultimately the news agenda, by controlling the flow of, and access to, important information (Stuart Hall et al., 1978). Schlesinger and Tumber (1999: 94) suggest more of a tug-of-war (or dance, Gans, 1979) in which sources compete for the attention of the journalist and for the right to define events. In each interpretation, news is a bone tussled over by those seeking to establish their right to define events ('symbolic' capital) and journalists (flawed or otherwise) who represent 'the public'.

The second approach moves beyond the binary power relationship between sources and journalists and considers the way in which space within the media is contested by organizations and individuals (Fraser, 1997). In this conception, journalists are not merely guardians of the public's 'right to know' but conductors of the information flow. This approach recognizes that sources have a democratic right to be heard and the focus here is on their strategies for representation. Voices rise and fall, as they attract the attention of the professional journalistic gatekeepers. Those with the most power will certainly attract the greatest interest but Manning (2001) and Davis (2002) describe the way in which competing sources have learned to operate within a mediated environment and to make use of the agenda-setting 'tools' (in particular dedicated public relations managers) so that they are capable of challenging the role of traditional primary definers.

Manning (2001) cites, for example, the effectiveness of Greenpeace in placing environmental issues on the public agenda. However, he points out that these shifts are also dependent on the fortune of the mass movements that promote alternative perspectives. In this conception of the field, improved public relations strategies do not necessarily make news less democratic. They may indeed enable greater public debate by making alternative viewpoints visible and challenging the right of elite sources to define symbolic capital, albeit within what Atton (2005: 349) describes as 'a hierarchy of credibility [...] based on power, legitimacy and authoritativeness'.

The task of this chapter is to consider the effect of the internet as a means of accessing information. Has its democratizing potential – its ability to bring the voices of ordinary men and women into the mainstream process of news construction – been realized? Are new channels of communication opening up the two-way conversation between journalists and elite sources to let in new, competing or simply different concerns? Or is it simply a case of elite sources accessing journalists via new routes: just the same old sources in new bottles?

Journalists in the 'Field'

A sample of 89, single by-lined, news stories was taken from a range of British elite, daily, national newspapers. The journalists who wrote them were interviewed in detail about the sourcing of each story. (In the context of this research 'sourcing' is interpreted in its journalistic sense as the sourcing of any information, whether from personal exchange, or via secondary media.) They were also asked to nominate an additional story that they personally felt had been important. This formed the core of the research but additional interviews were also carried out to verify and cross-check trends and a smaller sample, from regional newspapers in three different locations, was carried out for comparison.

Although the original intention was to find a representative sample of journalists working for the elite press, it became clear as the research progressed that structural changes within newsrooms – hastened by changes of ownership and the introduction of new technology – were having an uneven effect on the way in which journalists in different positions within the hierarchy and on different newspapers, were able to make use of new opportunities for selection of stories and sources. In order to analyse the use of sources, in the context of these broader structural changes, I have made use of Bourdieu's field theory which allows us to see not only how, but also why, changes are taking place in different ways, across different newspapers.

In Bourdieu's conception of the 'field', power in society is held not only by those who have economic capital, but also by those who wield cultural capital (and through it the ability to establish and maintain social norms which he refers to as 'symbolic capital'). Power within society circulates across and within defined 'fields' of influence (journalism, politics, medicine etc.). Within each of these fields, individuals operate according to a set of norms and assumptions (doxa) which are gradually internalized. Organizations and individuals in a field (and within organizations) are located along an axis. Those controlled by the state, or driven purely by the desire to increase dividends for shareholders, lie at the 'heteronomous' pole, of their professional 'field' whereas those driven more by the desire to maintain their cultural position and influence, lie closer to the 'autonomous' pole (Bourdieu, 2005).

In Bourdieu's own words, journalism is a 'weakly autonomous field' which is, 'structured on the basis of opposition between two poles, between those who are "purist" (most independent of state power, political power and economic power), and those who are most dependent on these powers and commercial powers' (Bourdieu, 2005: 41).

Within the 'field' of journalism, cultural capital (the ability to define and influence events) is prized. So newspapers are keen at least to provide the appearance of independence. In reality, with the exception of the *Guardian*, which is owned by a trust, all British newspapers are owned by large, commercially driven companies, but the logic of elite (as opposed to popular) newspapers requires that the need to please shareholders must always be balanced by the need to maintain influence. In the British newspaper field, elite newspapers, since the late 1980s, have each occupied a niche roughly corresponding to a segment of political opinion: their fortunes rising and falling due to various external events but maintaining equilibrium within the field. However, '[a] newspaper can remain absolutely the same, not lose a single reader, and yet be profoundly altered because its relative importance in the field has changed' (Bourdieu, 1998: 42).

In this paper Bourdieu was referring to the effect of television on French newspapers. A very similar – though more profound – change, is currently directly affecting newspapers in most developed countries and it is having a profound effect on the way journalists work. They are all adjusting working practices in response to new technology but also and far more importantly, because of new commercial pressures in a far more competitive media environment (see Freedman, this volume).

One of the newspapers in this study has recently changed ownership. From interviews both with those selected to discuss their news stories and those interviewed separately, it is clear there is now a new strategy pulling the newspaper (and the journalists who work for it) away from the position it used to occupy towards a far more commercial approach, more akin to a mass market popular newspaper's. This is profoundly affecting the way in which sources are used. Under the previous ownership, senior journalists were expected to be the experts in their subject and worked relatively autonomously. However the new management has used the excuse of technological change as a reason to undermine the position of senior reporting staff (a number of those approached had recently been made redundant or resigned). One senior member of staff quipped that his regular website checks included *Media Guardian*, 'To see who has been sacked'.

There was no evidence that it was an inability to adapt to new technology that was the key issue in staff retention. Rather it was the hunger created by the apparently limitless 'news hole' of the internet which was driving change. Increasingly the emphasis is now on speed rather than depth of work and this militates against follow-up and independent verification of sources. Every journalist interviewed was being affected to some extent by the need for speed and greater output (see Lee-Wright, this volume, for changes at the BBC), but journalists on this particular newspaper are working faster, producing more stories and are monitored more closely by news editors, than those on the other newspapers examined which lie closer to the 'autonomous' pole.

The Struggle for Autonomy

When asked to identify a story which they had written and they considered important, journalists interviewed (on both national and provincial press) always referred to ones which they had found themselves, which were original and usually followed up with a considerable amount of research. Bourdieu (2005: 40) suggests that this need to differentiate is critical for journalists' perception of themselves and their control of, or at least their role in, the production of 'symbolic capital'. 'To exist in a field is to differentiate oneself. [...] Falling into undifferentiatedness [...] means losing existence' (Bourdieu, 2005: 40).

The individual journalist struggling to stand out, is operating in tension within an increasingly 'heteronomous field'. He or she may be pulled towards the commercial pole dominated by audience ratings, circulation wars and the increasing importance of advertising but, within this field, it is not commercial success but originality and proof of autonomy which are admired. It is the reporter who steps out of line and scoops the best story who provides the paradigm upon which the mythologized vision of the journalist rests. One reporter explained how peer pressure pushes reporters to find their own stories:

> I know I'm interested when people bring in really good stories. And if they keep doing it you're slightly insecure about it, 'Oh you're getting all these good stories, where are you getting them from?' So it's an admiration but it's also a slight worry as well. (Interview 7: general reporter, national broadsheet)

This drive for differentiation may not be evident in the bulk of daily journalism but it should not be dismissed if, as Bourdieu suggests, the journalist's desire for differentiation and autonomy serves as the only real counter-weight to growing commercialization and homogeneity (2005: 43, 1998: 33). Across the range of newspapers, those journalists working at the 'autonomous' end of the spectrum (irrespective of their place in the hierarchy) were more likely to report a recent story which they had originated independently of either the news desk, or a news diary. On one newspaper more than half the stories randomly selected were either original or a 'self-generated' follow-up story. At the other end of the spectrum, where insistence on high productivity means that some journalists are asked to produce up to a dozen stories a day, nearly two thirds came either from the wires or were poached from another media outlet (see below).

Some journalists were working under such time pressure that they were not able to point to a single recent incident of a self-generated story although young journalists in particular (on all the newspapers), were prepared to work extra hours, on top of very long days, to find new 'off diary' stories and follow them up. This is not masochism. They know that, whatever the 'desk' might ask them to do in working hours, it is their ability to generate their own stories which will mark them out for promotion.

This provides rather more texture to the figures provided in research by Cardiff University (Davies, 2008: 5) suggesting that only 12–20 per cent of stories are generated 'entirely by reporters who write them'. Journalists need time to generate their own stories. Increasing speed and rolling deadlines dictate that only the most easily available sources will be used and that means the sources that the journalists already know. On local and regional newspapers phone calls from the public are still a key source of stories. On the nationals, even self-generated stories tended to emanate from, or be accessed via, known sources because they are trusted and more easily verified:

> I can't think of a decent story that I've got from somebody that I'd never met or heard of before. [...] maybe unsolicited in the respect that I'd not actually heard of them before but it was a part of a relationship I built up with people in the area generally. (Interview 7: general reporter, national broadsheet)

On national dailies, stories directed to specific journalists, from unknown sources, were rare enough to be remarked on:

> I received an anonymous envelope from somebody containing a two-page print out from a spreadsheet showing what had been spent. It's only the second time in my life I've had such a document sort of sent through the post. (Interview 5: specialist reporter, national broadsheet)

> I liked that story. You always dream of that happening to you, when somebody just rings you up and says 'guess what, this is going on'. (Interview 10: specialist reporter, national broadsheet)

Both these stories required extensive follow-up research and independent verification from authoritative sources to ensure that they didn't expose the newspapers involved to legal action.

Some stories originated on the 'net' but they tended to be found on the less well travelled parts of official websites, where internal documents, the agendas of up-coming meetings, Freedom of Information responses, or minutes of public meetings may be posted. Much of the material that in the past would have come via photocopies in brown envelopes, can now be found published on, or hinted at, in forums or websites of official, or semi-official organizations. Specialist journalists both locally and nationally (or those interested in building up a specialism) quickly become familiar with the relatively small number of related unofficial sites but they are becoming less useful as a means of finding original material because they are equally available to anyone with the knowledge to find them.

Although journalists said that they were finding stories on the net, they were often discovered via another newspaper or specialist magazine websites (a tried and tested source for national newspaper stories) rather than through trawling blogs or news groups. Only the political correspondents considered blogs to be of major importance (see Couldry and Davis, this volume); most other journalists dismissed them as mainly unsubstantiated 'gossip' though they may be consulted to get a general sense of the 'way the wind is blowing' on a specific topic. Although this was a small sample it is worth noting that not a single story on a national newspaper was initiated by a blog. This differs from American research suggesting that 'Weblogs have become a mainstream source for the traditional media' (Messner and DiStaso, 2008: 454).

User Generated Content (UGC) has been suggested as a new way of getting stories (Singer, 1997; Thurman and Hermida, 2008). Indeed some suggest that the future of journalism lies in 'allowing the public [...] to be part of the production' (Beckett cited in Marsh, 2008: 33). I found only two instances in national newspapers of a story being discovered via unsolicited material sent electronically to a newsroom. One was a case history and the other a significant source for a follow-up story. One section editor had given a reporter the job of checking incoming emails for stories and case studies. But although several said that they read comments posted under their own stories and often found them useful, on the whole, reporters did not trawl through UGC because it was perceived to be too time-consuming, untrustworthy and rarely produced genuinely new information. Most original stories were found the 'old-fashioned way' through talking to people, listening and following hunches. As one section editor observed:

> The people who spend the whole day sitting at their desks researching on the internet don't get the stories. They've broken the link between the unique relationship part of journalism, which is number one of what journalism is about, and the greater efficiency that the net can bring. It's only a tool and people forget that sometimes, they think it's the whole thing. And unless you have the relationships, you can't do it. (Interview 1: section editor, national broadsheet)

The Power of Public Relations

While the reporters identified the off-diary stories as the ones that seemed important, the bulk of reporting on all newspapers involves routine sourcing, analysing and structuring of information which is anticipated rather than random, offered freely by sources rather than being unearthed and produced under enormous time pressures, to relentless deadlines (Schlesinger, 1978; Golding and Elliot, 1979). Most of the time, rather than forcing information from those who are trying to hide it, journalists are sifting out which, of many competing voices, are sufficiently important to deserve space in a story and in what order they should be used. The rise of the public relations professionals (Davis, 2002) over the last 20 years has meant that journalists are faced with a great deal more information than ever before. As one specialist correspondent explained:

> Being a [...] journalist is rather like standing in the middle of a hurricane trying to pick out twigs. You're [...] constantly looking around to see what's significant. (Interview 5: specialist correspondent, national broadsheet)

One of the biggest changes brought about by the internet is the tendency of organizations concerned with a breaking story to send out emailed responses to an entire press list. In the past, organizations wishing to respond to a breaking story would have had to talk to a news agency, in the hope that their contribution, or part of it, would be circulated to all news desks via the 'wires'. Now they can bypass the agencies and go directly to the journalist's inbox with a complete and unedited statement. Journalists working on a breaking story can simply check their inbox for relevant names and will probably find that they have comments from a wide range of different parties without ever needing to make a call.

When they make follow-up calls, a specialist reporter will probably have a mobile phone contact with the major players, and be able to speak to them directly. It is clear that the more important a reporter is, the more likely it is that they will have direct contact, via email and mobile phone, with key sources. An experienced general reporter on a national newspaper will get 50 or 60 emails each day, most from PR companies. More junior reporters will have to spend time phoning around and asking for press releases – or checking organization websites in the hope that they have been published online. One specialist who had been promoted without being given time to research her 'patch' bemoaned the fact that to begin with press officers didn't know who she was and she found herself missing important statements.

Lewis et al. (2008: 20) found that:

> 41 per cent of press articles contain PR materials which play an agenda setting role or where PR material makes up the bulk of the story. As we have suggested, this is a conservative, baseline figure. If we add those stories in which the involvement of PR seems likely but could not be verified, we find that a majority of stories (54 per cent of print stories) are informed by PR.

This figure is almost certainly too low. In the day-to-day world of journalism, every single major public announcement can be classified as 'PR' and every organization wishing to address journalists will use public relations techniques. American research found that even when news is about unexpected events, 'the one predictable component of coverage is the presence of official sources' (Livingstone and Bennett, 2003: 376). Often these calls are to verify information or provide a right of reply so simply adding up the amount of copy which appears to have been initiated by PR, or in which PR has been used, tells us little on its own. Nor is there any reason to assume that the use of PR is 'by definition' evidence of a democratic deficit in the news media. It rather depends where the PR emanates from. Indeed, it could be argued that the improved understanding of public relations, by groups who are not powerful and do not have automatic access to journalists, has played a role in democratizing news (Manning, 2001; Davis, 2002) by challenging the position of primary definers. 'Pseudo-events' (Boorstin, 1971) such as demonstrations, pickets and 'stunts', for example, are used by non-governmental organizations to draw attention to events and ideas which are not in the mainstream and which might otherwise be missed.

However, as more and more organizations learn public relations techniques and use email and the internet to address journalists, old power relationships may be actually intensifying (see Fenton, Chapter 9, this volume). Specialist reporters, trying to deal with a 'blizzard' of information, will prioritize known organizations just in order to control the flow. Emails from unknown individuals will not necessarily be opened and according to one interviewee, are usually dealt with in about 'ten seconds'. Junior reporters using Google to find contacts will be faced with a mass of undifferentiated information. Their biggest fear is using information that turns out to be false so, particularly when working at speed, they will also prioritize known and therefore 'safe' organizations. The question of a 'safe organization' varies as issues (and their attendant lobbyists) move up and down the news agenda (see Manning, 2001).

Speed and Cannibalization

Lewis et al. (2008) also point to the growing role of news agencies in providing stories. National newspaper journalists interviewed for this research rarely referred to taking stories from the 'wires'. They didn't need to because they usually had the same selection of statements from all the major players in their own inbox (see above). What seems to be a rather more salient trend is direct cannibalization of copy. The 'pack behaviour' in which journalists are anxiously looking over their shoulders to make sure that they are not falling behind (or moving too far ahead) of their rivals, was first described by Crouse (1973) in his coverage of the

1972 American presidential campaign, but it has clearly been exacerbated by the pressure of online 24-hour rolling news.

As Bourdieu has observed, competition in fields of cultural production tends to increase uniformity (2005: 44; 1998: 23) and this has certainly been the case with the increased competition between news outlets on the internet. In daily print journalism, reporters didn't know if they had been 'scooped' by a rival until the next day's papers came out, when it was too late to do anything about it. Now every story goes on line within minutes and journalists are under intense pressure not to miss anything that has appeared on a rival website.

There is now a widespread practice across the news media, of reporters being asked to rewrite stories appearing elsewhere, in some cases without a single additional telephone call, and to lift quotes and case histories without any attribution. American newspapers apparently object to this practice and are therefore credited when material is lifted. One British publication that has also objected is *The Stage*. In a letter to *Press Gazette* (1 August, 2008: 14) *The Stage* editor, Brian Attwood, accused the *Daily Telegraph* of making use of unattributed material lifted from the magazine without asking for permission. But in general, British newspapers seem willing to tolerate behaviour by rival organizations that is clearly in breach of copyright law, and work is being attributed to writers who have no means of knowing whether anything they have 'reported' can be verified. Sources were not only (in some cases) not being checked, there were instances in which reports had been cobbled together so fast that they didn't actually make sense. One journalist said, of a piece written in fifteen minutes flat: 'The trouble is the news desk dictates what we write even if the facts don't stand up' (specialist reporter, national broadsheet). Another said, 'I was told that I didn't need to check sources because it came from the *Daily Mail*' (general reporter, national broadsheet).

This manic recycling of copy is reminiscent of a trend found in American research, of journalists quoting bloggers, who in turn derive their news information from other news media (Messner and DiStaso, 2008: 459). The same fear of missing something (and being called to account by the 'desk') means that editors and specialist reporters have become hyper-vigilant, regularly checking the BBC, Sky News and the one or two newspapers considered to be direct rivals. One specialist admitted speaking twice a day to the reporter covering the same patch in a rival newspaper. For many reporters there are only two kinds of stories: those you generate yourself exclusively and 'pack journalism' with stories being slightly re-angled to fit what one reporter termed the political 'G. Spot' of the newspaper. One specialist complained:

> There is a real problem when you're at conferences that if your colleagues are going to do the story you've pretty much got to do the story. In the past you would have been able to say to the news desk,

look, my colleagues are doing a flaky story, we don't do flaky stories, let's not do this story. And all that's gone. (Interview 12: specialist correspondent, national broadsheet)

The incidence of direct cannibalization of stories from another outlet varies across the field. The higher the number of stories being 'churned out' per reporter per day, the more likely it is that direct borrowing of copy, including case histories and unverified quotes, will occur. Those reporters with higher status may be able to maintain more control of their own time and therefore the quality of the work they do. As one remarked, 'The trick is to be bossy with the news desk. You have to own your own time' (interview 15: specialist correspondent, national broadsheet).

Improving Access to Stories and Sources

Time pressures are being felt everywhere and reporters are clearly turning round routine news stories at high speed but, at the more 'autonomous' end of the spectrum, follow-up phone calls are still the norm (if only to try and get a slightly different quote) and alternative opinions are sought. More importantly, for those who have the time to explore its possibilities, the internet is not just a machine demanding more and faster copy, it is also a means of improving the collection of information and greatly enhancing the quality of information gathering:

> I was able to get him to send his evidence direct to me by email which meant that process took, you know, fifteen minutes as opposed to arranging a meeting with him for him to give me a paper, which may take him an hour to produce and then, thanks to the new video part of the Parliament website, I could watch him giving evidence from my desk. So I can kind of cover a detailed hearing, but it also means I can do something else that day as well. I don't have to devote the whole afternoon to covering a story. It also means I can file it earlier. (Interview 6: specialist correspondent, national broadsheet)

Google, Factiva, and Lexis Nexis (or other 'cuttings' sites) are the most used tools. They are used to locate people and to find additional information – almost always from official sites or other trusted media. Official websites have massively increased the efficiency of fact-finding. Journalists can trawl the sites to look for reports, press releases, statements and other background information. Much of this would previously have been held in newspaper libraries where it could be accessed by trained librarians; but there is no doubt that for journalists trained to use web-searching tools intelligently, the speed and scope of the net and the ability to make connections between disparate pieces of information or names, makes it a very powerful tool. Three reporters mentioned original stories they had put together by following a hunch (or a tip) and cross-checking masses of data simply using Google. However, it must be said that very few journalists know how to use web-searching tools. Most simply admit that they write a name into Google.

Reporters who are trying to build up a specialist beat will regularly read online information from the organizations in the field just to keep on top of information and events. The web also allows them unprecedented access to dissenting voices. Press officers may dominate the field when a new product is launched but if it does not work, it is a work of moments to find a website, blog or Facebook group complaining about it. Such comments are fast taking the place of a 'vox pop' picked up on the street. Neither can be said to be verifiable, but the online version can be accessed in less than the time it takes to walk to the lift. Some reporters sign up to forums and participate in online debates in their field, listening out for the kind of chatter that heralds a concern worth following up.

A number of reporters mentioned signing up to a website called *They Work for You*, which sends out email alerts every time a particular MP makes a statement in Parliament: a rather more efficient use of time than trawling through the official transcript every day. The internet also provides a direct line to small organizations which in the past would have had much more difficulty accessing reporters and it allows reporters in a UK newsroom to read papers and journals from across the world alerting them to issues which may not yet have hit their shores.

Of all the web tools it is the 'people finding' and social networking sites that have had the greatest impact. General reporters regularly use people finding sites, including electoral registers and directory enquiries, which can be aligned to produce names, addresses and phone numbers (although at the time of writing there is debate about outlawing the selling of electoral registers):

> I mean if you're out on the road you'll see the likes of myself sitting there on the mobile phone to the researcher while I'm on the internet doing my own research. I'll take a laptop but that will get me the wires, it will get me emails, somebody can send me the electoral registers on there, and then I can cut and paste it [the result] into my sat nav. and it will take me there in my car. It's wonderfully Batman. (Interview 4: general reporter, national broadsheet)

They also use social networking sites of all kinds to track down individuals, and the friends of those individuals. One journalist told me that he had numerous accounts in several countries in order to access such information. Only one reporter expressed any scruples about the use of material that people would almost certainly consider private. Most felt that, if it could be accessed publicly, then it was public. If there has been a real change it is here and it is not an increase in democracy. Those whose Facebook sites are being trawled for information are rarely the great and the good (they know how to protect themselves). It is young people, often victims of crime, who have no idea how public their information actually is, who are being exposed to public scrutiny. It is hard to see how this has provided any extra power to the individual. It is the journalists who are in control of these interactions.

Face to Face Interactions

Most journalists questioned feel that the time they used to spend meeting sources has been curtailed by the higher speed of work and that this has impacted unfavourably on their ability to get good stories. Those who did manage to find time for meeting contacts were clear that this was important and several people referred to such a meeting as the original source for off-diary stories. It wasn't that these people whispered secrets in their ears; it was more that the informal chat and buzz opened up avenues of questioning which simply would not have arisen in a more controlled setting or via email. One specialist remarked that attending a briefing was worth the extra time because he regularly found three stories worth pursuing rather than just one. Following up press releases may be the bread and butter of daily journalism but it is 'exclusives' that provide the jam – the thing which makes the job worthwhile.

Conclusions

The availability of information is creating better opportunities for checking material, finding alternative sources and improving the reliability, independence and therefore the democratic and cultural relevance of newspapers. At the same time, the speeding up of news reporting and the need to be visible on the net is impacting directly on the quality of follow-up of routine news. It would seem from the evidence here that, far from broadening and democratizing, the internet is actually narrowing the perspective of many reporters.

Information that is publicly available on the web is being 'cannibalized' and re-angled with minimal verification. Journalists are being used simply to reorder copy or, in the case of large public reports, to look through and pull out the information which is most likely to 'hit the political spot' for their own newspaper.

Given the speed of work, and the sheer amount of traffic and noise that journalists are exposed to every day, it is not easy for ordinary citizens to make direct contact with reporters on national newspapers (although phone calls from members of the public are still a key source for local newspapers) and there was little evidence that reporters are actively monitoring UGC for new ideas and angles. It is not that they are refusing to pay attention to this material; they are simply overwhelmed with information, much of it aimed at them personally. In order to pick out the important information from the 'blizzard' they are forced to create systems of 'filtration' based on known hierarchies and news values.

With so little time at their disposal journalists tend to prioritize known, 'safe' sources, much as Golding and Elliot observed in accounts of television news production in the 1970s. At some newspapers, the combination of staff reductions and speeded-up production schedules mean that only the most established journalists, with the highest level of personal autonomy, will regularly have the luxury of phoning a number of different people to verify information, or probing for alternative views or contradictions. The youngest journalists, in some organizations, are barely leaving the office, making it difficult for them to make the face-to-face contact on which (there was almost unanimous agreement) all original stories are based and damaging their professional development.

The only significant movement towards a broadening of sources and contacts is in the use of social networking sites, electoral rolls and online directories by journalists. This 'virtual doorstepping' has made it very easy to find people who might in previous years have been able to maintain privacy. The overall effect, certainly in relation to general reporting, is that the power of the journalist has grown versus the power of other citizens, not the other way around.

This narrowing of source relationships is not an inevitable consequence of the use of the internet and the response to the speed-up varies according to the kind of organization journalists work for, and their place in the organizational hierarchy. Some reporters are trading speed of access to routine information, for time to work on new stories. However the effort this requires seems disproportionate. Right across the spectrum the sense was that reporters were fighting for the right to work autonomously, against news editors who seemed determined to chain them ever more tightly to their computers. One young journalist had filed thirteen stories the previous day. A dubious record if quality counts for anything.

Where journalists are allowed (or make) the time, there is evidence that alternative sources are making their voices heard. Some journalists are keeping in close 'virtual' touch with small organizations working in their field of interest. Inevitably, given the highly politicized nature of the British national press, reporters will only be keeping an eye on those which are of interest to their particular audience. There is also evidence that where journalists know how to use web search tools, some are using them to access and cross-check information which would formerly have been very hard to collect. This has certainly increased the scrutiny of politicians in particular. However, training seems to be concentrating more on the techniques of delivery (video and sound) than on routinely used techniques of research.

Newspapers that are too eager to embrace the speed of online news are in real danger of undermining the very point of reporting and the individuality of their 'brands'. The growing and unchecked propensity to 'cannibalize' copy from other newspapers is leading to a greater homogenization of news content. Online it is difficult to maintain 'difference' because stories will simply be stolen by every other outlet. If the commercial reason for producing exclusive material no longer exists then there is less incentive to invest in original reporting. But if news outlets are increasingly borrowing from an ever-decreasing pool of original material there is a real risk of damaging the very material upon which commercial news production is based. Unusually perhaps, the requirements of democracy and commercial survival seem to be pointing in the same direction, indicating a need for reporters to be allowed to move back towards a more autonomous place within the field. Until that happens, one is forced to conclude that the overall effect of the internet on journalism is to provide a diminishing range of the same old sources albeit in newer bottles.

Chapter Six

· ·

Liberal Dreams and the Internet

James Curran and Tamara Witschge

Introduction

The international public sphere is now regularly referred to as some-thing that actually exists (for example, Volkmer, 2003; Bohman, 2004; Calhoun, 2004).[1] It is invested with almost the same sense of reality as the World Trade Organization and the International Criminal Court. All are supposedly integral parts of the new global polity.

By 'international public sphere', most critical theorists intend more than just a synonym for international civil society in which organized groups seek to exert public influence on a transnational basis (something that dates back to at least the late eighteenth century when campaigns were mounted in Britain, France and America against the slave trade). What leading critical analysts like Nancy Fraser (2007) have in mind when they refer to the international public sphere (though they do not all agree)[2] is something more recent, and also less concerted: the bringing together of individual citizens and informal networks through intercon-nected global webs of public communication and dialogue. This is giving rise, they argue, to the creation of a new popular force in the form of *international public opinion* which is influencing both public and private structures of power.

The international public sphere has supposedly come into being as a consequence of multiple globalizing influences, including the growth of international social movements, the expansion of global markets, the increase of migration and foreign tourism, the development of global gov-ernance, and the communications revolution. This last development tends to be emphasized in particular because it is thought to be bringing the world closer together, and enhancing international communication and understanding. Satellite transmission, global telecommunications net-works and cheap air travel, it is argued, reduce both distance and time; international news agencies wholesale the same news across continents;

the global integration of media markets is promoting the consumption of the same media; and the rise of the internet is fostering interactive dialogue between nations.

All these different developments are allegedly forging a new cultural geography. Circuits of communication, patterns of public discourse, and the lineaments of imaginary life are all bursting out of the 'container' of the nation, and providing the basis for generating new global solidarities, shared concerns and common positions. These underpin, we are told, the emergence of international public opinion and 'global norms'.

In brief, the international public sphere is widely proclaimed to exist. It is said to be the product of globalizing tendencies, especially in the realm of communication. And it is bringing into being a powerful constituency of world citizenry.

Wistful Projection

Despite its mandarin eloquence, this critical theorizing has little connection to empirically grounded reality. The international public sphere does not exist, save in an embryonic – or at best, nascent – form.

This is partly because communication about public affairs has not been properly 'globalized'. The most important source of news in much of the developed world is still television. Thus, in Britain, 65 per cent said in 2006 that television was their main source of news, compared with just 6 per cent who cited the internet (Office of Communications (Ofcom) 2007a: 17; see also Freedman, this volume). Yet, television is oriented primarily towards national and local affairs, even if it also reports events from faraway places. Even in internationalist Finland and Denmark, domestic news accounts for around 70 per cent of their principal TV channels' main news programme content, while in the United States it accounts for 80 per cent (Curran et al., 2009). The same study found that foreign TV news tends to focus on parts of the world where the home nation has a connection. This is part of a broader process of 'domestication', in which foreign news tends to be interpreted selectively in accordance with the political culture, national interest and collective memory of the country where the news is shown (Hafez, 2007; Lee et al., 2005). Understanding of the world is still filtered through a national prism.

It is sometimes claimed that the internet is overturning this because it transcends place, and makes available a vast, shared storehouse of public information. However, the internet is used primarily for entertainment, correspondence and practical aid rather than for news and political information (Ofcom 2007b: 90; Hill and Hughes, 1998). The most visited *news* websites, as in Britain and the USA, are the websites of the dominant national news organizations (Ofcom 2007a; McChesney, 2008), which tend to have national news priorities. Nationalist cultures can also influence online interactions, as in Trinidad (Miller and Slater, 2000). Above all, the great majority of the world's population do not have access to the internet (Van Dijk, 2005).

While global consumption of the same media content is increasing, this trend is very much more pronounced in relation to screen drama and music than it is to news. Transnational satellite news channels like CNN have tiny audiences in most countries, indeed often so small as to be difficult to measure (Hafez, 2007). The trend towards global media convergence is also very uneven. The two most populous countries in the world – China and India – are in media terms still largely 'self-sufficient' (something that they have in common with the USA, which also has low media imports) (Tunstall, 2008). In addition, people in different parts of the world also tend to make sense of the same media content in different ways, as a consequence of the different national cultural and subcultural discourses that they draw upon (Tomlinson, 1999).

More generally, the world is divided and fragmented in ways that impede the development of global norms and public opinion. While EFL (English as a foreign language) is emerging as the shared language of elites, it is incomprehensible to most people. Chinese, not English, is in fact the language understood by the largest number of people in the world. The development of global consensus is impeded also by divergent cultures, values, economic interests, and affiliations. Indeed, empirical research tends to affirm the geographically confined rather than international nature of most people's primary orientation (for example, Couldry et al., 2007).

Yet if the global public sphere does not yet exist, it is much to be desired. Elected national governments have diminished control over their economies (Panitch and Leys, 1999). Yet, global financial markets, transnational corporations and the evolving system of global governance remain insufficiently accountable to the public (Sklair, 2002; Stiglitz, 2002). A number of responses to this democratic deficit are available.[3] One of these is to develop a communicative space between nations in which international civil society and international opinion become a growing political force, facilitating the reassertion of public influence in a globalized world.

This is why the subject of this chapter – an e-zine (website magazine) called *openDemocracy* – has an interest extending beyond its seeming significance. It is one of a number of new ventures that are using the web as the means of publishing international journalism. In the process, they are contributing to the creation of an international public sphere.

This study thus differs from the preceding two chapters which are concerned with the internet's influence on news-making within dominant news organizations in the UK. Here the focus of enquiry is on the internet's potential to support a different kind of journalism that crosses national frontiers.

Tufnell Park Phoenix

openDemocracy was originally conceived as a networking facility for British activists campaigning for constitutional reform. It then dawned on public intellectual and activist, Anthony Barnett, that the internet made possible something more ambitious – the launch of a virtual magazine of politics and culture – with only a limited outlay. He established a launch team of four (only one of whom was paid initially) in his garage in north London's Tufnell Park, created a wider network of volunteers[4] and, with some difficulty, secured small grants from charities and gifts from well-wishers, totalling almost £100,000.

When *openDemocracy* was launched in May 2001 as a 'pilot' project, it got off to a slow start. While it was free, and hosted some good writing, the e-zine remained virtually unknown. It had no promotional budget, and gained almost no media attention during its launch. Average weekly visits to its website in May–June, 2001 averaged a mere 1,750.[5] The new venture seemed destined to be yet another rags-to-bankruptcy failure that as feature prominently in the history of alternative media (Fountain, 1988; Downing, 2001; Coyer et al., 2007).

An unmistakable watermark of Britishness also permeated *openDemocracy*'s early content. The magazine's office was in London; all its paid employees were British; and their contacts tended to be home-based. However, the magazine aimed from the outset to be international, and to cover globalization issues. It was geared, therefore, to respond to an international event.

The September 11 attack saved the magazine, and altered its editorial trajectory. Todd Gitlin, the volunteer 'North America editor', posted on September 12 an impassioned article in *openDemocracy* urging his country to respond in a restrained way, with 'a focused military response – a precise one, not a revenge spasm'. Citing Hannah Arendt's dictum that 'violence happens when politics fails', he emphasized that the United States should not become involved in an indiscriminate jihad (Gitlin, 2001). Gitlin's article was accompanied by other instant responses, including contributions from Muslim Pakistan, commissioned by the home team working on an emergency basis in London.

Table 6.1   Average monthly visits to *openDemocracy*

2001	2002	2003	2004	2005	2006	2007	2008
30,000	60,000	196,000	105,000	441,000	233,000	179,000	224,000

Sources: The magazine's archives were dispersed, and largely discarded, when it moved offices several times during a period of growing financial difficulty. Consequently, figures for monthly visits relate to different months of the year, rather than strictly comparable periods, as follow: Sept–October, 2001 and 2002 (openDemocracy Board Meeting Statistics Report, 2002): November–December 2003 (openDemocracy Site Statistics since 2001), October–December 2004 and 2005 (openDemocracy 2005–06: Progress Report); July–December 2006, January–December 2007, Jan–May 2008 (*Google Analytics*).

This orchestration of an immediate, international debate about the implications of September 11 caused the magazine's audience to grow. Weekly visits to its website of around 2,000 before September 11 rose to over 8,000 in September–October, and to over 12,000 in November 2001.[6] Many of the magazine's new readers lived outside Britain. Indeed, by April 2002, the magazine's largest national contingent of visitors was American (44 per cent), while continental Europe (excluding the UK) accounted for a further 20 per cent.[7]

In effect, a growing international audience discovered the website. This raised the magazine's status and made sizeable grants, especially from American charitable trusts, much easier to obtain. This in turn increased the magazine's resources, enabling it to attract still more visitors. *openDemocracy* was re-launched, with increased staff and a broader range of content, in November 2002. Its post-launch audience was double that in the aftermath of September 11. Website visits increased still more in 2004, and soared to 441,000 a month in 2005. *openDemocracy's* audience contracted subsequently as it entered a period of economic crisis. Even so, it was still receiving a respectable 224,000 visits a month in 2008 (see Table 6.1).

A number of influences – which we will consider shortly – shaped the magazine. But it is worth stressing here that a global event, and a global technology, proved to be the making of *openDemocracy*. The magazine won a new audience, because its web-based accessibility enabled people from around the world to connect to a global debate about key issues in the aftermath of September 11.

Global Conversations

In line with the increasingly international nature of its audience, the magazine's editorial agenda also became more international. By 2002, its three most prominent debates were about the impact of globalization, the use and abuse of American power around the world, and the character of

Islam (a discussion that tended to emphasize its pluralism). As the magazine developed, the topics it covered extended across a widening spectrum of international themes from the politics of climate change and the regulation of global markets (long before the crash) to the future of multiculturalism and the impact of migration. The countries featured in the magazine also widened. In January–July 2008, for example, 69 articles published on three themes – globalization, democracy and power, and conflicts – covered 26 nations.

The magazine also recruited more contributors from outside Britain. In a sample of 134 articles, published in January–July 2008, authors came from 33 countries spanning five continents. Even well before then, authors were drawn, seemingly, from different backgrounds, persuasions and social networks (including different sectors of civil society). Foreign ministers and Third World activists, famous authors (like John Le Carré) and unknown journalists, business leaders and trade union organizers, public officials and poets, accountants and artists mingled, clashed and conciliated on its pages. Contributors also wrote from conservative, liberal, socialist, green and feminist positions. These manifold contributors reached a far-flung audience. In mid-2006 to 2008, visitors to the *openDemocracy* website came from 229 countries and territories, ranging from Albania to Ecuador (this last country generating 1,262 visits during this period).[8]

The e-zine also sought to further mutual understanding by the way in which it developed discussion through commissioned articles. In its early years, *openDemocracy* gave extensive space to set-piece debates from opposed positions on a major issue. These duels (for example, Hirst versus Held over the nature of globalization (Hirst and Held, 2002)) were usually evidence-based and deliberative, and were followed by discussion that generally became less polarized after 'seconds' had packed away their duelling pistols, and others joined in the debate. This format gave way increasingly over time to a less confrontational one in which authors offered different interpretations and responses to a common theme, such as the struggle for effective democracy in different parts of the world (for example, McGurk, 2006; Alavi, 2007).

This approach was overlaid in turn by a more event-driven rather than issue-driven format in which authoritatively voiced, 'balanced' contributions were published in relation to topics and places in the news. This placed the reader in the more subaltern position of being briefed, rather than, as before, being tacitly invited to arbitrate between opposed positions. But sometimes, the views of external experts on specific countries were challenged or supplemented by contributions from people in these countries (as in the case of China, Iraq, Kenya, Peru, Turkey, Russia and India) who offered different perspectives and sources of knowledge (such as in the case of the Tibet protests in 2008).[9]

The magazine's topical journalism also tended to be interpretive, and framed in terms of a wider context, rather than a record of discrete events in the tradition of conventional reporting. Alongside these threads of analytical debate and interpretation were also articles that invited a sense of solidarity, for example with women working in Asian 'sweatshops' (Khan, 2004) or migrants on an epic journey from Burundi destined for a cold reception in the west (Moorehead, 2003). These appeals to solidarity based on empathy were supplemented by those based on affinity, typified by two, early evocative articles celebrating a similar love of neighbourhood in Britain and the Czech Republic respectively (Baird, 2001; Pospisil, 2001).

In short, the e-zine appeared to be assisting people of different nations, backgrounds and opinions to come together to discuss issues of common concern, and to understand these better through informed debate, while at the same fostering, at an emotional level, mutual understanding and a sense of togetherness. It thus seemed – at least at first glance – to be in the vanguard of building a better, more enlightened world through the use of the internet. In the eloquent words of the magazine itself: 'We aim to ensure that marginalized views and voices are heard. We believe facilitating argument and understanding across geographical boundaries is vital to preventing injustice'.[10]

But while this self-conception is partly true, it contains also an element of delusion. In reality, the debate staged by *openDemocracy* was distorted by the external context in which it operated.

Global Inequality

In the late 1990s, the richest fifth of the world's population had 86 per cent of the world's GDP, while the poorest fifth had just 1 per cent (United Nations Development Programme, 2003: 425) – an enormous disparity that has broadly persisted (United Nations, 2006). This disparity is reproduced as a structure of access to the internet, with the world's poor being largely excluded. Their voice is muted, and their participation limited, by poverty. This is illustrated by the fact that the entire continent of Africa hosted fewer websites than London in 2000 (Castells, 2001: 264).

Economic inequality is associated with other forms of inequality, in terms of access to education, the acquisition of knowledge, language and communication skills, and links to global social networks. Poverty is associated, in other words, with diminished cultural and social capital. This puts the poor at a disadvantage compared with the affluent, who have greater resources and cultural competences at their disposal. The world's poor tend to be disadvantaged also by linguistic inequality. The population of Marathi-speaking India, for example, greatly exceeds that of Britain: yet an article in Marathi, however eloquent, will be under-stood by many fewer people in the world than one written in English.

So when *openDemocracy* sought to 'ensure that marginalized views and voices are heard', it set itself an enormously difficult task, especially for a magazine based in London, with limited resources, publishing only in English. How, then, did it respond to this challenge?

Its first strategic decision was to invest minimal resources in transla-tion. Unlike an interesting offshoot, *China Dialogue*, the e-zine translated only a tiny number of articles into English. It thus excluded, in terms of contributions, most of the non English-speaking world.

The magazine also raised a further barrier against the 'marginalized' by insisting on a high level of 'quality', usually defined in terms of clarity and eloquence of expression, insight and intelligence, and the appropri-ate marshalling of evidence. The threshold level of quality was high, with novelists like Salman Rushdie (for example, 2005) turning an elegant phrase, and the American philosopher, Richard Rorty (2004) offering intellectual firepower, and a legion of more frequent contributors from the sharply perceptive academic, Paul Rogers (for example, 2006), to the eloquent journalist, Caroline Moorehead (for example, 2003) setting a consistently high standard. Judged by these standards, the marginalized tended to be found wanting. As one senior *openDemocracy* journalist put it,[11] 'It is hard to find those people – you know, southern voices – without sounding too bad, writing well'.

Finding globally marginalized voices takes time, the cultivation of an extended network of contacts, and sensitive support for inexperienced writ-ers. This did happen, to some extent, especially during openDemocracy's most affluent years (2003–4), when clumsily written articles, in general, were heavily edited and when, on occasion, contributions were ghostwritten on the basis of interviews. However, the e-zine adopted a more topical edito-rial agenda, and accelerated the cycle of production, in 2005. Severe budget cuts were also made in 2005, and in subsequent years. This had the cumulative effect of speeding up the editorial process, increasing the volume of editorial output, and reducing the time and people available. Staff responded by relying on a coping mechanism: turning to predictable sources of good copy that tended not to include 'southern voices'.

This conjunction of global inequality, knowledge-based and stylistic definitions of editorial quality, and limited resources/time, had an entirely predictable result: a dialogue about the world in which one part of the world did most of the talking as well as most of the listening (see Table 6.2).

In the first half of 2008, 71 per cent of contributors came from Europe and the Americas. The poverty-stricken continent of Africa contributed a mere 5 per cent, and distant Oceania only 1 per cent, of authors. While *openDemocracy* did host, as it claimed, a dialogue across national frontiers,

Table 6.2   Geographical distribution of *openDemocracy* authors and audience

Continent	Europe	Americas	Asia	Oceania	Africa	Unidentified
Percentage of total						
Authors [1]	61	10	16	1	5	6
Visitors [2]	46	40	9	4	2	–

(1) Analysis of authors (N:102) is based on a sample of 25 articles on the three main themes 'globalization', 'democracy and power' and 'conflicts', and all articles on the other themes published in *openDemocracy* between 1 January and 10 July 2008 (a total of 134 articles). Biographical details about the authors were derived from the *openDemocracy* website, and the World Wide Web.

(2) Analysis of visitors is derived from Google analytics, and relates to the period June 2006–June 2008 (total number of visits during this time was 4,777,919, with a total of 3,093,096 unique visitors).

Note: all percentages have been rounded off to the nearest whole figure.

this primarily took the form of people in the affluent north-western hemisphere talking about the rest of the world. Those whose first language was English also dominated. Americans and Canadians accounted for 90 per cent of article writers from the Americas, while the British constituted 62 per cent of writers from Europe.

The geographical distribution of contributors was broadly similar to that of visitors. The e-zine had an international audience, with the United Kingdom generating only 24 per cent of total visits to the website. However, most of the remainder were concentrated in the affluent, English or EFL-speaking part of the northern hemisphere, with North America and Europe accounting for 83 per cent of website visits in 2006–8.

Social Inequality

If the external context influenced which national citizens wrote for *openDemocracy*, it also affected who *within* nations were invited to write. The disposition of knowledge, communication skills and time is unequal. This encouraged the e-zine to turn to the accredited rather than the marginalized, the expert rather than the ordinary citizen.

The first port of call was academics because they possessed specialist knowledge, flexible working hours and, as public salaried workers, would write for free. To use them was to take advantage of a hidden public subsidy. However, they also posed a problem because many academics have become accustomed to writing for specialist knowledge communities with a shared vocabulary and referential (a typical academic word) understanding, and are consequently unused to communicating with a public audience. The e-zine got round this problem in two

Table 6.3   Occupation of *openDemocracy* Authors [1]

Occupation	Academic	Journalist	Writer	Civil Society/ Activist	Politician/ Lawyer	Unknown
Percentage of total	48	20	10	14	3	4

(1) Sample   134 articles published by 103 contributors from 1 January to 10 July 2008.

ways: by investing considerable resources in sub-editing clunking academic prose (sometimes in a broken EFL form), and by developing a repertory of academics who were adept at public writing, and who were invited to write frequently. The second group the e-zine turned to were journalists and professional writers, usually with a special area of knowledge. Their attraction was that they tended to write well, and fast: their disadvantage was that they generally expected to be paid. The third group were people from the world of politics, especially public and NGO officials and civil society activists. However, *openDemocracy* staff – especially more senior ones – tended to be sharply critical of this last group's efforts, complaining that they were inclined to get 'bogged down in detail', to 'fight micro turf wars', to 'fail to see the big picture', and to offer a 'poor journalistic product'.[12] Rival e-zines were also criticized for being ready to publish 'NGO public relation stories'.

This congruence of influences had, again, predictable results. In the first half of 2008, eight out of ten openDemocracy authors were academics, journalists, or writers. Activists and those employed by civil society organizations generated only 14 per cent of contributors (see Table 6.3).

There is another significant way in which the external context influenced the editorial content of *openDemocracy*. While gender inequality has lessened, it is still manifested in multiple forms, from the distribution of life chances to pensions (for example, Strauss, 2006). The norms of traditional gender differentiation, ordaining that women should take the primary role in the home and the man the primary role in the economy and public life, have left a residual cultural legacy even though the economic division of labour on which this differentiation was based has been transformed. In Britain, for example, this contributes to a situation where women have long paid less attention to 'public affairs' in newspapers than men (Curran and Seaton, 2009), and where women still constitute only 20 per cent of MPs in the UK (Fawcett Society, 2005).

This gendered inheritance left a strong imprint on *openDemocracy*. Women writers were well represented in sections devoted to 'women and power', and 'arts and culture', but under-represented in the political sections (see Table 6.4). Feminist pressure within the office led to the establishment of the 50:50 section, 'a series of editorial projects designed to make *openDemocracy* a current affairs forum which is written, read

Table 6.4   Relative gender distribution of *openDemocracy* articles (as percentage of total per theme (1 January–10 July 2008)[1]

Theme	Women/ Power	Arts/ Culture	Globaliz-ation	Democracy/ Power	Conflicts	Faith/ Ideas	Other	TOTAL
Men	32	42	64	84	92	80	75	72
Women	68	58	36	16	8	20	25	28

(1) Sample   134 articles.

and used equally by women and men'. But in 2008, 72 per cent of the e-zine's contributions were still written by men.

The geographical, class and gender imbalance of article authors might have been redressed through the interactive dynamics of the e-zine. However, discussion forums were developed as a separate space within the website, and had a semi-detached relationship to its editorial content. One senior editorial executive confessed to 'rarely' looking at these forums during the period 2005–6. When users' comments were published below articles from 2007 onwards, there were relatively few of them. Even the most discussed article on the site in the first half of 2008 attracted just 36 responses.

In brief, the e-zine aimed to bring into play different perspectives, including marginalized ones, in order to foster international understanding. But in reality, it orchestrated predominantly elite, male contributions from the richest part of the world. Even so, the quality and intelligence of its articles, and its departure from a narrowly national perspective, makes this e-zine especially significant in the field of online journalism (see also Redden and Witschge, this volume).

Cultures of Production

If the external context strongly influenced the content of the e-zine, other factors also played a part. Thus, charitable funding exerted an influence, not directly on editorial policy but indirectly on strategy and personnel (with some changes linked to new pitches for grants). Stormy office politics also had an effect, contributing to the introduction of new topics and the exodus of some staff. The social and cultural networks that fed into the e-zine left an imprint: for example, a seminar series on 'Town and Country' at Birkbeck, University of London was a key recruiting ground of *openDemocracy* writers, including two out of its three editors. To focus on the alleged determining influence of new communications technology, as some studies do (for example, Stratton, 1997), is to overlook the range of influences that shape the use to which new technology is put.

Due to the limited space available, attention will be focused mainly on one of these influences here – the evolving 'culture of production'. Three distinct cultural regimes can be identified, though in reality each new regime incorporated elements from the past, and also had a continued 'life' after it had ended.

The first culture that shaped *openDemocracy* was primarily that of a political magazine but it changed over time by absorbing other inputs. The founding editor, Anthony Barnett (2001–5), was a charismatic man of letters and politics, who had been on the editorial board of the leading radical journal, *New Left Review*, written a number of books (including *Iron Britannia*), directed an influential constitutional reform group, Charter 88, and been a freelance journalist. The people he recruited to establish the e-zine were the founder of an experimental theatre group, a film-maker and a former college lecturer. The enlarged team at *openDemocracy* recruited people from still more diverse backgrounds, including international civil society activism and corporate business.

This heterogeneity bred innovation, something that was fostered also by the horizontal management structure of the organization, and the early ceding of considerable autonomy to different sections ('themes') which were allowed to develop in divergent ways. In 2001, *openDemocracy* was a print magazine in virtual drag: a cross between the *New Statesman* and *Encounter* (a political and literary belles-lettres magazine that had died in 1990). It even had numbered issues like a conventional print publication. Over the next four years, *openDemocracy* evolved into something that was original and different. Articles broke free from a common template, and came to vary enormously in length (some running to 5000 words or more). Parts of the e-zine were like entering a university symposium, with academics sparring with each other. One part was like entering an art exhibition with images rendered luminous by the light of the computer screen (for example, Robins, 2003). Still another resembled the 'comment' section of a broadsheet paper. Yet another was like entering a rowdy political meeting, especially in the run-up to the Iraq war, when an *openDemocracy* discussion forum took off. Other parts of the website synthesized diverse influences, as in the case of a remarkable series of articles on the different significations of hair as a source of beauty and fear, fetish and protest, universalism and localism, accompanied by a collage of visual images and quotations (the latter derived from poems, pop songs, sacred texts, novels and plays) (for example, Ossman, 2002; Dikötter, 2002). In a quiet corner, there was a quirky series of short articles on untranslatable words, illuminating the interior life of different languages and cultures, from Albanian to Japanese (for example, Kushova, 2004; Kamouchi, 2004). And all the time, the e-zine was evolving into a more cosmopolitan form, with more inputs from non-British writers. By the end of 2004, *openDemocracy* had ceased to be a replica political weekly, and had come to resemble only itself. It was a hybrid, drawing on different cultural forms – print journalism, photo-journalism, art installation, book, academic seminar and political meeting. It was like a caravanserai, laden with goods from different origins, travelling to an unknown destination.

The new editorial regime of Isabel Hilton (2005–7) imposed a culture of broadsheet newspaper journalism. Hilton was an assured, successful and clever journalist who had been a distinguished foreign correspondent, book author and BBC radio presenter. The talkative, decentralized, experimental and sometimes disorganized nature of the e-zine, in its first manifestation, was utterly different from the routine-driven, streamlined structures of professional journalism. She immediately set about embedding the disciplines, and conventions, of Fleet Street. A centralized structure of control was established, based on daily morning editorial conferences (as in a newspaper office). Staff members were instructed to listen to the radio news and read newspapers before these conferences so that they had something 'useful' to contribute. The editorial agenda of the website shifted from being issue-driven to being news-driven, and became more oriented towards the pre-scheduled events and cycles of the political calendar. Articles were published at a shorter, more consistent length, with few being allowed to exceed 1,200 words in line with British newspaper convention. Article output rose, shifting from a weekly to daily cycle of production. The composition of contributors also changed, with more professional journalists being used.

What emerged from this reincarnation was something much closer to the traditional linotype culture of print. The re-invented e-zine had greater quality control (with fewer weak articles). It was better written, more topical, and less eclectic. It was less cerebral, making fewer demands on the user. It was also less different from the mainstream media, less quirky and less original. In part, this was a consequence of the steep decline of the arts and culture section where budget cuts fell with disproportionate severity. But the website also innovated during this period, with the development of podcasts, and with the recruitment of good contributors from China and Latin America. Isabel Hilton had a difficult task in taking over a project with a greatly reduced budget. She re-stabilized the magazine, at a time of crisis, and reversed a precipitous decline of site visits.

The third reinvention of *openDemocracy* occurred under the editorship of Tony Curzon Price (2007–). He was constrained by still further budget cuts, and a skeletal (and shrinking) staff. But he brought with him a Californian, communitarian culture that offered potentially a new lease of life for the e-zine. Curzon Price had been a pilgrim to Silicon Valley, where he had worked as an internet entrepreneur during 2001–4. He took charge of an e-zine with a relatively low level of user interaction and one of his first steps was to symbolically relocate readers' comments beside the relevant article rather than in a separate space. A desire to forge an *openDemocracy* user-generating community not unlike that of *Slashdot*, though of a more diverse kind, led to the imaginative decision to establish an 'Ideas Forum' in 2008. A hundred people were invited – on the basis of their past significant contributions to the magazine – to participate online in proposing and discussing ideas for articles, and the selection of suitable authors. This went far beyond the very small group of mostly British external editors that Anthony Barnett recruited in the pilot phase of the magazine. It also went beyond the building up of a team of interns and volunteers (some operating from abroad) who had come to play a significant role in the administration, sub-editing and publishing of the e-zine. In effect, Curzon Price was seeking to use net technology to facilitate editorial commissioning as a collaborative process (while retaining final control to ensure quality). He was thus attempting to harness the network energy to be found in other web-based projects by 'wikifying' a central aspect of *openDemocracy*. Whether this will succeed or not, it is too early to say. But it represents a departure shaped by a communitarian culture different from the more hierarchical ethos of the previous editorial regime.

Yet even though all three editors drew upon divergent cultures to take the magazine in different directions, they have also in certain respects been similar. All three have elite educational backgrounds (with degrees respectively from Cambridge, Edinburgh and Oxford Universities, and, in the case of Tony Curzon Price, a doctorate from London University). The people they recruited tended to come from similar backgrounds (the small staff of *openDemocracy*, in mid 2008 for example, included people with degrees from Yale and McGill Universities). This shared educational background predisposed the e-zine, under all three regimes, to look for certain kinds of article – critically independent (whether on the right or left), evidence-based, and analytical.

Above all, at the very heart of the magazine, there has been a shared commitment to some version of internationalist humanism. All the central figures in the magazine, in its different phases – including the long-serving, influential deputy editor, David Hayes – have believed in the importance of being respectful to other cultures; of getting people in different countries to speak for themselves rather than be spoken for; and of developing a reciprocal exchange based on a relationship of equality. The investment made in improving foreign writers' copy through subediting was partly borne out of a desire to foster discursive equality between nations. Facilitating international dialogue as a way of promoting greater understanding has been the central *telos* of the magazine in all its incarnations (whatever its limitations in practice).

Technology and Money

The economics of *openDemocracy* has also been central to its development. Indeed, its history underlines the point that web-publishing –
beyond the modest blog – is far from 'free'.

The internet lowers costs by transferring print and reproduction costs
to the user. It opens up market access by bypassing wholesalers and
retailers (the last a major obstacle to minority magazines unless their
distribution is protected in law, as in France and Greece). The global
reach of the internet also makes new kinds of ventures possible
through the aggregation of minority audiences in different countries
(producing a situation that is analogous to art house film production).
openDemocracy benefited from all of these advantages – lower costs,
enhanced market access, and global aggregation.

But the e-zine still had to spend money. Its largest outlays were on the
salaries of staff to commission, subedit, and publish (i.e. code, lay-out and
present) content, and to administer its business; payments to contributors; and office overheads. In addition, it had miscellaneous calls on its
budget, for example £120,000 on website design and redesign in its first
three years (and on the commissioning of a less labour-intensive website,
in the subsequent period). The e-zine in fact cut a number of corners. It
spent little money on promotion and translation; paid its editorial staff
low salaries, and developed a network of volunteer and intern labour.
Even so, it spent around £4.35 million in 2001–8.[14] Part of this outlay was
admittedly misspent, since it was directed towards generating income
that failed to materialize. But a significant part of *openDemocracy*'s expenditure was unavoidable, given what it set out to do.

The real obstacle to net publishing lies on the revenue side. The world
wide web was given as a free gift to the world in order to foster inter-
connection and the open accessing of knowledge (Berners-Lee, 2000).
This legacy was supported by workers within the computer industry
(Weber, 2004), and reluctantly embraced by large media corporations,
nearly all of whom now provide free access to their online news sites
(partly in a bid to protect their offline business). Users have thus become
accustomed to *not* paying for web-based press content.

This made it impossible for *openDemocracy* to charge a website entry fee.
Its audience, though substantial, was too small in relative terms to generate
substantial advertising. The e-zine's lofty humanism was not like an urgent
humanitarian cause or a passionate partisan commitment propelling sym-
pathisers to reach for their credit cards. Yet, the e-zine made an undertaking to the Ford Foundation that it would seek to become self-funding
when it received a $1.6 million dollar loan. *openDemocracy* took on staff
to syndicate articles, market archived articles as e-books, sell institutional

subscriptions, solicit donations, and sell advertising. The new business personnel were expensive, and failed to raise significant revenue.

This plunged the magazine, at its peak with 24 employees, into a crisis that almost destroyed it. It received emergency charitable funding that enabled a soft landing in 2005–6. It then lurched into a near terminal crisis in 2007, after two major funders – Ford and Rockefeller – declined to help further. The magazine even moved for a time, in 2007, into the waiting room of a friendly NGO, after finding itself without an office, before eventually securing better accommodation. Its core staff dwindled to three people in 2008, with others employed in linked projects that contributed to overall overheads.

These projects included one devoted to cultivating an informed and critical dialogue about Russia funded by George Soros's Open Society Institute, and another devoted to British politics (and constitutional reform) financed by Rowntree. In effect, this development has come to represent a new funding model: the parcelling out of *openDemocracy*'s website into discrete projects that appeal to different charitable trusts. It also represents a move towards the partial Balkanization of the website into nation-centred enclaves that sits unhappily with the internationalism of the project.

Indeed, perhaps the most significant implication of this study is that the international space between commercial and state-linked media – between CNN and BBC World News, *The Economist* and Al Jazeera – is not sustained by an online revenue stream that will enable new ventures to grow and flourish. There is not a ready-made business model that will support worldwide online journalism of a kind pioneered by *openDemocracy*.

Partly for this reason, the building of an international public sphere is going to be a lot more difficult in practice than its magical realization has been in critical social theory. And, to judge from this case study, global inequalities of power and resources are likely to distort the international public sphere that will eventually emerge.

Endnotes

1. Other synonyms for the international public sphere are the 'transnational public sphere' and 'global public sphere'.
2. For divergent socialist, radical democratic and liberal interpretations, see respectively Ugarteche (2007), Fraser (2007) and Volkmer (2003).
3. For an especially illuminating discussion, see Held et al. (1999) and Held (2004) who argue that a more democratically accountable, multi-layered system of governance is the best way to reassert public power.

4. Both authors declare a personal interest: James Curran as an early volunteer, external 'media' co-editor with David Elstein and Todd Gitlin; and Tamara Witschge who is currently involved in the e-zine's strategic discussions. Both authors have sought to maintain, however, academic detachment in writing this essay.

5. openDemocracy Board Meeting Statistical Report, July 2001.

6. openDemocracy Board Meeting Statistical Reports, August, 2001; November 2001; December 2001.

7. openDemocracy Board Meeting Statistical Report, May 2002.

8. Source: Google analytics.

9. http://www.opendemocracy. net/editorial_tags/tibet_2008

10. http://www.opendemocracy.net/about

11. Interviews were conducted with nine *openDemocracy* editorial employees, past and present. These included the e-zine's three editors, and its long-serving deputy editor, as well as junior staff. Past and present staff have not been differentiated in order to preserve anonymity.

12. These quotations are derived from interviews with senior *openDemocracy* staff.

Part IV

....

New Media, News Sources, New Journalism?

Chapter Seven

Politics, Journalism and New Media: Virtual Iron Cages in the New Culture of Capitalism

Aeron Davis

Introduction

This chapter looks at the ways new media is influencing mediated engagement between politicians, journalists and their publics. Its starting point is a critique of the dominant research approaches that guide much enquiry here: the 'technological-determinist' and 'democratic-normative' lines. These merge democratic communication ideals with ICT potential to produce a blueprint for 'more democratic' forms of mediated public communication. New media enhances communicative exchange and thus brings stronger forms of 'social capital' (Putnam's 2000 definition). To date, in politics and journalism, such expectations have remained relatively unfulfilled. To investigate why, the research presented here takes more of a 'social shaping' or 'mediated' approach to new ICT adoption. Such work is actor-centred and records how individuals adopt, and change their everyday behaviours, in response to new technologies. Thus, it attempts to observe the daily communication-related practices of politicians and journalists and then asks how new ICTs are influencing these and, if so, in what directions.

Arguably, ICT-adoption in politics and journalism is being driven less by democratic imperatives or technological innovation, and more by rationalization and marketization. Like many other professions operating in 'the culture of the new capitalism' (Sennett, 2006), journalists and politicians are continually expected to be more productive – to be more cost-efficient and produce quantitatively more with less. The two professions are oriented around human exchanges, information-gathering and public audience connection. Both, accordingly, try to learn, deliberate and write about more policy issues in an increasingly complex policy sphere. Both attempt to have more human exchanges in order to facilitate this and to retain their fragmenting public audiences. Their adoption of new technologies is guided by these objectives. In trying to fulfil these increasingly elusive goals individuals are using ICTs to cut corners and to appear to manage the unmanageable (see chapters by Phillips and Freedman, this volume). In the process, information-gathering and human interaction is becoming 'virtualized' (Carrier and Miller, 1998). That is to say, public political engagement, between politicians, journalists and the public, whether online or via news media, is: more 'symbolic' than 'substantive', based on 'thin' rather than 'thick' communicative links, built on 'flexibility' and 'abstraction' in place of 'craftsmanship' and 'specialist knowledge'. Thus, new media is equally likely to be a contributory factor in weakening communicative ties, social capital and public engagement.

New Media, Politics and Journalism: Greater Engagement or Iron Cage-induced Virtualization?

Much new media research on politics and journalism has been concerned with fulfilling democratic ideals and ICT potential, rather than observing real actors and 'actually existing democracies' (Fraser, 1997) in practice. Whether the starting point is technology, media or politics, there is a clear normative agenda being put forward: existing political institutions and news media are letting down citizens and, at least in part, are responsible for declining levels of public engagement with traditional politics. In the UK, as with the majority of OECD countries (Dalton, 2004; Hay, 2007), there has been a long-term reduction in voting levels, political party membership, and levels of 'trust' in politicians and political institutions. Likewise, most national newspapers and terrestrial broadcasters have presided over a steady drop in audience figures since the 1970s (Tunstall, 1996; Curran and Seaton, 2003; Ofcom, 2007). MORI opinion polls for over a quarter of a century have placed journalists and politicians at the bottom in terms of professions that people 'trust'. All of which offers strong evidence for the thesis that the professions of journalism and politics have become disconnected and disengaged from ordinary citizens.

The proposed answer, in many cases, involves the use of new information and communication technologies. New ICTs offer the communicative potential for greater exchange and deliberation between politicians, journalists and citizens. Negroponte (1995) and Rash (1997) argued that the many-to-many, communicative network of the internet contained the potential for a renewal of direct democracy. Political and public sphere theorists (Dryzak, 2000; Norris, 2000; Putnam, 2000) have pointed out the potential for enhancing 'social capital' and a stronger, internet-enhanced direct and deliberative democracy. Empirical studies have sought to document or test the possibilities in a variety of ways (Coleman, 2004; Gulati, 2004; Trippi, 2004; Davis, 2005; Lusoli et al., 2006): 'e-con-sultation', 'citizen panels', a 'civic commons in cyberspace'. Studies of news journalism have similarly noted how the internet has made tradi-tional journalism more publicly responsive, and widened public partici-pation to bloggers and 'citizen journalists' (Gillmor, 2004; Pavlik, 2001; Allan, 2006; McNair, 2006; Fenton, Introduction, this volume). All these studies, in effect, view greater public participation, and engagement with politicians and journalists, as the way forward.

While such work has correctly identified substantive signs of a legitima-tion crisis in institutional politics, the causal explanations are faulty. Diagnoses and solutions are based on 'abstract' and 'ideal' rather than 'real' actors and 'actually existing' democracies. First, the 'agora' or 'public sphere' model of politics and public deliberation has never existed outside of small, elitist collectives (Calhoun, 1988; Behabib, 1992; Fraser, 1992; Habermas, 1996). Contemporary democracies are large and complex with multi-layered systems of government and civil society and a 'multi-dimensional policy space' (Bennett, 2003; Dalton, 2004; Crouch, 2004; Hay, 2007). The failings of institutional democracies are not simply reducible to a failure to obtain direct democracy. Second, any equivalent 'idealized' conception of media and communication is also outdated (see also Calhoun, 1992; Thompson, 1995; Sunstein, 2001; Curran, 2002; Garnham, 2007). Most news journalism in most democracies, regardless of its professional ideals, is privately-owned and market-driven. It is no more in a position to facili-tate wide access, engagement and deliberation than publicly-funded insti-tutions. Online forms of journalism, traditional, citizen or blogger based, have yet to produce a long-term sustainable business model (Cohen, 2002; Singer, 2003; Scott, 2005; Freedman, this volume).

Third, there is an assumption that ordinary citizens want to consume and engage with their news and politicians online. The majority do not. Lusoli et al. (2006) found that only 42 per cent could name their MP and only 8.5 per cent are 'net enthusiasts' when it comes to political engage-ment. Of those members of the public that do contact their MP, 48 per cent did so by phone, 20 per cent by letter, 11 per cent in person, and 12 per cent by email (Lusoli and Ward, 2005). According to Ofcom (2007b), in 2006, only 6 per cent of the UK public got their news from the internet, as opposed to television (65 per cent) or newspapers (14 per cent). In fact, most studies note that online news consumption and political participation is closely correlated to an existing predisposition to participate in real-world politics (Davis and Owen, 1998; Norris, 2001; Bonfadelli, 2002; Jensen, 2006). Fourth, such visions assume that journalists and politicians deliberately chose not to engage with ordinary citizens but have spare capacity to do so. As the discussion below points out, this is far from the case. Thus, the attempt to conceive of ICTs as making an intervention in this way ignores the many other social, organizational, commercial and communicative obstacles to such forms of direct public engagement with politicians and journalists (see also critiques in Polat, 2005; Brandenberg, 2006; Dahlberg, 2007).

Analysis of how new media is influencing news media and politics should, instead, begin by looking at current accounts of contemporary politics and news production. It should focus on the existing communicative practices of such professions and how new media may or may not be altering those practices. This 'recombinant' and 'social shaping' approach (Lievrouw and Livingstone, 2006: 4) views ICTs as 'more of a mutual shaping process in which technological development and social practices are co-determining'. Such socially-shaped adoptions of new media are, consequently, also likely to impact on the way politicians, journalists and their publics engage.

As the next section will argue in greater detail, the over-riding pressure being felt by politicians and journalists is that of greater productivity wrought by 'the cultures of the new capitalism' (Sennett, 2006). Weber (1948) first conceived of the modern state and its governing professions as being increasingly directed by 'rationalization' and the 'iron cage' of bureaucracy. Many core elements of the traditional 'iron cage' are to be found in contemporary commercial and public organizations of all sizes. Although structures and forms of labour have evolved considerably during the twentieth century, key elements of 'functional rationality' are ever present. For Ritzer (1998, 2004), Sennett (2006), Jamieson (1989), Carrier and Miller (1998), the combined logics of modern markets and bureaucracies offer up a range of contemporary variations. Each observes the shift of capitalist democracies to new forms of work and consumption but continuing demands for hierarchies and workforce control, predictability and quantification, efficiency and productivity. At the same time, each also recognizes new features influencing many newer professions in an era of globalization, post-Fordism and consumption. Transnational corporations get ever larger and more fragmented. Employees have to move jobs and learn new skills with greater frequency. 'Institutional knowledge' and 'craftsmanship', being able to build up experience and skills, and to spend time developing something well, is in decline (Sennett, 2006: 127): 'In a speeded-up institution, however, time-intensive learning becomes difficult. The pressures to produce results quickly are too intense [...] so the work-place time-anxiety causes people to skim rather than to dwell.' The emphasis is always on change, the new, speed, the consumer, and quantification of results – the 'audit society' (Power, 1997) (see Freedman and Phillips, this volume).

These issues also affect those at the organizational top who, in turn, have to accommodate a variety of alternative bosses, from anonymous international investors to auditors and consumer-citizens. They must themselves be flexible, adaptable, more productive, offer constant change and 'new' ideas (see Hay, 2007). Those in official power give it up to an array of external bodies, experts and corporations. According to Sennett (2006), it is by such means that power becomes disconnected from legitimate authority in contemporary hierarchies.

Running throughout this literature are two other themes integral to the discussion ahead: technology and 'virtualization'. For all these authors technology enables and facilitates new forms of rationalization and market flexibility. Information and communication (as opposed to industrial) technologies offer greater predictability, cost efficiency, flexibility, quantification, alternative hierarchies, organizational expansion and forms of non-human control of human activity (see also Piore and Sabel, 1984; Murray, 1989; Lyon, 1995; Herman and McChesney, 1997). As Ritzer states (1998: vii), 'McDonaldization involves an increase in efficiency, predictability, calculability and control through the substitution of non-human for human technology.'

At the same time, technologically-facilitated rationalization also contributes to a very modern by-product that Carrier and Miller (1998) label 'virtualization'. There are many elements of this such as the imposition of *'abstract' theory* and *'auditing'* on states and corporations. Another is the *weakening of direct social ties*; something Sennett (2006) develops in greater detail. Social relations involve time and investment, make difficult management decisions more complicated, and are thus an impediment to the new flexible, ever-moving workforce. Anonymous, computer-mediated transactions are more cost-efficient than personal relationships. Another is the rise of *symbolic promotion*. Companies, public institutions and individuals have to promote themselves and their products as consistent, ordinary and reliable but also, ever-new, changing and extraordinary (see also Wernick, 1991; Corner and Pels, 2003). Forms of virtualism, not to be confused with postmodern accounts of hyperreality, develop their own driving logic for individuals.

Thus, the successful professional, operating in 'the culture of the new capitalism' needs to: be numerically and technically proficient, be flexible and adaptable, be able to learn new skills and theory, operate in new work environments and with weaker social ties, increase personal and organizational productivity, and be able to promote themselves and their products. As argued below, each of these elements, tied to rationalization and marketization, can be linked to the adoption of new technologies within the professions of journalism and politics. New ICTs are not strengthening the communicative ties between politicians and journalists or between these professions and their publics. Instead, while news production and public political engagement become quantitatively greater and more 'productive', so they are also becoming 'thinner', more 'symbolic' and 'virtualized' in nature.

The Political and Journalistic Iron Cages of the Twenty-first Century

One over-riding impression from interviewing national politicians and political journalists is the constant pressure to be more productive. Recent interviews with 80 MPs and reporters at Westminster (as well as previous sets of interviews), convey an impression of extremely hard-pressed individuals caught between multiple taskmasters and professional demands. The majority of these on-site interviews were sandwiched between other appointments and were frequently interrupted by urgent calls, text messages and assistants looking for instruction or ushering the interviewee to the next appointment or news story.

The two professions share many characteristics. Both involve: rapid information collection in a diversity of subject areas, multiple contacts and exchanges with others, information summaries and presentations, evaluations and decision-making points. In effect, both professions are driven by human exchanges and information collection and production requirements. Consequently, the pressures of rationalization and marketization are applied to these professional functions. Technology, accordingly, has come to be adopted with these, rather than ideal democratic, objectives in mind.

Most politicians effectively juggle two jobs, spending half their time in their constituency dealing with local affairs, and half their time at Westminster dealing with parliamentary business (ministers have a third job in government). They have at least five constituent groups they have to communicate with and are, in various ways, answerable to: constituents, the parliamentary party, party members and workers, party funders and allied interests, and journalists. There are also a range of interest group representatives, think tanks and assistants (parliamentary, party and civil service) who present, compile and manage information and other contacts.

The average Member of Parliament (MP) has over 90,000 constituents they may potentially have to deal with. Conversely, since the 1960s their local party support structures and memberships have been in decline (see Webb and Farrell, 1999). Parliamentary existence is busier still. In 2004–5,

MPs had to deliberate and vote on 44 Government bills and 95 Private Members' bills were put forward, to which 7,668 new amendments and clauses were tabled. There were 421 standing committee meetings to discuss these and 1,286 Select Committee meetings, producing 190 reports. Many MPs were also a member of one or more of the 303 all-party groups and 116 country groups (Norton, 2007: 436). An average of 16 EDMs (Early Day Motions) were tabled each day and drew over 100,000 signatures in total from MPs (HoC, July 2005). The range of topics was extremely diverse. With the rising complexities of the 'multi-dimensional policy space', politicians have to be increasingly flexible in learning about issues, developing and delivering policy solutions and evaluating alternatives (Webb, 2000; Dalton, 2004; Hay, 2007).

All MPs admitted to being inundated with information and requests from constituents, interest groups, officials and their party. The large majority admitted to suffering an information overload problem which required drastic solutions. Many complained of the efforts required to keep up with their constituency caseloads. Many stated that they couldn't engage meaningfully with 80–90 per cent of the issues and legislation passing through Parliament:

> Maybe there's 80 new laws a year and another 200 statutory instruments, and I would guess that out of those you can only ever possibly know really the ins and outs of ten in one year. So you rely very much on your colleagues [...] just as they rely on you. (Labour MP)

The benefits of new ICTs have been relatively slow to be realized in Westminster. However, increasingly, parties and individual MPs are using new technologies to assist them in their tasks. Screens with meeting and debate timetables and other electronic reminders direct MPs when and where they have to be. EDMs and Parliamentary Questions are now more likely to be put forward electronically. When asked about how the internet had changed what they did, the most common answer, given by a majority of respondents, was that it aided them as a research tool. Nine out of ten said they used it to search for information on a regular basis, more than half of these said 'a lot'. This might involve using the internet to gain access to specific information sources, such as news sites, the House of Commons Library and interest group websites, or using it as an encyclopaedia to get basic information. It also helped with colleague exchanges:

> The full gamut of media and information sources, which include the internet now as a research tool, are the primary sources of information [...] I read a range of newspapers and websites every day ... (Scottish National Party MP)

> You know, you can set up a meeting with an exchange of emails in sort of ten minutes whereas doing the phone calls took forever, so that's much more efficient; circulating papers before meetings or bouncing ideas or drafts on to people, that all becomes much easier. (Conservative MP, former minister)

However, new technologies had also enhanced aspects of the political 'iron cage'. Party whips text and email their MPs telling them when and how to vote. MPs are constantly evaluated quantitatively and qualitatively. How many times they attend debates, vote, the way they vote, EDM signatures, committee memberships and public speeches (and now expenses), are all recorded, aggregated and accessible. New media has thus made the auditing and evaluation of MPs more publicly visible. Journalists, party leaders and whips, interest groups and constituents can all monitor their public performances and voting decisions. Of equal concern to politicians was that the internet had, in other ways, added to their workloads. Many complained that email had considerably increased the number of constituency and interest group exchanges they had. There was more information to digest, expanded 24-hour and online news media coverage to deal with, and more human interaction but with no extra resources:

> Just for the information that people send you, you can get overloaded by that, and it's actually getting into the remit of the internet as well because you get emails [...] You just can't, you know, you physically can't deal with them and, actually, even though you've got staff, you know, they can't either. (Labour MP)

Clearly politicians cannot come close to adequately fulfilling the ever-increasing productivity demands placed on them. They can only deal adequately with a limited number of constituent and interest group needs; only hope to gain a moderate understanding in a few of the many policy areas they talk publicly about, and vote on. ICTs have helped MPs do more but, at the same time, added to workloads in other ways.[1]

Political reporting, like news journalism more generally, has also suffered from the need to become more productive, rational and market-oriented. Over the last quarter of a century, the following trends can be observed with some consistency. There is substantially more news but also greater competition and fragmentation with fewer consumers per outlet (Tunstall, 1996; Franklin, 1997, 2005; Curran and Seaton, 2003; Davies, 2008). Global competition, market segmentation and entertainment alternatives have meant a steady decline of advertising revenues for most single, commercial news outlets. Consequently, national news producers have presided over a steady decline in audience figures since the 1970s. In an effort to remain profitable, papers have raised prices

well above inflation, increased outputs and news sections while simultaneously cutting back on staff (see Freedman, this volume). Tunstall
(1996) estimated that, between the 1960s and 1990s individual output
had at least doubled. More recently, Davies (2008) concluded that journalists now have to fill three times as much news space as they did in
1985. Such calculations may be over-estimates as it is difficult to work
out how much the use of freelancers or new technologies has filled the
gap. However, these and many other interview-based accounts strongly
suggest that more news is being produced quicker, with far fewer human
resources and under poorer working conditions. Critics have labelled the
new end product Newszak (Franklin, 1997), Infotainment (Delli Carpini
and Williams, 2001), 'junk-food journalism' (Ritzer, 2004) and, most
recently, 'Churnalism' (Davies, 2008).

A strong majority of journalists interviewed offered personal accounts
that tallied with this overview. Several described experiences of: declining employment security and job cuts, the hiring of cheaper, junior staff
replacements, decreasing editorial resources, an increase in output and
paper supplements, efficiency drives, the growing power of accountants
within firms, and a greater dependency on externally supplied 'information subsidies':

> There are two fundamental changes since when I first came here,
> which is almost thirty years ago [...] the news media is highly com-
> petitive, it's much more marketized than it was, and there's a lot
> more of it, notably 24/7 television [...] And all of this marketization
> of society and technical transformation of communications are
> both pointed to the same direction: enormously more speed and
> the need to get your message across rapidly. (Political newspaper
> editor, national broadsheet)

New ICTs have been widely adopted (or imposed) across all areas of
news production and dissemination. For most journalists interviewed
new technologies had many obvious benefits in terms of aiding the production process. Internet sources of information and the ability to access
and transmit information and news outputs over distance were useful.
Most importantly, the internet had rapidly become an invaluable
research and organizational tool. Committee reports, government bills
and speeches, information on individual MPs, local politics and internal
party matters could all be accessed instantly. Organization and information transmission was mentioned by more than a third of journalists
as having improved considerably:

> I think the overwhelming importance of the internet is as the knee
> jerk and accessible information source. I mean you can access every-
> thing from government documents to chasing down a quote or

> whatever in a matter of seconds, whereas before it would take you minutes if not hours. (Political editor, commercial broadcasting)

> Email is phenomenal [...] I didn't want to phone my guy and go through it. I just sent him the link to the bits, said this is what we're going to do, he looks at it, came back with the quote, you know. It just speeds things up. (Political correspondent, national broadsheet)

However, as discussions continued, it was also clear that new ICTs have added to the demands placed on journalists in various ways. The introduction of 'multi-skilling', the 'pooling' of journalists and sub-editors, merging of sister papers, and contracting out operations, were all facilitated by new media. More importantly, new media had contributed to an expectation of more output per individual and a perpetual need to keep ahead of the news pack. Twenty-four-hour news channels, the need for the same journalist to report in different formats, and the expectation that journalists should produce additional blogs, all spread the personal resources of reporters more thinly. In effect, online news production, which is yet to be supported by advertising (see Freedman, this volume), is further diluting the editorial resources available to news producers in general:

> At the moment PMQs finishes, George Jones has got to go over and file stuff, and he may even have to do an iPod broadcast as well as something for the blog. And that's all time when you'd normally go straight downstairs and talk to MPs ... it's draining people's already limited time for no particularly good purpose, because they all feel they need these platforms and have to be generating material on these platforms. (Political editor, commercial broadcasting)

Like many other professions, operating in the organizational 'culture of the new capitalism', journalists and politicians have been subject to contemporary forms of bureaucratization and marketization. New media has offered actors solutions for doing their jobs better and offered a sense of greater control. A majority of journalists were, on balance, more positive about how new media had helped them in their work. However, at the same time, ICTs have added alternative expectations and pressures. Many expressed strong concerns about the longer-term impact of new media on traditional journalism. While most politicians had positive things to say, they were, on balance, more ambivalent or even negative in their overall assessments of what ICTs brought to them personally in their working life.

New Media Adoption and Virtualized Political Engagements

In addition to delivering new forms of professional rationalization, ICTs have also contributed to types of 'virtualization': 'abstraction', 'symbolic promotion' and the 'weakening of social ties'. As stated above, the principle activities of both professions involve the need for multiple and intense human exchanges, and, frequent information collection and production requirements. The problem is, in the organizational 'culture of the new capitalism', gaining a full understanding of a subject takes time, deliberation with others takes time, and human face-to-face interaction takes time. Time is precious and each individual has to make a risk assessment about what they use their time for; what activities are more likely to produce useful results, gain a story, produce a working knowledge of a subject, or achieve stronger links to one's constituents or consumers. New media is seductive in its appeal as a means of stretching time by enabling more information collection and more individual exchanges. However, doing 'more' by such ICT-enabled means, also changes the nature of those same activities.

Politicians, overwhelmed by the information-gathering and human-interaction requirements of their job, have adopted many practical solutions in order to cope. These include the use of assistants, colleagues and advisors, to communicate with constituents, and collect and summarize policy information for them. Mass media use, to develop 'para-social' (Horton and Wohl, 1993) forms of public engagement, are obviously a productive means of symbolically communicating with many voters. New media provides other means of dealing with these objectives. The underlying theme of those advocating its adoption is that it enhances the communicative ties between politicians and citizens, and improves understanding and deliberation. However, the interviews suggest that over-stretched politicians are, instead, more likely to use new media in ways that make politics more abstract, symbolic and distanced from individuals.

First, ICTs enable politicians and ministers to quickly become knowledgeable about a wider range of policy areas. From one viewpoint this is a major advance in terms of being able to engage on more issues and question party or government policy. But, from another position, it also enables MPs to take on the appearance of expertise in an area. This is a 'pseudo' (Boorstin, 1962) expertise and semblance of technical knowledge and 'competence' that brings false expectations. It also offers public engagement of a promotional and rhetorical, rather than substantive, nature (Edelman, 1964; Wernick, 1991). Arguably, new media is, accordingly, facilitating a soundbite-level of knowledge for a soundbite news culture. Certainly such themes often came out in the interviews.

The decline of strong party ideologies, party leaders selected on grounds of competence rather than ideological vision, and the downgrading of MP expertise. Both mass and new media were in some ways implicated here:

> Some people undoubtedly have thrived because they've looked good on television. I mean the danger is the trivialization of politics, and it's associated with the kind of culture of spin and soundbite [...] where some politicians have felt it was enough, and indeed the only thing that they needed to do was to learn the official line and then repeat it [...] I think it increasingly shows where people haven't got a deep understanding of the subject but they're simply parroting pre-prepared lines. (Labour MP, former minister)

More significantly, new media adoption is proving more likely to weaken communicative ties between politicians and citizens and make politics more symbolic rather than less. This begins with the websites of MPs which are now the norm. By the end of 2004 (Lusoli et al., 2004) 76 per cent of MPs had individual websites. This percentage has since risen and during the research period more than nine out of ten MPs interviewed had a website presence. However, little more than a third said they had a direct input to their own sites. The rest either had no input at all or admitted it was all done by their assistant. Even for the third that did contribute directly it was unclear how much that was simply taking an interest in the site and/or directing their assistants. The vast majority of websites have also turned out to be used in an old, one-to-many fashion – they are simply used to promote information about the candidate and do not encourage actual exchange and engagement. Jackson and Lilleker's analysis of MP's websites (2004) found that only 7.1 per cent provided opinion polls, 4.3 per cent surveys, and 1.6 per cent used online discussion forums. They concluded that, with the exception of 'a few pioneers', 'the vast bulk' of such communications was 'asymmetrical'. The research here suggested little advancement on these figures with political websites generally performing mostly a symbolic function for constituents:

> People read it [my blog]. People tell me they've read it and they know what I'm up to and stuff. I think it's important for constituents to know what I'm up to, because one of the dangers is you come to the village, Westminster village, and if you're not seen for a couple of days in the community they will think, people may think where are you? (Labour MP)

Email is also no more likely to improve direct engagement between MPs and their constituents. Just less than one out of five MPs interviewed was calculated to have extensive e-exchanges with constituents (sending more than 20 emails a day and emailing their constituents directly). In fact, for each MP who was a constituency email enthusiast there were several more who voiced strong concerns about it. The strongest objection was over resource constraints. Many were concerned that the most vulnerable constituents did not have email access. Several actually regarded a large proportion of email, because of its ease and simplicity, to be trivial and unconsidered. The irony, apparent to several, was that much constituency case work had to be dealt with indirectly, through assistants. Since email had increased the individual communicative burden, the outcome was that a greater proportion of case work had to be dealt with by assistants using the politician's official email address:

> I mean the rise of email is a disaster for Members of Parliament, the workload is just out of, you know, it's just a disaster [...] I get 60–100 serious emails a day, which have to be responded to and dealt with in some way, on top of the normal post bag [...] to [continue to] cope with it we would have to employ staff to respond on our behalf, perversely making us more remote from our correspondents, while appearing to be more responsive. (Conservative MP, Select Committee Chair)

Similar problems were observed in attempts to develop forms of electronic deliberation or consultation. Overall, less than one in ten MPs had engaged with the public in this way with any frequency. In most cases the idea did not generate great interest or a positive response. Lack of consultation visibility, time and resource pressures, and the digital divide, were all put forward as reasons. Similar findings have been noted in respect to consultation with government departments (Chadwick, 2006). Despite some enthusiasm from officials involved (20 parliamentary clerks and civil servants were also interviewed), there was a general sense that such exercises were more symbolic than practical:

> The NHS 'Your Health, Your Say' last year was an example of that [a deliberative forum] and quite successful I think, and we put a lot of money into it of course. But [...] Government's got to be very clear what it wants to get out of these things, because the worst thing that can happen is that you do all this listening, you get people interacting a lot more, and then you just go off and do what you were going to do anyway. And then people become very cynical about that, and just say, 'Well look, it's just another gimmick isn't it?' The health one was criticised as a gimmick. (Civil servant)

In effect, new media may have thickened the communicative ties between politicians and their professional contacts but has not between politicians and ordinary citizens. Overall, they may possibly even be weakening them. Because politicians are already over-burdened, ICT adoption is not going to help if it increases the very causes of their overload. Like with existing mass media, it is instead becoming a means of signifying an image of politicians that cannot actually exist in practice: pseudo expertise and competence, impossible levels of constituency exchange, an ability to be in the constituency and at Parliament simultaneously. Thus, new media have helped reshape the political iron cage towards virtualism.

Journalists too have had to present a professional veneer that covers up the fact that, most of the time, they cannot possibly produce the kind of journalism they aspire to. Reporters, every day, must do instant research, gain an objective overview, and locate a balanced set of reliable sources, on a diverse range of news topics. Consequently, as media sociologists have observed (Tuchman, 1972; Gans, 1979; Fishman, 1980; Gandy, 1982; Schlesinger, 1987; Tiffen, 1989; Tunstall, 1996) a number of practical solutions have evolved for bridging the gap between reporting limitations and expectations. Set beats, diary stories, presentation of opinions rather than facts, the use of news wire and public relations material, and the recycling of news within and across formats (Franklin, 2005; Davies, 2008; Philips, this volume), have all become a naturalized part of news production. Thus, the professional, Fourth Estate ideals of journalism have, in many ways, come to be achieved more symbolically than substantively. Many daily practices are no more than short-cuts or proxy substitutes for what is required. As the twin logics of rationalization and the market have further tightened the journalistic iron cage, so journalists have been forced to find further short-cuts and proxy methods to make the existing short-cuts and proxy methods sustainable. News beats are narrowed, source exchanges limited, news agendas and story information copied from other journalists, political conflict and scandal stories substituted for detailed evaluations of policy and competency (see also Thompson, 2000; Brookes et al., 2004; Davis, 2007).

Once again, new media has made such activities seem much more achievable. As for MPs, the greatest benefit the internet has brought is its quick and wide-ranging research capabilities. However, they also suffer from online information overload and a need to construct reports from website sources with dubious credibility. Thus, as for politicians, there is a greater dislocation between the 'pseudo expert' presentation and the increasingly ad-hoc, under-researched and unreliably sourced (from PR and unchecked websites) nature of the production process:

In the old days you had to get up in the morning and read all the newspapers, listen to the Today Programme [...] Now, in addition to all of that we also have to keep an eye on websites, blogs of others, just in case stories crop up [...] As on the Internet what we have to contend with is hugely increased sources of information. (Political newspaper editor, mid-market national)

You could get something wrong from Wikipedia [...] when you're under those time constraints, the internet is fabulous but it's dangerous as well. And I think that's ... a lot of the times people get things wrong, particularly on 24-hour news channels, it's because they're relying on the internet. (Political editor, commercial broadcasting)

A key finding that emerged from the interviews was how much new media was encouraging journalists to watch each other and follow 'the pack'. Reporters have always watched each other to try and work out what is newsworthy. Rising pressures on journalists to be time-efficient, produce saleable copy, and not lose out on the big stories, means an ever-greater emphasis on news-monitoring. Here, 24-hour news channels, online news websites, and electronically-accessible news schedules, have propelled these trends even further. When journalists were asked about how new media had changed their practices, the second most common answer was its use in monitoring other news outlets (see also Quandt et al.'s, 2006, similar findings in respect of German and US journalists and Redden and Witschge, this volume). For many MPs and journalists, homogeneity in news agendas, as well as pack journalism, were thus now more prominent:

The first one [interview] I did was Radio 5 Live in the morning and they got a car around to my house, the radio car. Before I got into the radio car I'd had BBC breakfast radio, BBC Radio Wales and BBC Radio Scotland all on to me asking me could I do them in the same breakfast car because they'd found out the running order from BBC 5 Live, because, through computers they can see the running order of various programmes and they hack into them and steal guests basically. And what happens is that one organization will hear you on the radio and monitor it and think oh, that's good, we will have some of that, get him on. (Deputy political editor, national broadsheet)

The other noticeable trend coming out of the interviews was how much less personal contact there was between journalists and sources (see also Fenton, Chapter 9, this volume). Physical movement is time-consuming and general forays into Parliament that do not have a direct story purpose, are risky. Several interviewees on both sides commented on how 'lobby' exchanges, a traditional means of newsgathering, were now fairly rare. Instead, journalists pieced together politician-centred stories through websites, emailed information, quick mobile conversations, and recorded appearances of politicians on other news media. Thus, quite clearly, the actual physical relationships, which have been at the heart of traditional political coverage, have become distanced and filtered through new media:

> When you look at most of the debates, they're very poorly attended [....] I have the Parliament Channel on most of the time, and there's barely anybody in the Chamber [...] people don't need to go to the Chamber to know what's going on. They can just put the Parliament Channel on. (Political editor, public service broadcasting)

> They [journalists] don't even try to talk to you, they just watch breaking news upstairs. I pass them every day when I come in, I pass one of the rooms and I see them watching telly and they're banging away on the typewriters, all of them [...] When I first came here [...] it would be rare for that lobby not to include some journalists, and sometimes it could be as many as ten or a dozen or twenty. Now, the only people you see in the lobby are the fellas in the fancy breeches looking after the place [...] I think it's the advent of 24 hours news. (Labour MP)

Once again, new media has thickened the communicative ties between journalists and other journalists. However, it has also tended to replace rather than enhance relationships with political sources. This is significant because many publicly-reported insights on politics emerge from close journalist-source relations built up through direct contact over many years and, arguably, virtualized relationships are not the same (on this point, see also Phillips, Chapter 5 and Fenton, Chapter 9, this volume). Similarly, ICTs have also been utilized to paper over the ever-larger resource cracks that journalists struggle with. The 'pseudo expertise' of the reporter is spread ever thinner. The cannibalistic and herd-like tendencies become ever more enticing. Thus, new media has also helped to reshape the journalistic iron cage towards virtualism.

Conclusions: A Symbolic and Virtualized Public Sphere

Undoubtedly the internet and other ICTs have bought some very real benefits to those involved in politics and political journalism. In many ways it has helped those professionals to better research, communicate and engage in new fora. However, many of the prophecies and ideals of technophiles and democratic theorists have not been realized. This is not, as some have argued, because the technologies need further development or, because politicians and journalists are apathetic or lazy. Indeed, a strong majority of those interviewed appeared to work exceptionally hard and hold to many of those same ideals. The less they achieved them the harder they tried.

As argued here, it is the very nature of the demands and expectations on them which have been the main driver of new media adoption. Politicians and journalists operate in very modern 'iron cages'. The nature of their work revolves predominantly around human exchanges and gathering information with a view to reporting and/or making decisive evaluations of political issues. As they have been driven to become ever more 'productive' in these tasks so they have found new media uses to help in this. Such uses have both assisted and altered those professional practices and, consequently, the nature of their 'iron cages'. One overall shift identified here is towards 'virtualism': 'pseudo forms of expertise', 'abstraction' and 'presentation' over 'craftsmanship', 'symbolic' rather than 'substantive' forms of news and politics, and 'thin' rather than 'thick' communicative ties. Individuals, in the spheres of institutional politics and political journalism, are becoming more distanced from their publics rather than being brought closer to them. As Jamieson (1989), Carrier and Miller (1998), Ritzer (1998) and Sennett (2006) have argued, such contemporary developments are not to be simply labelled 'postmodern'. They are not merely cultural, abstract and apolitical shifts. Politics and markets continue to evolve and reshape human relations but just do so under an alternative layer of ICT-enabled mystification.

Endnotes

1. See Fenton, Chapter 9 this volume, for a similar discussion in relation to NGOs.

Chapter Eight

·····································

New Online News Sources
and Writer-Gatherers

Nick Couldry

Introduction

This chapter is about those outside mainstream UK media institutions who, through the networking and information-gathering resources of the web, seek to be new news sources. What are their values? Do they intersect with journalistic values, and so extend journalistic practice? Is this extension stable, or liable to be undermined? This chapter's topic is wider than 'online journalism' (Deuze, 2003) since not all those followed defined themselves as journalists. Nor is its topic the huge recent expansion of opinion-giving online ('blogging') as such. Opinions, after all, are hardly a new element in journalism, and online opinion may generate hierarchies as sharp, if not quite as rigid, as those around conventional op-ed pages (Park, 2004); while the potential new news sources in which we are interested may not operate through opinion at all, but through news aggregation.

Given media's intertextuality, which is intensified online (Bolter and Grusin, 2002), a story source can be anything (including another story), but there remains a clear distinction in practice between a story and a person or site (what we might call a 'source-actor') that is regularly regarded as reliable enough to make further inquiry unnecessary. Is the online world throwing up new types of source-actors for journalism? If so, this matters: sources are fundamental to the types of stories that journalists can routinely produce (Hall et al., 1978, Schlesinger, 1990). By this standard, many blogs written with the aim simply of giving a point of view, not to challenge mainstream news's modes of production (Rosenberg, 2007), may matter less, even if some blogs become so authoritative and fashionable that their opinions are reportable as 'fact'. By contrast, *opinion-less* websites – such as the site founded by Brian Stelter, TV.newser.com, subsequently absorbed into www.mediabistro.com, which in 2006 became regarded by the US TV industry as 'a trustworthy source of information' precisely 'because he posts everything'[1] – may represent a more important sign of structural change.

So the broader question is: 'What happens when people at the edges participate in the news-gathering and dissemination process' (Gillmor, 2004: 25)? Here too there is a choice of focus to be made. We could concentrate on alternative media online that aim to be full rivals to mainstream news but that space has already received some attention (Atton, 2004). We are interested more in those source-actors – lying between individual web-posters and fully fledged news organizations – who through the web are expanding the news landscape, either directly or by altering the sources from which mainstream news typically draws.

We call these source-actors 'writer-gatherers'.[2] This term is preferable to the US term 'citizen journalist' which does not necessarily play well in the UK context and (like 'user-generated content') is sometimes used to include anyone who posts even one story or photo on a mainstream news site.[3] Citizen journalist as a term also brings with it an implausible claim of automatic democratization (Jarvis, 2008). In any case, the UK lacks the larger-scale 'self-organizing newsrooms' (Gillmor, 2004: 146) of those regarding themselves as citizen journalists found in the US or Israel.[4] The term 'writer-gatherer' by contrast is intended as a non-evaluative term to capture those engaged in a regular practice of writing and/or information aggregation outside mainstream media institutions.

Inevitably the space of writer-gatherers is fragmented, and not a clearly defined 'field' in Bourdieu's sense (Bourdieu, 1993), that is, a competitive space organized around a common set of resources and practices, even if some writer-gatherers approach or overlap with the borders of the journalistic field. In spite of this fragmentation, it was important nonetheless to approach these actors through a common question: if there is potentially a democratization of journalism under way, are its likely preconditions being met in the practice of those writer-gatherers? This chapter concentrates on four such preconditions; is there

1. an extension, even if in new language, of something like journalistic values, or the development of new sources on which journalistic practice can rely;
2. the time for actors to carry out such a role;
3. the money and resources to carry out such a role;
4. legitimacy and recognition for such a role.

Our argument will be that the fulfilment of these preconditions is mixed and, where achieved, likely to be unstable. Predictions of a wider democratization of journalistic practice through an expanded range of internet source-actors are therefore premature. However, some new types of writer-gatherer may be newly enabled by the web, with positive consequences.

Methodological Note

The heterogeneous, fast-changing space of online writer-gatherers means it is impossible to achieve a 'sample' in the statistical sense. At best, we could hope to interview a satisfactory *range* of producer *types*, sufficient to give a sense of this space's complexity.[5] In addition, access was often difficult. Sometimes the only access-point was an email address on a website or blog; this led to many no-replies and some interrupted access (for example a police sergeant blogger who proved too busy to keep up his blog or email correspondence with me). The sample was built slowly. Gradually we had to accept that certain types would prove too hard to reach, and perhaps for a good reason: a strong concern over anonymity (police bloggers)[6] or primary involvement in other practices to which the website was less essential (campaigning websites).[7]

In spite of these difficulties a sample was built of 19 writer-gatherers: some opinion-givers, some pure aggregators; some on the edge of mainstream political news, others on the edge of celebrity industry; some individual professionals and others close to community media.[8] Because of our project's broad news focus, we avoided bloggers or aggregators in the domain of cultural taste, as well as types inadequately represented in the UK: general aggregators without any editorial identity (reddit.com, dig.com) and very large-scale, already mature aggregators such as the Huffington Post or the Drudge Report. Other interesting groups emerged too late to be pursued, for example the 'blogging mums' recently followed by UK publishers and newspapers.[9] Professional blogs, a site of huge expansion recently, could have been a study in themselves, but we did not attempt to cover the full range of professions.

Analysis

The range of writer-gatherers is huge. Reliable figures for comparing website audiences are notoriously difficult to obtain, but our sample ranges from those reaching self-reported audiences of 250,000–750,000 unique users per month (political blogger, and celebrity gossip sites) to 25,000 per month (one professional site) and probably much lower in the case of some other individual sites. In terms of scope and legitimacy, there is a huge span too: political bloggers and celebrity gossip sites, whether liked or not, are an established part of the political/entertainment media industries, whereas some local and professional sites we interviewed worked in relative isolation, with any status derived from mutual linking with similar sites.

Difference in size and status however does not necessarily equate with differences in significance, if it is a genuine expansion of the source landscape underlying news production in which we're interested. Take the case of leading political bloggers (interviewed by Aeron Davis): they certainly offer more than just opinion, crossing over into journalism when, on the basis of the wide attention secured through their opinions, they lead factual stories of political significance and so extend the range of sources on which mainstream political news relies. A similar case can be made for celebrity gossip sites such as Holy Moly which work closely with the tabloid press. But such relationships are better seen as extending the flexibility and speed of mainstream journalism (by outside *agents,* as it were), rather than representing a completely different type of source entering the news landscape. They represent a lowering of the entry-barrier, if not to the mainstream media, at least to the buffer zones which link journalism to politics/celebrity, but hardly a democratization of news itself, in spite of claims, for example, by the founder of celebrity news site Popbitch to be 'democratizing gossip' (quoted in Aitkenhead, 2006). Both political and celebrity writer-gatherers realize this:

> nothing's going to really change is it, you know […] there's [just] another bit of competition for them [politicians] that's going to make them a little bit wary, and it's going to change at the margins. I don't think it's going to dramatically change things. (Guido Fawkes, interviewed by Aeron Davis)

> ultimately the publications are business. And there are only so many ways in which that business is going to succeed. One of the ways being you sell scandal and you've got to be unpleasant to people. […] a newspaper and a publication […] they're very powerful things. […] a blog […] causes them to enlarge their vocabulary of defence that's how I would put it […]. [while] journalists on these mainstream papers are turning into bloggers. (Celebrity site A)

By contrast, much smaller sites may represent a more important long-term shift in the *types* of people and interests represented in the space of public comment. We will look at professional bloggers in this light below.

At the same time, the celebrity websites (whose authors worked or had worked in mainstream media) regarded the possibility of independent unofficial production, combined with the web's speed, as changing the celebrity news cycle significantly:

I could never have imagined when I started as a journalist, when I used to actually write things out on a fucking Remington typewriter and it was two weeks for editors to get back to me by post or phone, or a carrier pigeon that I now can think of an idea at half-past two and get a piece up by quarter to three. And have comments by three. (Celebrity site A)

Meanwhile writer-gatherers outside the media industries often saw themselves as part of a broader expansion in media content: 'I think that all the mainstream press will now refer to bloggers as another thread coming in. It's certainly given people like me a voice they wouldn't have had before' (professional site C). At one level this was seen as working to expand awareness of professional zones previously closed to the media and the general public: 'it's giving people who don't have a window into the armed forces [such] a window' (the army rumour and information exchange site ARRSE). At another level, and more boldly, some saw a radical shift under way in the sites of cultural production, with varying opportunities for influencing news, depending on whether you were a writer-doctor, a community news producer or a new entrant to the London celebrity-news market. Not all however were optimistic looking ahead: two websites linked to the Manchester blog aggregator Manchizzle were pessimistic about influencing news agendas or in one case about surviving at all: 'I'm not confident, I think tomorrow the web is all going to change [...] the small guys like me are going to be swept aside and it's all going to be Google and Yahoo'.

Let's now turn in more detail to the values which motivate the writer-gatherers we interviewed.

Values and Aims

In the hybrid space of writer-gathering, private and public motives inevitably intersect, but it was only at celebrity websites that private motives were dominant, either in the form of commercial motive or personal expression for an otherwise constrained working journalist: '[my site] has become its own kind of news site and gossip site and personal performance [...] because I have fairly well developed ideas about life [and] I don't find them reflected anywhere else' (celebrity site A).

Most sites interviewed had a distinct public aim, but this could take many different forms. For some, their site's public role used individual expression to influence public debate: 'it's pamphleteering all over again. [...] I'm trying to influence the agenda' (local personal A). Doctor bloggers were consistent in their aim of 'bearing witness' to National Health Service conditions at a time of intense government pressure for reform to doctors' contracts and hospital provision:

Currently as a doctor I feel totally misrepresented and distorted by the press. Blogging levels up the playing field, and if I can present the doctor's side well and get enough readers/leverage then I can make a very positive difference to my profession. (Professional site F, email to the author, 25 February 2008)

The aim of increasing awareness was shared by The Magistrate's Blog, although without the context of current disputes with government: '[Magistrates are] ordinary people, we have real lives, we live in the real world, and so I wanted to try and dispel that by trying to explain how we make our decisions, the rules we work by'.

Others, by contrast, saw the public role of their site in a non-individual way, whether gathering a pool of information for citizen journalists to use however they wished (TheyWorkForYou) or, in more targeted fashion, providing a focus-point for the information needs of a particular group of campaigners ('bringing all the data to one place': Tescopoly). Still others saw their site as a direct expression of 'community' at a time when communities were difficult to build because of modern living conditions (Vision News) or difficult to sustain because of dispersed working conditions (ARRSE on the armed forces).

Not surprisingly therefore, given this variety, such public aims did *not* translate easily into what we might recognize as journalistic values for a number of reasons noted shortly. There were however exceptions. Some sites described methods of checking sources or information accuracy that were clearly oriented towards journalistic values. Political bloggers and celebrity gossip sites worked in close proximity to the media industries and under similar legal constraints, while the local government information site Mayorwatch aimed to correct information faults in mainstream media coverage of local government: 'there's nothing worse when you know something very well and you see it misreported elsewhere. So it's that very sort of thing that drives [my site] really [...] to [be] accurate, authoritative, informed' (Mayorwatch).

With the exception of these sites, however, journalistic values were generally confined to a broad desire to avoid distortion (indeed Tescopoly hadn't previously thought of themselves as operating in the space of journalism at all). Some sites took up a non-objective position aimed at what Pharmagossip called 'not quite neutrality', while others, particularly doctors, distanced themselves from journalistic values as actually found in media:

'Values [...] guiding mainstream journalists'. You have to be joking. Have you ever read the *Daily Mail*? (Professional site A)

My own values are at least as high as those of the average journalist [...] I think of myself as a blogger – but doing a better job than some journalists. (Professional site B)

Indeed *correcting* journalistic values was seen as part of the doctors' blogs' point – 'there would not be a need for bloggers like me if the journalists did their job properly' (professional site B) – a view expressed in more muted fashion by The Magistrate's Blog (concerned with tabloid coverage of law and crime) and TheyWorkForYou:

> I hope we are seen as a trusted source by journalists and the wider public. We always link back to the source of our data, so people can check it if they want [...] I wish mainstream media and independent news sources were as trusted and always linked back to the sources of their data. :) (TheyWorkForYou, email interview)

Given this variety, it is perhaps surprising that most of those interviewed saw themselves, even if in different ways, as providing a *new news source*. Mayorwatch expressed this through a contrast with political bloggers: '[Guido Fawkes] is a personal opinion based, personal experience based [site], and mine is I guess a step removed from that [...]. I don't see it as a blog; I see it as a legitimate news source' (Mayorwatch). Yet political bloggers themselves, along with most of the rest of the sample also saw themselves as news sources. The only clear exception was a financial advice site, Abnormal Returns, aimed at serious private investors, against the background of an already well-developed financial news industry.

The term 'citizen journalist' by contrast split those interviewed and there were few, if any, for whom it had an immediate resonance, even if, like Dr Blue, they could 'accept' it as 'a label'. Either or both of the words 'citizen' and 'journalist' failed to fit:

> I don't like the idea really of citizen journalist, [...] I mean I'm not really a journalist. (Local personal site A)

> I don't like the expression [citizen journalist] and never use it. Can't decide if it is rather Stalinist sounding, or just tacky. (Professional site A)

The whistleblowing site Pharmagossip which had strong US links was perhaps the site for whom the term citizen journalism resonated most as part of its vision of how 'Web 2.0' was changing media so that content was now driven by those outside media institutions.

Actual Practice

To sum up so far: we found little evidence amongst citizens interviewed of an alternative source of journalistic practice emerging, even if most saw themselves as 'new news sources'. To what extent then is writer-gatherers' belief in themselves as new news sources justified, when we look at their sites?

Even from a brief look at the contents of the sites whose producers we interviewed, the limits to this potential transformation are clear. At one end of the spectrum lie the high-profile political bloggers and celebrity gossip websites offering a new, generally more strident, less consensual voice. The clarity of the shift under way is linked directly to its *limits*: these are new voices inflecting already well-established spheres of political and entertainment media, rather than an expansion of the news landscape into a new domain. At the other end of the spectrum are local personal bloggers who offer respectively, personal opinion or image portfolios with the potential under certain favourable circumstances to feature in mainstream news agendas, at least at the margins, but have a limited chance of influence otherwise.

In between lie a number of partly institutionalized voices, some of them offering something new and potentially significant, others perhaps not. Professional blogs and armed service rumour sites are not news sites; they insert streams of individual opinion, often highly forceful in language, into the wider ambit of public debate. While such sites sometimes offer detailed reasoning and professional knowledge,[10] they may also be abusive or at least very informal in tone, with a limited chance of influencing journalists, let alone wider public opinion. Nonetheless the *potential* of such professional sites to be a new news source is clear, and it is illustrated further by industry-based sites such as Pharmagossip and more risky whistle-blowing sites such as the former www.wikileaks.org (closed down by US court order in February 2008). Similarly, a campaigning site such as Tescopoly, by collecting information on a mass of small campaigns across Britain and beyond, shows how a well-resourced site can transform the information landscape not only for journalists but for interested citizens too. Aggregator sites like TheyWorkForYou (UK national parliament) and Mayorwatch (local government in London) constitute a parallel innovation, but without any campaigning stance.

By contrast, local news web-TV sites (Felixstowe TV and Vision-News) have, as yet, few independent investigative resources for becoming a genuinely new news source, and at most work as a site of exchange for local information and promotion, although they are too recently formed to draw any final judgements on their potential.

It is certainly not the case, therefore, that the news source landscape is standing still even if the signs of a genuine expansion of journalistic practice are limited. We need however to look closely at how far such changes as are under way are likely to be sustainable.

Time

If the identified expansion of news sources is to be sustainable, certain preconditions need to be met. The first is time: those involved need the time to act as effective sources and, if this time is subsidized, the subsidy needs to be stable.

With the exception of one celebrity site (already working full-time as a journalist and drawing on that practice in a blog which took no more than 30 minutes a day), all those interviewed reported significant time spent on their site. Two sites (one celebrity site and one local TV news site) involved a number of full-time staff within a wider business model that allowed for cross-subsidy of time costs from other income streams: a general media content business and a media training business. In three other cases, the significant amounts of time spent on the site were 'loaned' from a separate organization, whether under a formal secondment arrangement (Tescopoly) or more informally in accordance with the underlying organization's objectives (They Work For You, linked to My Society) or by personal choice of the business founder (Mayorwatch is run by the owner of a broader web business).

In other cases the time subsidy was potentially less stable, since it involved work done in the spare time of someone fully employed or self-employed. The time reported in such cases varied from 3 hours per week to approximately 2 hours per day. Clearly these are significant amounts of time and effort to sustain over long periods. While this is not difficult for the semi-retired (professional site C) or those returning to work after a period of sickness (two cases), it was difficult to sustain in other cases: so the two full-time doctor bloggers reported difficulties in sustaining their blogs and needed to withdraw their commitment for significant periods:

> I don't time it. I do not consider it work. Ideally I would do it just when I wanted to do it but it got out of control and that was when it became a burden. Because it was taking up too much time I backed off and currently I am not spending much time actually writing for the blog. (Professional site B)

So if such blogs do represent a positive development (see Conclusion, below), the time subsidy on which they are based is unstable.

Finance/Resources

Another basic condition for sustainability is of course adequate finance and resources. The main costs for the sites contacted was time (just discussed) but for the more ambitious sites the cost of buying a content management system (and the related data skills) was also significant. How were these resources provided? Some sites, as just noted, were made possible by the loan of time from other businesses or non-profit organizations, and so were as stable as the finance underlying those wider entities. When, as with Mayorwatch, that related business was website management, web-related skills and resources were not a separate cost.

With the exception of the sites reaching large audiences (one celebrity site and one political blogger) there was little evidence that web advertising was a significant present or future income source. Some sites implicitly dismissed advertising's importance:

> I get a few hundred pounds a month from advertising but it does not compensate for the time commitment. I don't have anything to sell. Of course [...] it's wonderful to see all these hits, you know, go into Google analytics, oh Alaska's big today. It's satisfying on a sort of ego level but quite frankly if ten people came into my site on one day and if 10,000 came in the next, it makes no difference to me – maybe $3 on the Google ads, that's all it makes, you know.

For local web-TV sites seeking to establish a full-time business model, it was not yet clear whether advertisements would be sufficient to generate a significant income stream, but it remains possible that in the long-term local business advertising will become significant. For individual sites run by those without independent economic capital or resources, Google advertising was a potential significant source of income, but increasingly unstable, with impacts on future development:

> the Google advertising revenue started to climb during 2007, and I carried out some optimization, added some more content, and it climbed steadily and it peaked at [] a month in July. And by that stage I thought well that's it I've made it now because my [...] that's enough to live on [...]. But unfortunately that income dropped and dropped and dropped and dropped and dropped month on month, and it bottomed out at about [] in December. [...] that was a great shock to the system.

From a financial point of view therefore, there are good reasons to doubt whether the suggested extension of the news landscape is stable unless it occurs in tandem with a wider business model or corporate (NGO) objective.

It is possible of course to run a low-tech blog that is 'economically neutral' (for example, most professional blogs), but in each case the site-owner's real income was provided by independent employment or self-employment (that is by independent economic capital), generating in some cases, such as full-time doctors, the problem of unstable time-subsidy already noted.

Legitimacy and Recognition

A more subtle precondition of sustainability is legitimacy. In the long-run, new news sources will fade away unless they secure from somewhere a degree of legitimacy and recognition to motivate their efforts. At this point the splits within the space of writer-gatherers become particularly clear.

For those in our sample with symbolic capital within the journalistic field, that is, journalistic capital, established through media work (such as the celebrity sites), that was not an issue. Celebrity site A's relationship to tabloid journalists was close: 'I can pick up a phone to all of them, they all take my calls, and they're also another good source checklist. They're also good for running stories by'. Legitimacy was also available to those without journalistic capital who relied on their symbolic capital within other professional fields, such as doctors. It is not surprising they chose to keep a distance from mainstream journalists. Indeed one doctor-blogger believed that he had the reputation to write in his own name and influence public debate directly:

> in fact if I write it under my own name with my own authority and put all my degrees and all my connections and all the jobs I hold, I'm a very powerful character and I immediately establish my credibility. And in fact once I start doing that then I also become a lot more referenceable. (Professional site F)

For others (The Magistrate's Blog and Tescopoly), their independent professional standing was quite compatible with having a good working relationship to mainstream media. So the NGO staff running the Tescopoly site commented:

> we do get a high volume of media looking at the local campaigns, which is why we do try and keep [that part of the website] as up to date as we can [...] I think the overall role of Tescopoly is one of the first ports of call for some media. [...] and I think we can fulfil that quite well because we've got a broad knowledge and lots of contacts.

ARRSE (the army rumour site) lay in the middle: being able to rely on independent professional capital as members of the armed forces, they felt no need to make any particular adjustments to attract journalists;

journalists in any case were in the habit of signing on to the ARRSE site
to pick up what was going on.

For those without journalistic or separate professional capital, however,
legitimacy was more difficult. The local web-TV sites both operated at
some distance from the local press who appeared, perhaps not
surprisingly, to see them as potential rivals: one referred to 'blocking
mechanisms in place'. Instead they sought legitimacy through 'community'
links but in the long run this was likely to require establishing themselves
economically as well. For others such as Mayorwatch, Google rankings
offered an alternative source of potential status:

> it allows me to put my content, my headline and précis on the same
> page as something on the *Telegraph* or *The Times*. You do a search
> for, you know, Cross Rail, or whatever it might be, and you might
> get twelve stories, and one of them will be from MayorWatch, and
> one will be from Transport Briefing, and the others will be from the
> BBC and the *Telegraph*, and how else, at no cost, could I put my
> news in the same shop window?

In the long run search engine rankings may be an alternative source of
status also for local news sites. But for others operating outside
traditional media brings the risk of lacking broader legitimacy. There
was little evidence that loose communities of bloggers (for example
around the Manchizzle blog aggregator in Manchester) provided an
effective alternative form of cultural capital: 'there is a community of
Manchester bloggers, but it's like bloggers being bloggers, it's not like
they meet' (local personal site A).

Conclusion

What signs exist here of specific transformations of potential long-term
significance? We have seen reasons for scepticism about the general
sustainability of many new source-actors, but at the same time, there are
two potentially positive developments which must be noted, first in
improving the communications within professional and campaigning
groups and second, more boldly, in extending the range of people who
can operate as regular source-actors.

The first development, while not constituting an extension of news
broadcasts as such, does facilitate communication among those who might
in the future become actors in the news. The existence of professional
gossip sites (in the armed forces and elsewhere) enables a disparate but
significant group of people to be registered as a public actor, even against

the wishes of government, forming potentially a new form of pressure on related professional elites, at least in the public services:

> I think the Department of Health read us. I think the Department of Health have got spotters and scanners, and in fact I know that, for instance, when the Deputy Chief Medical Officer was getting grilled by the House of Commons Select Committee about the MMC [Modernising Medical Careers] fiasco he made reference to the various unkind comments about him on blogs. (Professional site F)

The links from improved 'internal' communication to increased action within the news are subtle and long term, but should not be dismissed. Tescopoly plausibly suggest that their online information-gathering has mobilizing potential:

> the sort of feedback we've had from local campaign groups is [that] it's great to have our campaign linked to because we feel part of something. I think that's really interesting because a lot of them actually don't need that support from us, it's just that feeling of being linked somehow [...] as being part of a national or international network.

A rise in professional militancy may develop from becoming more 'present' as a group on the national scene, as suggested by the organizer of the ARRSE site: 'I think people generally are more politically aware [...] or more willing to campaign [...] on issues, and certainly that's what we've noticed'. If so, then there is something to support Ed Mayo and Tom Steinberg's recent claim (2007) that the web is changing the information flows of UK civil society (as with nineteenth-century friendly societies): the significance of NGO information strategies is discussed in more detail in Chapter 9.

Second, and more speculatively, it is possible that we are at the very beginning of a transformation whereby, out of the disparate space of writer-gatherers, some new types of source-actor are emerging. We are not referring here to celebrity gossip sites whose relationship to the existing media industry is close, not to say parasitic; nor do we mean the rise of authoritative political bloggers, who use their institutional independence to carry on the opinion-dimension of journalism more freely than can be done within media institutions. Nor do we refer to the hyper-local websites whose long-term economic viability is as yet unclear. Instead, we mean individual professionals, acting independently whether out of personal interest (The Magistrate's Blog) or out of dissatisfaction with their own institutional representation (many doctor blogs). The evidence that such professional bloggers are influencing media and through media the institutional forces with which they are competing is as yet thin: for all their vociferousness, doctors' blogs have not yet been reflected in any successful media-based campaign against the UK government, although the ARRSE site is perhaps a more plausible example of maintaining the profile of its members' working conditions in the UK news. However, the strategy of The Magistrate's Blog, of influencing opinion not only through an anonymous blog but through good working relationships with mainstream journalists, and so aiming to 'influence the whole debate nationally', is interesting as a sign of what might be possible for skilful and time-rich source-actors.

As noted above, the emergence of such new source-actors depends on independent professional capital, but that does not make it any less striking a development, contradicting somewhat the pessimistic views of Geert Lovink (2008) and David Leigh (2007) that the commercialization and fragmentation of news and comment in the digital era will be unable to generate a critical public culture. Whether these shifts hold within them the seeds of a wider democratization of news, however, must remain a matter for further, appropriately sceptical, enquiry over the coming years.

Endnotes

1. *New York Times*, 20 November, 2006.
2. This chapter draws on the interviews conducted by Nick Couldry between November 2007 and March 2008 with *political news and information aggregators* (Mayorwatch (http://www.mayorwatch.co.uk), TheyWorkForYou (http://theyworkforyou.com) and Tescopoly (http://tescopoly.org)); *local community news-sites* (Felixstowe TV (http://www.felixstowetv.co.uk) and Vision-News (http://vision-news.tv)); *professional bloggers/aggregators* (Pharmagossip (http://pharmagossip.blogspot.com), Dr Crippen (http://nhsblogdoc.blogspot.com), Dr Blue (a member of the http://www.drrant.net site), Dr Grumble (http://drgrumble.blogspot.com) and The Magistrate's Blog (http://thelawwestofealingbroadway.blogspot.com)); *the armed forces information exchange sites*, ARRSE and RumRation (http://www.arrse.co.uk and http://www.rumration.co.uk); *local personal commentary sites* (Rentergirl (http://www.rentergirl.blogspot.com) and Aidan, a photography site (http://www.aidan.co.uk)); *celebrity gossip sites* (Holy Moly (http://www.holymoly.co.uk) and Madame Arcati (http://madamearcati.blogspot.com)); and a *financial advice site* (AbnormalReturns at http://abnormalreturns.com).
3. For debate on the term in September 2007 see: http://www.pressgazette.co.uk/story.asp?sectioncode=1&storycode=38718

4. For the US, see www.democracynow.org and www.publicintegrity.org; on Israel, see Reich (2008).
5. Initially, anticipating major difficulties of access, we included US producers in our fieldwork. This later proved too cautious (we had a 50% success rate from approaches for interviews), but it explains why there is one US producer – www.abnormalreturns.com (a financial analyst) – in the sample.
6. See those listed under Further Reading.
7. Such as www.medicaljustice.org.uk and www.pricedout.org.uk
8. In order to protect confidentiality, quotes will be identified either by site name only, or (in the case of more personal sites) with a generic attribution (such as, celebrity site X/Y, professional site XYZ, local personal site X/Y).
9. See the *Daily Telegraph*, weekend section, 10 May 2008.
10. See The Magistrate's Blog throughout and the 9 July 2008 post of Dr Rant at www.drrant.net

Chapter Nine

· ·

NGOS, New Media and the Mainstream News: News from Everywhere

Natalie Fenton

Introduction

This chapter looks at one type of news source – the NGO – and the nature of its relationship to the professional journalist in a new media environment. It draws on a range of interviews with a variety of NGOs and journalists conducted throughout 2007/08.[1] Publicity – both for campaigning and for fundraising – is a central aspect of all NGOs' work. For many, particularly the large, resource-rich organizations, responding to a media-saturated environment has meant a growth in press and public relations (PR) offices increasingly staffed by trained professional journalists. These professionals apply the same norms and values to their work as any mainstream newsroom albeit with different aims and intentions; they use their contacts and cultural capital to gain access to key journalists and report increasing success in a media-expanded world. The resource poor however, far from finding a more levelled playing field with new media increasing access, as proclaimed by many early exponents of the advantages of new communication technologies (see Klein, 2000; Norris, 2002; Rheingold, 2002), are forced to rely on long-standing credibility established by proven news-awareness and issue relevance. They find it much harder to keep up with changes in technology and the explosion of news space; and much harder to stand out amidst the countless voices online all competing for journalists' attention. As journalists are now required to do more in less time (Davies, 2008; Phillips, this volume) so their interactions with news sources dwindle. In news terms, NGOs may be getting more coverage (often online), but the nature of that news remains firmly within pre-established journalistic norms and values – referred to in this chapter as 'news cloning'. The opportunity to explain complex issues in detail in the hope of shifting news agendas is waning. The increased pressures on journalists from the marketization of news,[2] combine with the pressures of non-elite news sources to maximize news coverage, resulting in NGOs feeling frequently compelled to give journalists what they want – ready-made copy that fits pre-established news agendas.

But before moving on to the empirical data that explains these findings, it is critical to appreciate the changing socio-political context of the status of NGOs in a neo-liberal global order. To understand the way in which NGOs are positioned as news sources, their subsequent relationship to professional journalists and the impact of technology, we must also take account of the altered nature of NGOs as organizations and their changing position in society.

Over the last two decades there has been an exponential growth in NGOs worldwide though the majority are still in developed nations (Albrow et al., 2008). NGOs have not only increased in number but have become an essential part of society. In the UK this is manifest in a vastly enhanced role for NGOs as service providers making a significant contribution to welfare. In the process of expansion many NGOs have become more professional in outlook. The sheer expansion in numbers has increased competition between NGOs to garner the attention of both policy makers and donors alike. Consequently, the fundraising and campaigning roles of the press office have gained in importance. In 1989 Knapp and Saxon-Harrold noted that NGOs had greater diversity of income sources, social programmes and organizational complexity; enhanced advocacy and more extensive media attention related to more professional fundraising, management and the use of marketing than ever before. In the 20 years since this study it would appear that this trend has continued.

The contemporary role of NGOs and their relative prominence in civil society is indicative not only of national political and economic changes but also of the rise of non-state actors and their relationship to global changes under neo-liberalism. As the work of nation states moves and combines across national borders, the presence of non-state actors not accountable to electoral state-bound constituencies is beginning to 'reformat the political field' (Dean et al., 2006: xxviii). New ICTs enable relatively easy networked communication between NGOs and by NGOs with other political actors on a global platform. Local actors have become part of global networks, intervening in international concerns such as human rights and environmentalism, further increasing their credibility and enhancing their relationship with journalists who are more likely to perceive them as newsworthy.

The enhanced social and political role of NGOs has occurred alongside diminishing public confidence in traditional political elites and systems. People are increasingly disengaged from mainstream politics (Park, 2004). The extensive literature that discusses people and politics falls largely into two camps: one that talks of disaffection and the other of citizen displacement (Loader, 2007). In the former, studies speak of the decline of (particularly young) people voting in conventional party political elections as indicative of extensive alienation of people from society's central institutions (Wilkinson and Mulgan 1995). In the latter, an engagement with traditional politics based on a sovereign nation state is displaced. People may not be any less interested in politics than before, but traditional political activity no longer appears appropriate to address their concerns (Loader, 2007). Rather, certain parts of civil society are foregrounded as alternative arenas of public trust, information and representation. It is argued that politically motivated people tend to look to non-mainstream political arenas frequently populated by NGOs and New Social Movements (NSMs) – alternative forms of political engagement that work at the margins of the dominant public sphere (Hill and Hughes, 1998; Kahn and Kellner, 2004, 2005; Bennett, 2005). It is claimed that these forms of political participation better fit the experience of social fragmentation and individualization felt by citizens (Loader, 2007) as well as being compatible with the structure and nature of the internet. Declining levels of trust by the public in established institutions seem to be giving way to increased expectations of and a strong belief in the organizations of civil society (Gaskin et al., 1996).

NGOs have been accepted as service providers and as legitimate voices and informed campaigners on public concerns and political matters. These new sources of political legitimacy offer a diversity of values and compete in the media sphere for their share of attention. Through strategic positioning of their organization and their issue profile and through being reflexive about their modes of mediation and means of representation (Deacon, 2004) NGOs can further boost their credibility and become 'authorised knowers' in the eyes of journalists. As DeChaine (2002) highlights in relation to MSF:

MSF's emergence as a major NGO on the international stage represents a specific historical trajectory. In its early years, MSF lacked resources, in terms of both money and bodies [...] In the 1980s, MSF experienced a massive growth in both membership and resources. The continued proliferation and globalization of media communication aided the group in its efforts to publicize humanitarian crises, as well as its aid missions [...] It has grown to become the largest independent medical relief organization in the world. (MSF, 2000, 2). [...]Through its construction of a public image of neutrality, its focus on media, and its discursive construction of a 'humanitarian space' for social action (Paupst, 2000), MSF conscripts the powerful ethos of the social imaginary (Appadurai, 1991) in an attempt to forge an imagined global community uniting individuals, governments, NGOs, and international institutions. (DeChaine, 2002: 354)

The re-positioning of MSF on a global stage was only made possible through increased resources, thereby allowing them to invest more heavily in communication and publicity that in turn swelled their resources yet further. Far from being less relevant, resources have gained in importance in a world of new ICTs – just as it is easy for anyone with a personal computer to have an online presence, so it is harder to catch the eye of the increasingly deskbound journalist in a vastly expanded news marketplace. Face to face or even one-to-one interactions with journalists are spread ever thinner. To be seen, NGOs are now expected to embrace all of the opportunities available to them in the digital world – from blogging, podcasts, and social networking sites to their own online news platforms and beyond – what is referred to below as both the seduction of space and the tyranny of technology – all requiring investment of time, money and technical skills; resources that are not equally available to all. Importantly, to gain widespread acceptance by the mainstream media MSF also had to project a 'public image of neutrality' not so far removed from the journalistic ethics of objectivity and impartiality. Rather than release the potential for increased advocacy through publicity, new media seems to have amplified the pressure on NGOs to emulate mainstream news, encouraging them to act as pseudo journalists in simulated newsrooms.

Cloning the News

The large, resource rich organizations now often have substantial press offices staffed increasingly, though not exclusively, by trained journalists all peddling copy that fits the requirements of mainstream news agendas. A survey of the voluntary sector by Deacon (1996) noted that 31 per cent of organizations had press/publicity officers and 43 per cent used professional PR agencies. In those organizations with annual budgets over £250,000 the figures rose to 57 per cent with their own press officers and 81 per cent who used external agencies. Davis (2004: 31) also notes how research on various campaigning organizations (Miller and Williams, 1993; Anderson, 1997; Manning, 1998; Allan et al., 2000) all point to increasing use of professional press and publicity methods for political and economic gain. As this interviewee notes:

Certainly everyone in a particular section [...] were journalists and intentionally so. When I was there I was the first one, I think to have been a journalist. It was something new anyway [...] that's changing now and they are wanting more journalists to come in [...] When I went for my interview the boss was like it's all changing and we're very excited about media. (Interviewee A: press officer of a large international NGO talking about their previous job in a similar organization)

Although this study has not undertaken an extensive survey of communication's resources every interviewee reported an increase in media-related activity with the larger organizations having experienced a steady increase in paid press officers over the last 10 years, mostly from journalistic backgrounds. These NGO news professionals spoke frequently of how they knew intrinsically what makes a news story:

I like to think I could bring a certain kind of instinct to it. (Interviewee A: press officer, large international NGO)

Of how they used their network of journalist friends to shift stories:

The football team that I play for is the Press Association. Not that they actually work for the Press Association any more but they work on the *Daily Mail*, the *Independent*, they're all hacks and we play other hacks. It's, how easy is that [...] It's not like the well meaning press office that sends out a press release like, oh this is really important, rubbish. (Interviewee A: press officer, large international NGO)

And they told of how they perceive themselves as journalists:

Because I like to write the story. Because, having been a journalist, I want to do all of it. So I want to get the quotes and, apart from obviously the quotes from other sides. So they tend to, often it's used word for word or it's word for word but with the third paragraph of it put first and then the second paragraph fourth or whatever. Which is quite satisfying but I guess it makes it easier for them as well. (Interviewee C: press officer, large international NGO)

These organizations 'work' the news on a daily basis and seek to provide ready-made copy to fill the ever expanding space available to news. This may make these organizations very news-friendly and ensure they receive more media coverage but we found little evidence of NGOs managing to change news agendas and challenge normative conceptions of news criteria. On the contrary, pressures to reproduce these normative conceptions are increasing. This has resulted in what I refer to as 'news cloning':

> There is definitely pressure to kind of move onto something that might be more, perceived to be more newsworthy. (Interviewee H: press officer, small international NGO)

Those who do news cloning can be seen as 'political entrepreneurs' (Schlesinger, 1990) and their ability to be entrepreneurial is determined by the resources available to them. These resources include the financial (the capacity to maintain a press office and employ specific staff), but they also include the cultural capital associated with class, professional status and expertise as well as the legitimacy and credibility gained through previous activities within the political and media fields. In the world of new media this extends to being able to provide podcasts, pictures and video clips. In this way some NGOs have followed a 'media logic' (Altheide and Snow, 1979) that conditions how they behave – how they provide news gatherers with material that conforms to the pre-established criteria of what news is.

> I'm a proper old hack [...]. I used to be on the other end of these things [press releases] and they just went straight in the bin, not a chance. And if someone rang you up to chase them then you got angry with them because you were busy doing your job. But the reason it didn't work is because what was in them wasn't interesting. If you get the right story then yeah, we send out press releases...but you can't do that unless it's good stuff [...] it's a good story [...] you just put your journalistic hat on and you think well, if I got that as a story then would I run it or not? (Interviewee E, head of media, large international NGO)

Today, in a vastly increased competitive market, news is widely accepted as being commercially determined and entertainment driven. The NGOs in this study clearly recognized the need to focus on the personalization of issues and celebrity endorsement. As NGOs place more and more relevance on mediation and adopt a media logic they run the very real risk of pandering to the market and encouraging, albeit implicitly, the demise of autonomous investigative journalism (see Phillips, this volume).

> ...celebrities have so much currency, and there's good arguments that if you want to engage with people the best way of doing it is to do it through celebrities they like or the programmes they like... I'm doing

some work with the *Observer* at the moment and it's interesting that two things they've asked me for are both celebrity-related. (Interviewee B: head of press office, large international NGO)

As the news space has expanded so dramatically the onus upon 'political entrepreneurs' to reach and penetrate all of the various news platforms also increases. The ability to do this consistently and with rigour, though not necessarily difficult with a cloning mentality, is time-consuming. Only those organizations with adequate numbers of suitably trained personnel can sustain the levels of activity necessary to blog, inhabit social networks, develop their own news pages, contribute to online forums etc.:

So some of this [media work] actually is driven by individual staff members, because there aren't so many of us [...] we can't just hire in things, and we're on quite tight budgets so it's not we've decided we want a new e-campaigning strategy for getting stuff out onto blogs or whatever [...] it's largely who do we know? Can we do it in-house? Can our person who does membership databases spend some time doing this sort of thing? (Interviewee D: press officer of a small national NGO)

Smaller, resource-poor organizations cannot keep pace with the information onslaught on mainstream news sites and platforms of their wealthier counterparts. They have small press offices with staff that have often come up through the ranks. As Davis (2004: 34) notes, more resources 'mean more media contacts, greater output of information subsidies,[3] multiple modes of communication and continuous media operations. Extreme differences in economic resources mean wealthy organizations can inundate the media and set the agenda while the attempts of resource-poor organizations quickly become marginalized.' So, far from ICTs expanding access and representation amongst resource-poor groups as much of the early literature envisaged (for example, Putnam, 2000; Norris, 2001), resources, in particular the ability to spend time and money on keeping up-to-date with the technological advances and feeding an insatiable news space, still on the whole, structure access and determine levels of representation. Several PR agencies have stepped into the breach to try and sell their services to NGOs that lack adequate in-house media/communication sections:

...at least once a month for the last year I have people ringing me up and telling me about an exciting new way of getting my stories out, which is by making my own video of news and sending it to news desks [...] I listened to it to see what the spiel was, but it's basically

> that the news rooms are incredibly pressurized and haven't got any time to make their own films so if you send them a film they'll pop it on. I mean it's a horrible idea, even my version of the news, because I know that if I'm at work I don't point out all the deficiencies in X's arguments do I, because I don't get paid to do that. (Interviewee G, head of policy and communications, medium-sized national NGO)

Smaller, resource poor NGOs are undoubtedly disadvantaged in terms of access to the mainstream news. But NGOs of all sizes have learnt that they will only get their voices heard if they subscribe to journalistic criteria of expertise and professionalism. Smaller organizations can get mainstream coverage and they do use new media. Those that do get coverage talk of the importance of establishing credibility over several years as professional researchers and experts in their own right. For example, one small international NGO interviewed insists on all their information being checked and filtered by legal professionals before it becomes public. This in turn, gives the journalist a degree of confidence in the material provided.

The mounting media know-how amongst NGOs has occurred alongside efficiency cuts in news organizations, including a cut-back in journalists, particularly foreign correspondents (Davis, 2004), increasing opportunities for NGOs to insert themselves into the news production process. This was well recognized by our interviewees. International NGOs can now offer international news that news organizations are no longer well placed to provide. Here, a press officer of an international NGO talks about how one of his colleagues researched a story about a family separated by war overseas for the Saturday *Times*:

> One of my colleagues [...] she went out with the Saturday *Times* and did some research on her own stories [...] she found one kid, a heartbreak story. They found him and took him out, did some counselling with him, contacted his family, are you ready to take this guy back [...] the story turned horrible because the family were happy we could take him home [then] on the way his father died, oh shit a brick. So media-wise, it's brilliant. You know, I mean the journalists were in tears, like hardbitten news hacks – now that's amazing. Forget about the emotional side, it's a great story so we used that to tell that story.

Another international NGO talks of how access has increased:

> ...we might just get more space in that paper because they need that foreign news, they haven't got their own people on the ground. We're a trusted source of information so they might give us that space. (Interviewee B: head of press office, large international NGO)

Similarly, in countries where NGOs may have a presence but journalists are forbidden or their freedom curtailed, the NGO has an added news advantage. One NGO talked about the uprising in Burma and how they were able to get footage out before any journalists gained access, thereby securing their place in the news. Their role in global politics as adjudicators, translators and mediators clearly speaks to the increasing authority of international NGOs and a global communications system.

Seduction of Space

The limitless *potential* of the internet was recognized across the board, both with excitement because of the possibilities it offers; and with resignation on the basis that they lacked the resources to invest in it fully. The seductiveness of the space available creates a kind of tyranny – a never-ending process of mediated reflexivity and a feeling that they can never do enough but must always keep trying:

> ...we also started using photographs in reports, but that's now moved on. There is a sense there is a need to do, not just have decent images for reports that illustrate graphically what you've written about but also to have short clips, testimonies, if it's possible from the people that you're interviewing but if not then from the researcher [...] the aim was that those clips could be used by media organizations who don't have the wherewithal to call in. (Interviewee H: press officer, small international NGO)

The days of a couple of phone calls, a few press releases and maybe a press conference are over. This world of source-journalist relations is faster and greedier than ever before. This is leading paradoxically to forces that reproduce existing power hierarchies on both sides. All news outlets are content hungry and NGOs need to feed the space relentlessly if they are to gain coverage. The seductiveness of space invites recognition of the huge potential for coverage but it is only realizable for those with resources and well-established relations with journalists and for those who fulfil normative news criteria. The sheer amount of information online and the endless bulk of emails sent by all news sources to all journalists means that established contacts are ever more important if you want to creep to the top of the pile or stand out in the email inbox.

The majority of NGOs felt that because of the space that journalists are now required to fill and the time pressures in which to do it, their copy gets picked up more readily and more rarely gets changed:

...journalists are now expected to write copy for the newspaper and write copy for the website and maybe to blog and maybe actually to produce podcasts now as well. So what we are looking at is how we can make, I think, you know, the PR's job fundamentally to try and make the journalist's job as easy as possible is still what's driving us [...] one of the things we're looking at at the moment is actually gearing up more to be able to feed audio and video material to journalists [...] They will take what you, exactly what you give them. I think that has changed from before. You know it as very much you gave a journalist, you know, a press release as the idea of a story. It would then be worked up. Whereas I think now we see much more of our stuff appearing verbatim. (Interviewee J, head of communications, large national NGO).

The sheer amount of news space and multiplicity of news platforms has also led NGOs to seek out the traditional, trusted news forms. They do this for two reasons: one, they believe that the high profile, high status news platforms (the *Today* programme on BBC Radio 4; the Press Association; BBC 1 evening news; the *Guardian* and *The Times* followed by the BBC website) will provide a springboard to all other forms of news dissemination including all online news as other news organizations feed constantly off these sources; and two, they believe that these outlets are still the news sites most trusted by the general public and the most closely watched by the powerful. Only two of the organizations interviewed showed any active awareness whatsoever of alternative news sites and even then these were sidelined in favour of the 'big hitters'.

This has one obvious consequence – as the NGOs target traditionally powerful news outlets with more and more professional adeptness and news know-how, established news values remain as dominant, and one could argue even more entrenched than ever before. In other words, the internet may provide constant *possibilities* for the fracturing of dominant discourses but on the whole these remain unused and untapped. NGOs use new media simply as different ways to get the same story out. And the story is written to fit all the normative dimensions of mainstream news as closely as it possibly can.

The Tyranny of Technology: 'Because We Can, We Do' (interviewee D: press officer, national NGO)

No organization could not have a website could they? I mean you couldn't not have a website because you would look stupid. (Interviewee I, head of communications, small national NGO)

In the larger, resource rich NGOs, once new technology has been accepted as part and parcel of one's media presence then there is an endless process of revamping and updating. This is no small task and frequently organizations reported a growth in staffing to deal with new roles created out of the capacity of new technology. Contrary to claims of new technology breaking down communication barriers due to ease of access and relative low cost, the relentless marketization of new software and new communication fads and fashions puts ever more onus on NGOs to maintain technological faculty, at no small cost. Every organization we spoke to reported the current revamping of their website:

> One of the things we've actually put a lot of money into is improving our website [...] If you're a serious organization you have to have a website and that's it, or else you're not in the game. (Interviewee G: head of communications and policy, medium-sized national NGO)

The endless amount of space available, the multiplicity of news channels all requesting information and material along with the need to 'keep-up' with new technology trends was felt as a substantial pressure by many:

> ...with new media, I mean we currently have a sense in the organization that we do need to be venturing into that but we're held back by once again, resources and time. (Interviewee F, press officer, small national NGO)

And the small press offices simply couldn't keep pace with the demand of 24-hour news, putting them at an immediate disadvantage:

> The other major thing I see happening now is obviously the 24-hour rolling news programmes are in themselves a problem. They almost discourage things because as soon as you get a news item then somebody else will pick it up and then somebody else will pick it up and so everybody wants another quote. (Interviewee G: head of communications and policy of a medium-sized national NGO)

Thin Interactivity

One of the positive arguments in favour of the democratizing potential of new media is that it increases the interactivity between journalist and source and journalist and reader/viewer (for example, McCoy, 2001; Pavlik, 2001). However, in this study we found that on the whole, new media has reduced the interaction between the journalists and the NGO source. Whereas the instinct of a journalist trained prior to the internet is to talk to someone, it is felt that the instinct of the new breed of journalists is to send an email. The increase in journalists' workloads and the increasing pressures on them (see Phillips and Davis in this volume) all render a much thinner level of interactivity between journalist and source – what Davis (this volume) refers to as the 'virtualization' of news production. NGOs in this study all claimed that it is much harder to get a journalist to leave their desk than it ever used to be:

> I've been out for a coffee, not a lunch, with one journalist in the last year and that's not because I've not been particularly trying to but so many people are just resistant to leaving their desk. So we had the Czech Shadow Foreign Minister over to talk on missile defence in January, and any journalist could arrange for his office to speak to him at any point if they wanted to, telephones and emails exist, so we thought the interesting thing was he is in the UK, you can come and talk to him. But we had people who wanted to talk to him from the *Guardian* offices on Farringdon Road, through a phone call on a mobile in Westminster rather than come down because that takes too much out of the day. (Interviewee D: press officer, medium-sized national NGO)

As a consequence they are less likely to use publicity stunts, photo-calls and press briefings because they simply cannot get the journalists to turn up. Of increasing importance is the distribution of professionally produced reports on-line and pre-packaged news material that can be downloaded with a single click. Similarly NGOs use social networking sites because they know that journalists frequent them and this increases the likelihood that items will be picked up. Social networking sites also cater for the personalization and dramatization of potential news stories, increasing their appeal to the journalist. The journalist never has to leave their desk or pick up the phone. Despite journalists' insistence that they still do speak to people this was clearly not the impression of the NGOs who were insistent that talking to a journalist was a rarity. The exception to this was where good relations with a particular journalist had been established over time, suggesting that in a world of information overload and news-savvy sources the trusted book of contacts is ever more important.

The level of interactivity between the news professional and NGOs at best can be described as thin but when it comes to interaction with their own supporters and members there was clear evidence of substantial extension and intensification of interactivity. The internet has enabled resource poor NGOs to gather information and disseminate their work more readily than ever before, particularly within and among their own publics. In an investigation into the websites of international and national environmental NGOs in the UK, Finland, Spain, Greece and the Netherlands, Tsaliki (2002: 95) argues that the internet is most useful for intra and inter-organizational networking and collaboration. And that rather than bringing in new forms of communication, on the whole it complements existing media techniques for issue promotion and awareness raising:

> The thing here as well is that this is what [this organization] is about. It's about people taking action and people doing things and the web's really important for that. So a lot of what goes on the website will be geared towards, and our blog as well actually links back to some of the letter writing that I mentioned has become, so the emails or clicking on an on-line petition and doing those kinds of things, and so a lot of what's going on on the web is facilitating that, it's actually facilitating people going to participate. (Interviewee B: head of press office, large international NGO)

There is also a growing literature on the use of the internet by new social movements for oppositional political mobilization; much of this agrees that although it may not point to identifiable new political projects it does point to unprecedented political activity of a global nature (Fenton, 2008a, 2008b; Benkler, 2007). This form of networked technopolitics links marginalized groups and builds counter-discourses but endlessly resists the construction of a one-size-fits-all politics by insisting on the preservation of a multiplicity of political identities. Many of the grassroots groups involved in these new social movements consciously reject the mainstream media and seek to establish other, alternative means of communicating their message (Fenton, 2008b).

As with other established communities (such as politicians and interested political groupings in the inner circle of Westminster, (Davis, 2007)) so with the voluntary sector, the use of the internet for intra and inter-organizational debating and sharing of information does seem to have increased sociality and interactivity, augmenting communicative ties. Internal communities of interested people are built and reinforced through the networks facilitated by new communication technologies:

> We did some work on internet repression, a very high profile campaign on internet repression which caught the eye of a lot of bloggers and gave us a good reputation with them. So we started reaching out to the bloggers. We have now what we grandly call the e-Action Task Force where there's about 200 or so bloggers that we regularly send information to, encouraging them to blog about those issues on behalf of [this organization]. (Head of press, UK division of large, international NGO)

NGOs in this study recognized that they had to relinquish a certain amount of brand control to embrace the interactive elements of Web 2.0 on their sites; unleashing increasing possibilities for losing control of their message as members and supporters contribute their own views on internal and external platforms – a cause of concern for many of the press officers interviewed. At the same time pressures on journalists to produce copy also offer more opportunities for the NGOs to dictate content to journalists as long as they conform to established news criteria that are ever more at the behest of the market. The people with the potential to disrupt the monotony of news cloning are the audience/interested others. However, as reported by Redden and Witschge in this volume, the instances when this occurs are few and far between. Occasionally, the 'internal' communities of interest do extend outwards and 'go viral' as links online reap multiple connections. It is these instances that are more likely to be picked up by journalists as newsworthy than any regular interactivity. In other words, the internal spaces (or public sphericules) of communities of interest experience enhanced interactivity through ICTs, but this rarely spills over to impact upon the dominant public sphere as interactivity with journalists is curtailed through pressures and scales of production.

Conclusion: News from Everywhere

Elsewhere in this book we have discussed how news organizations are making economic decisions to cut staffing and increase investment in technology in order to survive and expand online news platforms (see chapters by Freedman; Davis and Lee-Wright in particular). This has reaped the consequences of a more desk-bound, internet-captive journalism. While it appears that the internet has given NGOs more opportunity to peddle their wares and get their voices heard, those voices have been trained to deliver what mainstream organizations are crying out for – news that conforms to established news criteria and provides journalistic copy at little or no cost. The line between the professional PR agency and the large-scale campaigning NGO has blurred into near extinction. On the one hand, this would appear to be further evidence of what Blumler (1990) refers to as a 'media-centric model of pressure group activity'. On the other hand, this is countered to a certain extent by the use of the internet to enhance intra and inter-organizational communication and also, importantly, by the growth in grassroots pressure groups that reject wholesale any relationship or connection with mainstream media on the grounds that they will distort and misrepresent their views and who use new media for the dissemination of alternative news and views that openly conflict with the mainstream media. A media centric model is also oblivious to the sophisticated and strategic political lobbying and campaigning that takes place outside of the parameters of the mainstream media, often with great success.

For those that do seek coverage in the mainstream media, the expansion of news platforms has resulted in the tried, tested, trusted and thereby credible NGOs rising to the top of the pile. Tried, tested, trusted and credible amounts to NGOs who can provide journalistic copy and have learnt the rules of the game. The NGOs in turn focus on the traditional powerhouses of news journalism for coverage – the *Today Programme*, PA, BBC and the quality press. Gaining coverage with any of these means that your message will come through the morass and be picked up readily. As news now comes from everywhere, conforming to normative news values is crucial for gaining coverage.

This chapter raises a critical question: if NGOs are simply doing the job of journalism – putting together well researched, legally tight, impartial and objective stories – does it matter that it is them and not the professionals in news organizations that are making the news? Does it make any difference? There are three important rebukes to this line of argument: Firstly, we need NGOs to be partial, occasionally illegal and passionate about their cause – if they continue to mimic the requirements of mainstream, institutionalized news then arguably they will fail in the role of advocacy, become no different to elite sources of information and lose the position of public credibility (that comes by dint of distinction from elite sources (Gaskin et al., 1996)) that many are now enjoying. If all NGOs conform to the dominant 'media logic' then they are all journalists and everybody's story is newsworthy and of course, by definition, then nobody's is. This is a pluralism that succumbs to the rule of the market where multiplicity merely translates into more of the same, albeit packaged in different ways designed to attract the journalists' attention – an attention that is increasingly preoccupied with market conditions. Secondly, in the competitive environment of news sources those with established positions of advantage and 'bureaucratic affinity' (Fishman, 1980) are likely to retain a level of dominance. In the end, new media is just a different way to get the same stories out and being able to get it out is still, on the whole, a privilege of the well-resourced. Thirdly, rather than conveniently ignoring or maybe even welcoming news cloning, we need paid journalists in news organizations to expose the inadequacies and shortfalls of thoroughly mediated democracies if we are to retain a journalism that can be said to be for the public good and in the public interest.

Endnotes

1. NGOs come in very many different shapes and sizes from the large-scale, global charity to the small-scale local pressure group. The term NGO covers a vast range of organizations from trade unions to service providers to groups

of radical political activists. Over-generalizations are not helpful (Anderson, 2004; Deacon, 2004) and disguise very real material, ethical, legal and structural differences that may have a direct impact on the ways in which they use and interact with media and ICTs. Nonetheless NGOs do share common characteristics: they are non-governmental, value-driven and mostly reinvest any financial surpluses to further social, environmental or cultural objectives. The sample of NGOs interviewed for this chapter was stratified by purpose (both those whose main purpose was as service providers and those whose main purpose was acting as pressure groups); geography (whether local, national or international) and size (calculated on the basis of annual income); although it was by no means a fully representative sample. Interviewees included both general and senior managerial staff in departments/units aligned with media relations/ publicity; but did not include those with prime responsibility for online communication (often of a technical persuasion) where these differed from those involved primarily in media relations.

2. This is particularly true for newspapers where a decline in advertising revenues and in audience figures and/or sales has led to increased competition in unit costs, larger newspapers and less journalists. See Davis (this volume) for a fuller explication of the marketization of news.

3. Gandy (1980) uses the term 'information subsidies' to refer to external sources that provide pre-packaged, ready-to-go stories for journalists who, facing the increasing pressures of less staff, less time and more news space to fill are more inclined towards and become more dependent upon external information sources.

Part V

....

New Media, News Content and International Context

Chapter Ten

A New News Order? Online News Content Examined

Joanna Redden
Tamara Witschge

The study on which this book is based has raised several concerns relating to the nature of news production. It has focused primarily on journalism, since news is what those who produce it make it. But we cannot fully investigate the claims for new media and the news without an analysis of news content. In this chapter, we examine some of these claims and further interrogate the issues uncovered in the production study reported on throughout this volume, directly in relation to the nature of online news content. Following on from the themes outlined by Fenton in the Introduction we question arguments that the internet would lead to the production of more news (because of its speed and space), more diverse news (through multiplicity and polycentrality), and allow greater public participation in the production of news (due to interactivity and participation).

This chapter is based on the analysis of five different types of stories. These stories and their development were tracked within a range of internet spaces – those which include 'traditional' online news spaces (BBC Audio & Video; *BBC News*; *Daily Express*; *Daily Mail*; *Daily Mirror*; *Daily Star*; *News of the World*; the *Daily Telegraph*; the *Guardian*; the *Independent*; the *People*, the *Sun*; *The Times*), search engines (Google and Yahoo), alternative news spaces (Current TV; IndyMedia; openDemocracy – introduced below) and social sites (Facebook; MySpace; YouTube).

The 'traditional' online news sites include most of the UK press with national reach (both broadsheet and tabloid) as well as the BBC. The alternative news sites selected for analysis represent different types ranging from broadcast to text focused and include both 'established' and 'new' online platforms. Firstly, there is Current TV, established in 2005 by Al Gore and broadcast in the UK from 2007. Calling itself 'the first television network for the internet generation', the channel targets 18- to

35-year-olds and allows viewers to post and rank content. Secondly, the IndyMedia network is one of the oldest online alternative media networks and dates back to the 1999 Seattle protests. IndyMedia.org.uk is UK-based and aims to present an open and accessible posting process. Finally, openDemocracy tends to follow a global news agenda and aims to include a diversity of voices and facilitate argument and understanding across geographical boundaries (see Curran and Witschge, this volume). The search engines (Google and Yahoo) and social sites (YouTube; Facebook; MySpace) selected for analysis are consistently ranked among the most popular in the UK.[1] Analysing news coverage as returned in search engine results and on social sites provides us with insight into the content, construction, and responses to news coverage within non-news spaces.[2]

Five news stories were chosen specifically to include a diversity of types of news issues:

1. Prince Harry in Afghanistan (28 February–5 March 2008). A domestic and celebrity story. The UK media agreed to keep Harry's positioning on the Afghan frontline secret in exchange for media-pooled material. The story was eventually broken widely online by Matt Drudge (although it had been published in Australia and Germany previously).
2. The Tibet protest story (10 March–20 March 2008). This international/foreign affairs story concerning the uprising of Tibetan monks and other Tibetans provided insight into the global circulation of news where access to information was an issue.
3. Knife crime (29 March–4 June 2008). A domestic crime story tracked from the day the UK government launched an anti-knife crime campaign. This story provided an opportunity to consider news of direct relevance to young people, allowing us to explore whether and how young people engage with news stories online, particularly on social spaces such as YouTube, Facebook and MySpace.
4. The Sichuan earthquake (12–18 May 2008). This international disaster story provided an opportunity to consider the way in which global information travels in response to a natural disaster. Of particular interest here was the use of eyewitness intervention/representation.
5. The Northern Rock crisis (13–19 September 2007). A complex financial news story that provided an opportunity to consider how a complicated financial issue is explained online and how this type of story 'lives' on news and social spaces outside of the mainstream.

For each of the news sites (both traditional and alternative) we used the site's archive to gather our sample. The search terms used were 'Tibet' (with related stories selected), 'knife crime', 'Sichuan and earthquake', 'Prince Harry and Afghanistan', and 'Northern Rock'. The same search terms (Tibet was replaced with 'Tibet protest') were used to search YouTube, Facebook and MySpace and the search engines Google and Yahoo. All texts within our specified date range were analysed from the

Table 10.1   Number of articles in the sample

Issue Outlet	Prince Harry in Afghanistan	Tibet Protest	Knife Crime	Sichuan Earthquake	Northern Rock	Total
BBC Text and Audio and Video	45	70	32	98	62	307
The Daily Mail	29	10	16	14	47	116
The Daily Mirror	22	6	8	3	11	50
The Daily Star	6	5	16	1	8	36
The Daily Express	4	4	24	3	20	55
The Guardian	34	78	19	43	141	315
The Independent	21	25	13	19	66	144
The News of the World	7	0	9	0	2	18
The People	2	0	4	0	1	7
The Sun	32	8	15	9	20	84
The Times	40	38	21	33	40	172
The Telegraph	80	50	33	48	163	374
Current TV	9	26	5	46	1	87
IndyMedia	2	9	0	1	1	13
openDemocracy	2	6	0	2	1	11
Facebook	3	10	11	10	1	35
MySpace	10	10	10	10	10	50
Google	10	12	11	11	10	54
Yahoo	10	12	11	10	10	53
YouTube	68	106	16	155	15	360
Total texts	436	485	274	516	630	2341

news sites and from YouTube. For the social networking and search engine sites only the results from page one were included in the analysis.[3] Table 10.1 details the number of texts that comprised the sample for each case study.

In relation to coverage of these five news stories we asked: Is content diverse or homogenous (within and between platforms)? To what extent does online news dissemination expand the sphere of news? Does online news offer a diverse range of content? What possibilities do sites offer for the public to participate?

Speed and Space: Homogeneity of 'Traditional' News Sites Examined

One of the early claims about online news asserted that the limitless space available allows not only for more news to be produced, but also for new ways of presenting the news (Fenton, Introduction, this volume). In our study we found an abundance of news online, particularly on mainstream 'broadsheet' sites and BBC News online. However, much of this content is homogenous – news organizations often covered stories from the same angles and different news organizations repeatedly presented the same information in their stories be they images, quotes, or descriptive passages. In other words, homogeneity was common within as well as between mainstream news sites. Levels of internal, within-site, recycling varied by story. In the case of the Prince Harry story, over half of the articles on the BBC, and in the *Daily Mail*, *Daily Express*, *Sun*, *The Times*, and the *Telegraph* contained images, quotes, or text recycled from other internally produced stories. In the case of the Tibet protest story the BBC and the *Telegraph* had the highest percentages of stories with internally recycled elements, 42 and 40 per cent respectively. The high level of recycled content in the Prince Harry case reflects the repeated use of images and text. For example, the BBC repeatedly used a quote by the Prince stressing how happy he was to be in Afghanistan and to 'finally get the chance to do the soldiering that I want to do'.[4]

In the case of the *Daily Mail* and the *Telegraph*, it was common practice for stories to be updated by adding new information at the top of the articles and moving blocks of text, images, and quotes from story to story. The focus on speed and the idea of constant live news updates creates the need for a continuous uploading and updating of stories, which, due to lack of resources (and lack of actual new information), leads to the incremental updating and reusing of material (see Phillips, this volume). The Project for Excellence in Journalism (2008) similarly found high levels of homogeneity in American media. We also observed high levels of content homogeneity between sites – stories that had the same angle and/or specific content that also appeared on other sites. Levels of content homogeneity vary by story, as indicated in Table 10.2.

Table 10.2   Percentage of texts with same story angle and/or specific content that also appears on other sites

Story Outlet	Prince Harry in Afghanistan	Tibet Protest	Knife Crime	Sichuan Earthquake	Northern Rock
BBC Text and Audio & Video	51	58	56	35	35
The Daily Mail	72	60	62	71	44
The Daily Mirror	40	66	87	100	63
The Daily Star	83	100	93	100	100
The Daily Express	75	100	66	100	70
The Guardian	58	39	42	48	21
The Independent	23	56	46	63	16
The News of the World	71	No stories	77	No stories	50
The People	100	No stories	50	No stories	100
The Sun	90	75	73	88	65
The Times	65	60	57	69	40
The Telegraph	63	48	60	58	41

At one end of the mainstream news spectrum are the *Daily Express* and the *Daily Star*, owned by the same company – Northern & Shell – both of which often posted identical stories. At the other end of the spectrum are sites containing parts or elements found in other stories. In general, the national tabloid press contained more externally homogenous material than the national broadsheets. To phrase it conversely, broadsheets had more original content. Images from wire services were some of the most recycled elements in stories. For example, in the Tibet protest case an AFP (Agence France-Presse) image of tanks and chaos on a street in Lhasa was used in a BBC article, a BBC picture gallery, a BBC video, two *Guardian* articles, and one *Independent* article. Although there were high levels of material recycled between sites in all of our case studies, the Prince Harry story contained the highest levels of content homogeneity, likely due to the media's reliance on pooled material.

Content homogeneity does not only pertain to the recirculation of images, quotes and blocks of texts: many of the news angles presented on mainstream news sites are similar.[5] The duplication of similar material and a focus on similar stories can in some cases be explained by the event itself; press conferences, release of reports, etc. However, ethnographies and interviews conducted for this study in general (reported on throughout this volume) show that quite a considerable part of the activity in online newsrooms involves a reliance on press releases and wire material (such as that of PA and Reuters). This is in accordance with Paterson's (2005, 2006) content analysis of international news coverage which credits high levels of content homogeneity to a reliance on wire material. In the Northern Rock case, 7 out of 12 of the traditional news sites sampled had stories profiling Northern Rock's chief executive, which were similar in content.[6] A Press Association profile of Adam Applegarth entitled 'Tough day for Northern's Chief Executive' preceded the publication of these texts and it is likely that this profile provided impetus and content for these later articles. Of course, journalists have long since relied on the news wires and press releases for stories, but in the current environment where speed of news production is greatly increased and the space for news greatly expanded, the time available to check these stories is severely restricted.

A year after the Northern Rock story broke, some journalists have provided reflexive accounts of their reporting of the credit crunch and its significance. These accounts suggest that the story's complexity and journalistic practices limited journalists' abilities to forecast. When asked why many City journalists did not see the financial crisis coming Dan Bögler, Managing Editor of the *Financial Times*, argued it was because they believed bankers who said derivatives were making the world safer (Robinson, 2008). *Daily Mail* City Editor Alex Brummer has also argued that too many journalists are influenced by manipulative PR operations or fear losing access if they are too critical (Robinson, 2008). Bögler argues that many financial journalists and experts did not really understand the sub-prime market or the credit crunch (Robinson, 2008). This latter point was echoed by Michael Wilson, Business and Economics Editor of Sky News:

> It's not something I'd have cared to admit a while ago, but, having had it verified by my peers and rivals, then confirmed by the real off-the-record operatives in the City, I can tell you a collective, painful truth. We all have little or no idea what's going on. The who-what-why-when-where of the story we're trying to tell is impossible to define. Some of us have been treading the canyons of capitalism for years and still we don't know. It's as if all we see are, if I may borrow a bit of Plato, reflections and shadows, and from these we compose our myths and fables. (Wilson, 2008: 57)

The scenario painted is one in which those in need of investigation were looked to as trusted sources, and confusion dominated. This would suggest that the speed of news production does not facilitate investigation and deliberation and the multiplicity of news sources encourages constant return to tried and trusted voices (often of the elite).

In our analysis of Northern Rock coverage we found a great deal of homogeneity in tabloid coverage, and lower levels of homogeneity in BBC and broadsheet coverage. The diversity found on these latter sites was generated by the reports from specialist reporters and editors who were relied upon to explain the story and offer commentary. It is likely that cross-media monitoring contributed to homogeneity, as ethnographies and interviews conducted for this study (reported on throughout this volume) show that journalists spend considerable amounts of time checking other media for stories (Phillips, this volume; Witschge and Nygren, forthcoming). The suggestion is in accordance with findings by Boczkowski and De Santos (2007) who suggest online media monitoring has increased levels of homogeneity in Argentinean news coverage.

As indicated in the above example, where content at times did differ between outlets it was clear that informed commentators and specialist correspondents played a crucial role in providing unique information, supporting the view that specialist correspondents increase the quality and range of information available. In the Tibet protest case a number of mainstream news sites had correspondents reporting from China, including the BBC, the *Guardian*, the *Independent*, the *Telegraph*, *The Times*, and the *Mirror* (but note that the *Mirror* had only one related story). Reporters in China after the Sichuan earthquake and during the Tibet protest provided coverage that translated and personalized events. In each case the journalists on the ground were able to provide first-hand accounts of what was happening in various parts of China. In relation to the Northern Rock story, as noted above, analysis and discussion provided by business editors and commentators explains the much higher levels of content diversity in broadsheet coverage for this case. This finding comes at a time when there has been an overall scaling back on investment in news gathering and foreign correspondents to cut costs (House of Lords, 2008a).

The overall findings of this study, however, reinforce concerns that there is a lack of diversity within mainstream news spaces. Given that the internet is the fastest growing platform for news and other information (Ofcom, 2007b), the finding of an homogenous 'interconnected web of meaning' (Boczkowski and De Santos, 2007) is cause for concern. A lack of content diversity online is significant particularly if we think of the internet as a public sphere which presents not only a potential site of interaction, but also figures as a cultural and informational repository of ideas and projects that feed public debate (Castells, 2008: 79). Homogeneity in news content may delimit the way representations and opinions online are formed, de-formed, and re-formed which in combination 'provide the ideational materials that construct the basis upon which politics and policies operate' (Giddens cited in Castells, 2008: 80). Such findings are relevant given that the internet is increasingly a key site for the articulation of social issues, a primary information source, and has become embedded in the daily lives of much of the Western world (Mautner, 2005).

Homogeneity is reinforced by a lack of external links on mainstream news sites. Our research shows that most mainstream news sites rarely provide links to external sites in connection with their own coverage. The BBC and the *Independent* are exceptions. The availability of links is important given research suggesting that most people looking for information and opinions online about a certain topic rely on search engines, links, or recommendations from other websites (Zimmerman et al., 2004). In not providing external links, mainstream news sites can be viewed as collective actors operating as gatekeepers (Zimmerman et al., 2004), a role they have long held that does not seem to be changing in this new mediascape.

The BBC and the *Independent* warrant discussion as exceptions. In the Tibet protest coverage external links accompanied 60 per cent of BBC articles, while the *Independent* provided a link to Wikipedia content at the bottom of all of its texts. The BBC example illustrates the role external links can play in directing the meaning potential of stories. From 10 to 14 March 2008, as protestors were marching to commemorate the 49th anniversary of the Tibet Uprising Day, BBC articles most often linked to the Tibetan Government in Exile site, the International Campaign for Tibet site, a Free Tibet Campaign site, and the Chinese foreign ministry's site (also often in this order), thus providing direct access to different and disagreeing actors on the issue. The common practice of the *Independent* to link to Wikipedia is unusual. As a web-based free content encyclopedia the site provides a wide range of material and content collectively authored and legitimated by volunteers. No explanation for this practice is offered on the *Independent*'s website, but it may be related to Wikipedia's consistent ranking as one of the most popular sites on the web and to the encyclopedia's practice of providing a list of related external links on its content pages, making it a directory of sorts.

While homogeneity on mainstream news sites is the norm and would seem to suggest little expansion of the news sphere at all, the archiving of news stories on the internet does have profound implications. All of the traditional news sites under analysis provided a search engine that readers could use to search their site. This tool provides an opportunity for readers to track and follow an issue, return to and pause and reflect on material. The online news world, then, is very different in this way from broadcast and print news. The archives increase the depth of available coverage and also provide an opportunity for stories to be read and compared, and for readers to contextualize articles themselves.

We found some news organizations use the increased space afforded by the internet to provide additional background information or other related material, both of which increase the depth of coverage. For example, in the BBC coverage of the Tibet protest story news articles were often accompanied by links to additional BBC content, including related stories, a profile of the Dalai Lama, a background document detailing both China's and a Tibetan view of the Tibet issue, a Q & A, a background document detailing key places and events, and eyewitness reactions to the protests. The addition of internal links in this case provided readers with the opportunity to contextualize stories and add information where desired.

Within the online news sites analysed there was an overall emphasis on text (YouTube and MySpace were exceptions). Multimedia use is common on the BBC site, to a lesser extent on the broadsheet sites, and on the *Sun*'s site. The most common use of multimedia is the attachment of picture galleries and videos. The *Guardian* and the BBC also posted audio. The same galleries and videos are often used repeatedly to accompany different text-based stories. Some uses of multimedia illustrate how such material can provide an additional layer of depth to content. Correspondents' ground-level footage during the Tibet protests and Sichuan earthquake provide visual eyewitness accounts. In the Sichuan case, video after video personalizes and reinforces the human tragedy detailed in text-based coverage by showing us survivors being pulled from fallen buildings. Also notable is the posting of material shot by citizens in relation to the Tibet protest and Sichuan earthquake stories. The BBC in particular posted video, comments, and images submitted by eyewitnesses. This eyewitness coverage contributed to diversity in both form and content.

Multiplicity and Polycentrality: Alternative News and Non-news Spaces Examined

We argue above that the sheer amount of space available and the perceived need to constantly update texts leads to an abundance of news on mainstream news sites, with homogeneity rather than diversity of content being the outcome. In this section we interrogate claims that the internet, in light of its virtues as a medium, would increase the multiplicity of content and polycentrality of the news. Such claims are based on arguments that easy access and the low costs of online publication would lead to an internet environment where wider discussions become the norm and where the dominance of transnational corporate monopolies could be countered. It was hoped such developments would lead to a reinvigorated democracy (Rheingold, 2003). Our sample, comprising some of the most popular news and non-news sites reinforces earlier concerns that offline patterns of corporate dominance and power structures would be replicated online (Dahlberg, 2005; McChesney, 2005; Salter, 2005). Transnational and monopoly ownership remain an important issue. In our sample *The Times*, the *News of the World*, the *Sun*, the *Independent*, and the *Daily Mail* are all owned by transnational corporations.[7]

Our results do suggest, however, that alternative and independent news sources online are providing different perspectives from those represented in mainstream news coverage. Of the three alternative news sites analysed each had a different ownership model. openDemocracy operates as a not-for-profit and has been supported by trusts, foundations, and individual donations. Current TV is owned and operated by Al Gore and Joel Hyatt. It was initially funded through affiliate fees and advertising, but in January 2008 it was announced that the company would also begin selling shares. On the IndyMedia.org.uk site the organization seeks individual donations and states that they are not owned by anyone or funded by large commercial conglomerates.

There were only a few openDemocracy and IndyMedia texts with regard to the stories examined. However, the limited content that was present was unique.

openDemocracy's Tibet protest coverage was salient. One story provided a detailed discussion of how and why Tibetans were protesting, while another was written by a Tibetan exile. Another article detailed Chinese government responses to Olympic organization, the Tibet protests and the Sichuan earthquake to draw conclusions about 'the nature of modern governance in China'. In the case of Northern Rock there was an engaged discussion online following an editorial arguing that the Bank of England should not have bailed out Northern Rock. Within this discussion the editorial writer responded directly to criticisms posted. In this way the level of communication transcends that found on mainstream news sites where interaction is often limited to an individual posting a comment in reaction to a news item, an interaction Schultz categorizes as one-way communication (1999). In contrast, the chain of interrelated messages and communication in this open Democracy example transcends reaction and achieves a higher level of interactivity as both sides send messages and respond to each other.

IndyMedia's coverage was unique in its emphasis on activism, particularly in connection to the Tibet protest story. In this case stories and posts encouraged people to get involved with protests, often providing details of event locations and times (part of the raison d'être of the organization). Individuals also posted images and text of the protests they had attended, and there were updates of events happening in India and in China. IndyMedia coverage of the Prince Harry story was highly critical of the mainstream media. Neither openDemocracy nor IndyMedia.org.uk had any stories about knife crime in our sample period, suggesting how their news agendas differ from (and do not necessarily follow) the mainstream news agenda.

Current TV is unique in its reliance and recontextualization of mainstream news sources. In relation to the Sichuan earthquake, the site became a central location where people posted updated information as mainstream sites released it. Although mainstream news content dominates, news stories are placed in dialogue with each other and links are more often than not followed by readers' comments. For example, in the knife crime case one person posted a summary of the government's anti-knife crime advertising campaign including an image and then asked: 'Some of these [images] are likely to shock us. Do you think this campaign will be effective?' Her question was followed by eleven responses with links to mainstream news coverage and the government's campaign site (intended to target youth). This example demonstrates online engagement with the news, and the use of news texts to fuel discussion. Nothing of this nature was available in mainstream news sites in relation to the stories analysed.

While independent and alternative news content is more easily accessible online than offline, it has still proven difficult for such content to reach a wide audience. The exception to this may be Current TV in that it provides service through mainstream television outlets in the US and the UK. When searching Google and Yahoo for our five case studies, no alternative news sources were returned in the first page of search results. Mainstream news sites dominate Google's page one results for four of the five stories searched: Prince Harry (11 of 11), knife crime (7 of 11), Northern Rock (6 of 10) and Tibet protest (7 of 11) versus Sichuan earthquake (3 of 11). Mainstream news sites were returned on page one of our Yahoo results but to a lesser extent (the exception being the Prince

Harry case where 7 of 11 returns were links to mainstream news articles). As most internet users in the United States and Europe do not venture beyond the first page (Jansen and Spink, 2005, 2006; iProspect, 2008), this does not bode well for opening up the news sphere. Search engines pre-structure access to information (Koopmans, 2004), and in the cases examined, provide a limited palette of what is available.

Despite there being a number of alternative perspectives available online and the potential to engage in debate on many issues, interested people must commit considerable time to actively seek out such sites. Traditional news outlets (as well as search engines such as Google News and Yahoo News) are still the news outlets most frequently visited (ABC Data; Ofcom, 2007b), countering early hopes of smaller news providers being on an equal footing with transnational conglomerates, and of a move to many-to-many communication.

Given the popularity of social sites such as YouTube, Facebook, and MySpace, their role in news construction and dissemination and as platforms where people can respond to the news are also considered in this study. It is worth pointing out that transnational ownership and oligopoly are issues here as well: MySpace is owned by NewsCorp: YouTube is owned by Google: and Facebook is owned privately, with Microsoft possessing a small share. Although these are all non-news sites, they are sites of interaction where individuals engage with the news directly and with issues covered in the news. A YouTube search using the phrase 'Tibet protest' returns re-broadcasts of mainstream news stories, but footage of protests from various locations, seemingly shot by the protesters themselves, dominates. Through this alternative coverage protesters from around the world can communicate with each other as well as with a wider community. In the case of the Sichuan earthquake, YouTube presented a large number of videos where images of the disaster and text were set to music. These videos were posted from locations around the world including Australia, Canada, China, Germany, Hong Kong, the UK, and the US. Analysing the social platforms Facebook and MySpace with regard to knife crime also provided interesting instances of user participation. A Facebook search using the term 'knife crime' returned 138 results. The first page included links to discussion based sites categorized as common interest (5), group organizations (2), a student group, and a site titled 'stop knife crime'. These sites in combination have over 40,000 members (as of October 2008). Levels of engagement and content differed. Content ranged from comments and condolences about knife-crime victims, posts about upcoming events such as a concert to raise money for an anti-knife crime charity, and homemade videos related to the issue. Outside of our sample period, several Facebook groups became involved in organizing a knife crime protest march that was covered by the mainstream media. These examples illustrate that political discussion and local organization are taking place on this site.

On MySpace, a 'knife crime' search returns sites with creative content and innovative presentation. Four of the eight results contained links to homemade or independent videos, including a performance (dance) video about gang culture and knife crime. Another link was to a documentary aimed at young people, titled 'Knife Lewisham', described as a 'documentary about the disturbing yet complex state of knife crime in London'. This content has the technological potential to reach a wide audience, but in reality has only limited reach: at the time of analysis the performance video had just over 400 views, and the documentary 163. It is of course possible such content is being used and shared in other ways. Greater interrogation is needed into how these types of sites connect to the wider public sphere as well to decision-making bodies.

The above examples illustrate how social media are being used to organize, to communicate experiences and thoughts, and to respond to events that are in many cases brought to their attention by the mainstream news. Thus these sites can provide a location for interaction, necessary for a functioning public sphere. An important caveat to the above discussion is that the use of the internet for political purposes is minor, as noted by Dahlgren (2005: 151), when compared to activity connected with consumerism, entertainment, non-political networking and online chat. Degrees of involvement also vary by story. The lack of content on Facebook and MySpace in relation to the Northern Rock issue, is in stark contrast to the knife crime examples detailed above and speaks to the demographics of people using these sites, but also potentially to what kind of stories generate activity.

The way people are using these platforms is what is being noted here as unique and potentially transformative, rather than the platforms themselves. There are widespread concerns about the commercialization of Facebook, and about the influence of corporate control on sites such as MySpace and YouTube.

Interactivity and Participation: Considering the News Online

The potential for the internet to enhance democracy by increasing public engagement has been a subject of much discussion. All the mainstream news sites in our sample provided an opportunity for readers to interact with articles at some point, largely through posting comments. Some news organizations also posted questions to solicit reader comment and opinion in relation to a news topic. The BBC received thousands of comments on its 'Have Your Say' pages in response to questions the organization posed in relation to the Prince Harry, Knife Crime and Northern Rock stories. The *Sun* and the *Mirror* both have discussion boards on their sites, and in some cases stories directed people to these discussion pages.[8] The BBC, *Daily Express, Telegraph,* the *Sun,* and the *Star* all have a 'have your say' page, while the *Guardian* and the *Daily Mail* have debate sections. In relation to the knife crime story, the *Sun* posted an option for people to add their name to a petition calling for the government to prosecute those who carry knives – a type of 'passive interaction' that required no more than an individual fill in their name within a pop-up window. No details were provided about how the petition is to be presented, when or to whom. As of October 2008 the *Sun* was reporting more than 30,000 names on its petition. Many mainstream news sites also provided readers with the option to further disseminate stories through email and by posting on other shared sites. The above examples illustrate that for the most part the public is only able to participate in the last phase of the 'traditional' news production process by interpreting texts and commenting upon them. We found no evidence of individuals involved in any of the decision-making stages in news production. Similar analysis of American and European news sites suggests limited interactive options are the norm (Quandt, 2008; Schultz, 1999; Domingo et al., 2008).

Of course, readers have always recommended stories, provided eyewitness reports and figured as sources in stories, and this has only become easier with e-mail and User Generated Content (UGC) technology. With these new technologies, however, the balance of power has not shifted to users. Journalists and editors still ultimately decide what makes a 'good' news story, who gets to speak, and what gets said (see Phillips, this volume). In our sample, the Prince Harry story was the only case in which technology was used to seek readers' opinions on the production of a story (albeit post-publication) by seeking the public's verdict on its decision to withhold information. It is difficult to determine to what extent solicitation of the public's views after the fact bears influence.

We did find a blurring of content producer and reader/viewer on YouTube and the alternative news site Current TV. Mainstream news content from the BBC, *CNN, SkyNews* and others is posted on these sites and re-purposed by the audience. These postings put various news pieces, from different organizations and locations around the world, in dialogue with each other. Moreover, mainstream coverage is posted alongside alternative content such as individual commentaries (as we found in relation to the Northern Rock case) and more creative responses to the news (such as the young adult's music video on knife crime on YouTube). Both YouTube and Current TV present environments where the authoritative voice of the journalist is diluted and where we can observe a blurring of producer/consumer distinctions.

Early predictions suggested that the interactive and participative nature of the web would mean that with the proper tools everyone or anyone could be a journalist. As with alternative media, the ability for citizen journalists to reach a wider audience is a challenge. In our sample there were significant examples of what can be referred to as citizen journalism; for example, Tibet protest coverage on IndyMedia.org.uk, the posting of homemade documentaries on YouTube and MySpace in relation to knife crime, and video clips of Sichuan earthquake experiences uploaded to YouTube.

Also, mainstream media providers often used images and eyewitness accounts provided by citizens as elements within news stories, particularly in relation to coverage of the Tibet protests and Sichuan earthquake where access to information was difficult. In these cases, new media made it much easier for people to contact media organizations such as the BBC and to post footage on YouTube. One YouTube video, entitled 'Earthquake in Sichuan China', posted on 12 May 2008, shows footage of the earthquake as experienced by a college student in his residence. This clip, returned on Google's page one results, was used in the BBC's and the *Telegraph's* video footage. The video has been viewed over 1.5 million times on YouTube, and shows how media from social sites such as YouTube can at times influence mainstream news content. Whether user generated content in the long run shifts the balance of power between journalist and reader or mainstream and alternative news outlets is a question that cannot yet be answered. But current journalist and audience practices suggest there would be an incremental change in power dynamics if at all.

Conclusion

Even though most news consumers get their news from traditional media and the television in particular, the internet is the fastest growing platform for news and other information (Ofcom, 2007b). In this chapter we examined claims that the internet would democratize news production and reinvigorate democracy, specifically expectations that the internet would lead to the production of more news, more diverse news, and increased public participation in news processes.

Our overwhelming conclusion is that there is an abundance of news online, but the content of mainstream news outlets is largely the same, with different outlets – often with a very different ethos and editorial stance – using identical quotes, images, and very similar text. Further, the news angles provided are often similar. These sites paint, for the most part, a one-dimensional picture of online news homogeneity. A startling outcome, in this so-called space of plenty.

Further, we found that new media technologies have changed how the news is presented on 'traditional' news sites, but not dramatically: The emphasis on most news sites is on text, to date there is limited use of multimedia (the BBC is an exception), and most news sites rarely provide external links to outside sources of information. <u>There is, however, a great deal of emphasis on images, giving a lot of power to the visual.</u> The heavy recycling of images within and between mainstream news sites further contributes to content homogeneity.

News presentation has changed significantly in the use of web space to provide access to media archives, and in the addition of supplementary contextual material to articles. Further, where multimedia is used it can and does provide an additional layer of depth to textual content. These practices increase the accessibility of information.

Mainstream sites offer little opportunity for the public to participate beyond interpreting and responding to stories. When the public are asked to respond to an issue rather than a specific story the response can be overwhelming, as has been the case with the BBC 'Have Your Say' page. Such response suggests much untapped potential. We found readers were almost never offered access to sources, and the lack of external links to outside websites on most sites further limits any potential to widen the news agenda and its participants. Where public submissions were incorporated into news items these were largely as witness / personal accounts and can be read as part of the larger trend toward personalization within news coverage. How interactive the news 'should' be is an ongoing debate and a mainstream news organization may choose to provide excellent service to its constituency over interactivity (Deuze, 2003).

As mainstream news sites are still the most popular in terms of news consumption, and the most popular search engine Google returns mainstream sites for the most part when searches are conducted, the potential for the internet to open up the news media sphere seems limited. However, alternative news sites do provide unique content. Moreover, mainstream content is, through user participation, being re-purposed and re-contextualized online as at Current TV. Alternative news sites are also being used as tools for organization and communication, as with IndyMedia.

<u>The way people are using and responding to news coverage on social platforms such as YouTube, Facebook and MySpace reveals a blurring of news and non-news spaces.</u> The extent to which this impacts on notions of authority and the role of journalists as experts is still an open question. In the knife crime case Facebook helped people communicate and organize in response to news events and coverage. The example demonstrates how people are using online communication in ways that do enhance political participation, but this was an exception rather than the norm in our sample. On sites such as YouTube and MySpace communication efforts were often met with limited or no response. Further, the contributions on non-news spaces are often responses to news and involve a repurposing of

mainstream news content, underlining rather than challenging the position of the mainstream media as gatekeeper.

Endnotes

1. Hitwise, July 2008; Alexa.com, August 2008; and Nielson, January 2008.
2. We chose deliberately not to focus on the specific news sites of the search engines (such as Google News), as we wanted to consider what types of information non-news sites would bring up regarding news items.
3. We acknowledge that this provides a particular, limited picture, but users typically view only the first few pages (Jansen and Spink, 2005, 2006; iProspect 2008) and hence their news return when searching these issues would be equally limited. We do, however, note that search engine results are not straightforward or static and that the results presented here are not necessarily representative (see, for instance: Wouters, Hellsten, and Leydesdorff, 2004).
4. This quote appears in a number of BBC stories including: 'Prince Harry on Afghan Front Line'; 'Harry's Excitement Over Posting'; the video 'Harry on Fighting Prospects'; 'In Quotes: Prince Harry in Afghanistan' (all published on 28 February 2008).
5. Boczkowski and De Santos (2007) concluded the same in their online news analysis; see also the American Project for Excellence in Journalism 2008.
6. The *Guardian*, 14 September 2007: 'Northern Rock's shaven-headed chief executive'; *Daily Telegraph*, 14 September 2007: 'Adam Applegarth: the man under the spotlight'; *The Times*, 15 September 2007: 'Uncertain future for the cashier who got the top job'; *Daily Mail*, 15 September 2007: 'Northern Rock: from cashier to youngest Footsie chief in just 18 years'; the *Independent*, 16 September 2007: 'Millionaire boss who joked he couldn't make the tills balance counts the cost'; *Daily Mail*, 16 September 2007: 'The £1.4m golden boy now facing an uncertain future'; *Daily Express*, 17 September 2007: 'Whizz kid caught between the rock and a hard place'.
7. House of Lords, 'Communications – First Report', June (2008a) <http://www.publications.parliament.uk/pa/ld200708/ldselect/ldcomuni/122/12202.htm>
8. The *Sun*, the *Telegraph*, the *Daily Express*, and the *Daily Star* have attempted to provide personalized services by allowing people to customize content through their *MySun*, *MyTelegraph*, *MyExpress*, and *MyStar* pages. These specific sites are not analysed here as they did not show up in connection to any of the content we retrieved.

Chapter Eleven

· ·

Futures of the News: International Considerations and Further Reflections

Rodney Benson

New Media, Old News offers a fascinating, in-depth look at the state of media as it moves online in the United Kingdom. What strikes me as most unique and important about this book is that it highlights structural features of media systems in the context of a richly detailed portrait of multiple types of communications practices. This approach is evident, for instance, in Phillips, Couldry and Freedman's well-supported insistence (in Chapter 3) that journalistic ethics are only achievable on a mass scale if also supported by structural reforms (as opposed to, say, Roger Silverstone's individually-oriented ethics in *Media and Morality* (2007)). It is also evident in several chapters where mainstream journalism is situated in relation to the variety of alternative media, writer-gatherers, and NGOs who are attempting to influence the newsmaking process. Finally, and this is no small achievement, the book consistently adheres to a careful analysis of what is and is not 'new' about new media.

In this essay, I'd like to try to pick up where the Goldsmiths contributors leave off. In the first half of this chapter, I address the empirical puzzle. To what extent does this portrait of the UK also hold for the US, the rest of Western Europe, and indeed, the rest of the world? In the second half of this chapter, I tackle the thorny questions of ideals and solutions. To paraphrase Jay Rosen (1999): What is journalism for? Of course, there are many different answers to this question. What the answers have in common is a concern with democracy; where they differ is how they conceive of democracy. The main thing is to put these cards on the table. This I intend to do with a brief overview of democratic-normative theories of journalism and an assessment of how current trends in new media are quite democratic in some ways and less so in others. Solutions will differ depending on which aspect of journalism we value the most. I conclude by suggesting how various types of journalistic best practices may be institutionally secured.

As Great Britain Goes, So Goes the World?

New Media, Old News first of all documents the familiar litany of the internet's 'affordances' (Kress, 2003; Adams, 2007: 10–11), that is, the kinds of communication practices that online media uniquely afford: archiving capabilities that increase depth of coverage, multimedia formats that draw readers into complex topics, easy access to a multiplicity of voices and viewpoints outside the mainstream, and opportunities for ordinary citizens to ask questions of political and cultural elites via chat rooms and forums or even to create vast activist networks such as the one that played a key role in financing and helping get out the vote for Barack Obama's presidential bid. In their content analysis of a wide range of British elite, popular, and alternative media websites, Redden and Witschge (Chapter 10) show that at least some of the time, and in some media outlets, these potentials are realized.

But *New Media, Old News'* 'techno-optimism' is quickly tempered by a strong dose of 'techno-pessimism': the dramatic decline of newspaper circulation and advertising revenues, due at least in part to the flight of classified advertising to the internet; the sharp increase in online media audiences accompanied by the failure to find a way to make online media pay for itself, even as the parent traditional media companies often remain quite profitable; the fragmentation of news audiences across multiple media outlets, both offline and online; massive newsroom layoffs and cost-cutting, with especially deep cutbacks in foreign and investigative reporting, and greater job insecurity for those who remain; and finally, intensifying time pressures on journalists to produce news 'content' across multiple media platforms, contributing to the increasing homogenization of content (as shown by Redden and Witschge in Chapter 10) and the use of pre-packaged 'news' provided by public relations professionals.

To what extent do these trends extend beyond the UK? In what follows, I draw attention to some of the scattered evidence that is emerging about global trends, all of which of course may have been interrupted (or exacerbated) by the exceptional worldwide economic crisis that intensified during the winter of 2008–9.[1]

Audiences: In the 'Anglo-American' world, at least, it is first of all important to stress (as does Freedman in Chapter 2) that the decline in newspaper circulation did not start with the internet and has been going on for several decades. Between 1960 and 1995, before the rise of the internet, circulation per 1,000 adult habitants fell significantly in the United States (from 326 to 226, a 31 per cent decline), the United Kingdom (from 514 to 317, a 38 per cent drop), Australia (from 358 to 185, a 48 per cent decline), and Canada (from 222 to 191, a less dramatic fall of 14 per cent).[2] Not all countries, however, suffered from such declines: during the same 35-year period, circulation per 1,000 actually increased in countries such as Finland (52 per cent), Japan (45 per cent), and The Netherlands (10 per cent). Likewise, since 2000 when internet competition could conceivably have played a major factor in any decline, less advertising-dependent, politicized press systems – Hallin and Mancini's (2004) so-called 'polarized pluralist' systems of southern Europe – have tended to experience smaller circulation declines from already smaller bases. Thus, while US and UK per 1,000 circulation fell 9 and 18 per cent, respectively, from 2000 to 2006, in Italy, there was only a 4 per cent decline. Since 2000, newspaper circulation has remained steady in some high circulation, state-subsidized countries such as Sweden (there was a 0.4 per cent increase from 2000 to 2006), while in the 'developing' world, including the former USSR states and Eastern European satellites, circulation increases have been substantial. From 2002 to 2006, raw circulation increased 25 per cent in Poland, 8 per cent in Estonia, 53 per cent in Kyrgyzstan, 54 per cent in India, and 16 per cent in China (from 2002 to 2005). In aggregate, due to growth in Asia, Latin America, and Africa, it is simply not accurate to say that there has been a worldwide newspaper readership 'crisis'. Global circulation of paid-for dailies increased by 9.5 per cent between 2002 and 2006, and when free newspapers are included, there was an increase of almost 15 per cent; likewise, the global number of newspaper titles increased from 9,524 in 2002 to 11,207 in 2006, nearly an 18 per cent increase.

At the same time, even declines in newspaper print circulation are misleading to the extent that they do not necessarily indicate a decline in actual news consumption (Saba, 2005). For example, while the *New York Times*'s daily print circulation has fallen to just over 1 million (representing approximately 4.7 million readers), its online version now claims a readership of nearly 13 million monthly users (*New York Times*, 2007; Westerdal, 2007). While these online readers tend not to spend as much time reading as their print counterparts, at least some of the *New York Times* content is reaching more people than ever before.

To what extent are news audiences becoming increasingly fragmented? It is obvious that the number of media voices available, in principle, to audiences is on the increase. Even if the internet increases choices exponentially, it is nevertheless important to emphasize that audience fragmentation is not something new (Meyer, 2004). Throughout the nineteenth and into the early twentieth century, most US cities had two or more newspapers, and millions of immigrants relied on a diverse array of foreign-language newspapers. Magazines have targeted diverse constituencies long before the arrival of radio, cable, and the internet. Fragmentation is the norm, historically speaking. What is atypical is the media systems that emerged in the post-World War II period in Europe and the United States and indeed across the world in which a handful of national broadcast television channels were able to garner majority audiences. The current situation is thus a return to the normalcy of divided attention, with the important caveat that a select few of the now established 'brands' – leading national newspapers and television channels such as the *Guardian*, the BBC, the *New York Times*, CNN – have transferred and even augmented their agenda-setting power on to the net.

Advertising: Generally, newspaper print advertising revenues are down, while online advertising revenues have increased. In most cases, the print loss tends to be larger than the online gain. For example, despite significant gains in online advertising every year, overall advertising revenues in Germany declined by nearly 21 per cent between 2001 and 2005 (WAN, 2007: 336). Some countries' news media are managing the transition better than others. In Norway, total newspaper advertising revenues actually increased by 4 per cent in 2006, bolstered by a 42 per cent rise in online advertising (WAN, 2007: 545); likewise, a dramatic increase in online advertising offset print advertising losses in Canada, keeping overall newspaper revenues virtually steady in 2007 (CNA, 2007). Even in the US, a handful of the most-viewed online news sites, such as CNN, have been paying their own way for several years and expect eventually to be the dominant profit-generator for the company. CNN officials estimated that their website, whose audience already far exceeds that of its cable channel (and in fact is the world's number one news website, with an average of 1.7 billion monthly page views), would nevertheless not surpass the television channel in revenues for at least '10 to 20 years from now' (Stelter, 2009: B-1, 2). Outside the industrialized West where newspapers remain less reliant on online platforms, overall advertising revenues have in some cases increased quite dramatically: in India, for example, newspaper advertising revenues increased 90 per cent between 2001 and 2005 (WAN, 2007: 377).

Profitability: Even as offline audiences and advertising revenues have declined for newspapers in most industrialized countries, many large news media companies – at least until the economic crisis of 2008 – continued to be quite profitable. Certainly, this has been the case in the United States. Net profit rates (net income as a percentage of total revenues) have declined since the beginning of the 1990s when they often exceeded 25 per cent, but even in 2007, they ranged from 6.5 per cent at the New York Times Company and 6.9 per cent at the Washington

Post Company to 14.2 per cent at Gannett (owner of 85 US newspapers, including *USA Today*) and 12.0 per cent at Rupert Murdoch's News Corporation (which now owns the *Wall Street Journal*, the *New York Post*, Fox News, as well as, of course, several major British and Australian media properties). These respectable profit margins have been maintained, in part, by aggressive cost-cutting. But the sense of crisis, among media owners, is driven less by current profit rates than by shareholder expectations that 'offline' media, especially newspapers, are a dying breed, which has led to a virtual freefall in share prices. Gannett shares which traded at $85.71 in January 2004, near historic highs, had fallen to $7.59 in early January 2009; likewise, New York Times Company shares peaking at $51.50 in 2002 were trading at $6.41 by January 2009. Even the Washington Post Company, insulated to a certain extent through its ownership of the highly profitable Kaplan educational testing service, has seen its share price fall from a peak of $983.02 in December 2004 to $408.24 in January 2009.[3]

The shift of news to the internet – the specific ways in which it is transforming journalistic practice – cannot be understood solely in relation to so-called technological 'imperatives'; rather, the internet has become an 'iron cage' for many journalists (see Davis, Chapter 7) because owners and advertisers have long favoured such economic rationalization and have sought to develop the internet in ways to maintain and extend the existing 'social formation' of power relations (Williams, 2003). In the United States, the conventional wisdom is that the publicly-traded corporation is to blame, since its legal charter requires profit maximization for shareholders, and virtually all leading news organizations are now part of publicly-traded corporations. While the UK also has its publicly-traded media organizations (the *Daily Mail*, the *Independent*, and Murdoch's News Corporation-owned the *Sun* and *The Times*), what strikes me about the British situation is the intensity of competition in a highly-centralized, multi-newspaper national journalistic field, and how this has been amplified by the 24-hour internet news cycle. The degree to which media outlets are economically directly competitive, or perceive themselves to be, also needs to be taken into account as a factor contributing to a decline in news quality.

Newswork: Similar to Great Britain, in both Canada and the United States the full-time journalistic workforce has been decimated in recent years (PEJ, 2008; Ray, 2009); at the *Los Angeles Times*, for example, successive layoffs between 2001 and January 2009 have halved the editorial staff from 1,200 to 600 (Agence France Press, 2008; Bensinger, 2009). In the aftermath of such cutbacks, US freelance journalists working under incredible pressure are increasingly being used to fill the news hole, similar to the process described by Phillips, Couldry, and Freedman (Chapter 3). This transformation of journalism into yet another form of flexible labour has also occurred in Canada (McKercher, 2002), and across Asia and Latin America (IFJ, 2006). Nevertheless, it should be emphasized that increasing job 'precarity' for journalists had been observed in countries such as France (see, e.g., Accardo, 1998) even before the shift to the internet was well under way. Reduced overall staffing combined with the need to provide content for multiple platforms (online print, audio, and video, as well as the original 'offline' print, audio, or video versions) is creating a time-squeeze that stretches well beyond the Anglo-American (Klinenberg, 2005) world, affecting newsroom working conditions across Europe and the developed world (Deuze, 2008). This 'multiskilling ... leads to increasingly pressurized arrangements, to higher stress levels and burn-out rates, [and] an ongoing recasting of specialists into generalist reporters' (ibid.: 154). In this volume, Phillips (Chapter 5) describes how competitive pressures are leading British journalists to spend more time monitoring and even 'cannibalizing' without attribution news stories written by their colleagues at other media outlets. Cannibalization hasn't been adequately studied in the US, but if it is perhaps less prevalent, again, it may be due in part to the more fragmented character of the US journalistic field (with leading media outlets spread across the country) which could mitigate, even online, the kind of intense competitive pressures produced by the UK's London-based media.

Finally, given the PR industry's own self-conscious expansion across Europe (Burton and Drake, 2004) and indeed the world (Sriramesh and Verčič, 2003), coupled with a global trend toward newsroom job cuts and the use of flexible labour, it is certainly likely that there is also a global increase in the predominance of PR-produced 'news'. Unfortunately, there has been little systematic research on this question in the US or other western democracies to match the impressive UK-based research in this book as well as previously published studies by Davis (2002) and Miller and Dinan (2007).

In sum, *New Media, Old News* paints a portrait of the press under siege in the age of the internet, but in some ways it seems to be a self-inflicted wound, bound up in its reliance on an advertising-driven model of mainstream journalism. As Barnhurst and Nerone (2001: 285) observed in their global survey of online news media, 'the most striking quality of online newspapers is the dominance of promotion [and] advertising, much of it self-promotional [which] completely overwhelms the other content'. The crisis of the journalism business, offline or online, should not be so quickly equated with the crisis of the journalistic vocation. There is no automatic correlation between a news media industry's economic success and its contributions to democratic life. On the other hand, economic failure can open up a process of reflection and self-questioning that could ultimately make the media more democratic.

But what, precisely, do we mean by democracy? Before we can determine the best way forward, it is essential that we acknowledge the complexity of the term and its cross-cutting, potentially contradictory elements (Ferree et al., 2002; Baker, 2002; Schudson, 2008).

Journalism and Models of Democracy

In democratic theory, three broad schools of thought have emerged: elitist, deliberative, and pluralist.[4] How we evaluate journalism in the era of the internet depends crucially on which of these democratic models are emphasized and valued.

The elitist democratic model is most often associated with Walter Lippmann (1997) and the ideal of a 'watchdog' press. The primary duties for the press are to examine the character and behaviour of elected officials, to monitor closely their activities for corruption or incompetence, to critically analyse policy proposals, and to provide reliable, in-depth information about social problems. It is largely against this standard that the contemporary press – both offline and online – has increasingly been judged inadequate. Of course, some elite print-based journalistic organizations continue to provide in-depth reporting and investigations of official wrongdoing. But as Davis, Phillips, and Fenton show in their contributions to this volume, commercially driven online news media tend to emphasize the latest breaking information and thus operate according to a rhythm fundamentally antithetical to slower-ripening, depth reporting;[5] moreover, as also noted, the pressure to produce news content for multiple platforms shifts time from reporting to repackaging.

Whereas in the elitist model, the press largely acts on behalf of the public, in the deliberative model, the press works alongside the public to 'support reflection and value or policy choice' (Baker, 2002: 148–9). In the deliberative model, mainstream media like the BBC and the *Washington Post* are not valued so much for their well-funded capacity to investigate as for their status as 'inclusive, non-segmented media entities that support a search for general societal agreement on "common goods"' (ibid.: 149). The deliberative model, most closely identified with Habermas's ideal public sphere, provides a benchmark to evaluate both journalistically-produced and non-journalistically-produced discourse on the net, including such aspects as civility, direct engagement of opposing viewpoints, and reasoned argumentation.

Increasingly, the major news websites facilitate debate and dialogue. When readers engage with each other, the quality tends to be lower than when they engage with journalists or other expert contributors. Unmoderated reader forums on nytimes.com became such 'sewers of profanity' that the newspaper was forced to close them down in 2006 (Robinson, 2007: 310). Another detailed content analysis of reader postings on the French lemonde.fr and wanadoo.fr open forums found that they tended to be dominated by a few, often aggressive readers, some of whom displayed 'the effects of some form of intoxication or mental illness perhaps' (Adams, 2007: 193). The same study, however, found that in conversations that were effectively structured by journalists, as with the reader comments to a *Libération* blog, the quality of discussion was significantly higher. NYTimes.com now has a regular feature called 'Room for Debate' in which 'knowledgeable outsiders' are invited 'to discuss major news events and other hot topics'. Reader comments are welcome, but are moderated. One January 2009 debate concerned 'bonuses for bad performance' on Wall Street and featured a novelist, a law professor, a professor of labour economics, and responses from 798 readers (often outraged, but all free of profanity!).

Finally, the pluralist model emphasizes ideological diversity, popular inclusion, citizen empowerment and mobilization, and full expression through a range of communicative styles. Measured against this pluralist standard, there are certainly signs that some online news media are enabling greater democracy. For instance, nytimes.com now has a 'TimesExtra' version that adds links at the bottom of news articles to a wide range of other news media (including British) and diverse types of blogs. On January 23, 2009, there were Extra links to various independent writer-gatherers (e.g., Brooklyn Vegan) as well as more established blogs (Huffington Post, Politico, etc.). On the 'Blogrunner' website linked to nytimes.com (and also owned by *The Times*), mainstream media articles tended to dominate, but there were also prominent links to blogs by a University of Oregon economist, the liberal filmmaker Michael Moore, and the obscure blog Sadly No! whose contributors include its founder Seb, a French-Canadian financial analyst living in Germany, and various scattered graduate students, writers, and designers.[6] Likewise, *Le Monde*'s website (lemonde.fr) has at various times featured links to a range of blogs produced by the kind of writer-gatherers described by Couldry – judges, financial experts, amateur art aficionados, ordinary citizens concerned with the quality of urban life – as well as more occasional 'chronicles' written by individual *Le Monde* subscribers and even videotapes of professors' lectures delivered at the prestigious École normale supérieure.

Certainly, there is an upper-middle class, professional bias to the non-journalistic voices (paralleling the newspapers' readership) that tend to be permitted inside the journalistic tent. If writers from the developing world appear relatively rarely on openDemocracy.net (as Curran and Witschge show in Chapter 6) they are surely all but absent on nytimes.com. We need more research to see whether the range of online 'linked' viewpoints significantly extends the amount of ideological diversity found on print newspapers' editorial and op/ed pages (in a careful study of the *New York Times* op/ed articles and letters to the editor, Benjamin Page (1996) found that these tended to closely straddle *The Times*' official position as represented in its editorials). Building on the more optimistic observations of Redden and Witschge (Chapter 10) and Couldry (Chapter 8), though, it seems clear that the best online newspapers are moving in the direction of more, rather than less, openness toward civil society. There is reason for techno-optimism here.[7]

In sum, democratic normative theory helps clarify the problems and potentials of new media, at least within the industrialized western democracies. How we define the problem crucially shapes the appropriate response. I now turn to the question of solutions.

Policy Solutions: Private and Public

For the most part, the 'crisis' discussion has tended to presume the elitist model, which should not be surprising since this is the standard most closely associated with journalists' own self-conception, at least in the United States and the United Kingdom. While this is surely a crucial role of the press, and worthy of serious attention, it is important to keep in mind that it is not the only democratic function it performs.

To illustrate this point: the dominant journalistic frame for understanding the current crisis is that the 'old model' of advertising supported media isn't transferring well to the online environment. As Freedman reports (Chapter 2), there is a strong journalistic nostalgia for this 'arrangement' that supposedly benefits the public, 'whereby advertisers have been happy to pour money into bulletins and titles that provide them with desirable audiences while these audiences are in turn provided with public affairs-oriented material ...'. While there is certainly some truth to this claim, it too quickly elides the many ways in which the public has also been short-changed by this particular arrangement. For one, critical reporting of the business world, whose power has increased exponentially over the past half-century, has been mostly non-existent. For another, advertising funding has led the press to conceive of their readers more as consumers than citizens, and this has been a major obstacle to a press that is more deliberative and pluralist.

It's not even clear that advertising support is the best guarantee of the kind of journalism most valued by the elitist model: investigative reporting of government, foreign reporting, and in-depth examinations of social problems. Good journalism has sometimes been good business, of course, but there is no necessary connection between the two. The Gannett chain headed by *USA Today* has been spectacularly successful at making money and just as spectacularly unsuccessful at producing high-quality journalism. The best journalism – again, as defined by elitist democracy – has required not only resources but a civic and intellectual vision and the commitment to pursue it even when it is not profitable.

One key word that often comes to the fore in this discussion – it certainly has in this book in several chapters (see especially Phillips, Chapter 5) – is the notion of 'autonomy'. Autonomy is usually understood in a negative sense, that is, autonomy 'from' something, usually the market. Yet, such autonomy can't simply be asserted through the actions of journalists within the field, it has to be 'secured' by something else, that is able to underwrite the accumulation of cultural capital (Benson, 2006).

At the *New York Times*, for more than a century, that 'something else' (or someone) has been the family that owns the newspaper, the Ochs and Sulzbergers, that have treated it as a public trust (Tifft and Jones, 1999; McCollam, 2008). On a recent PBS 'Frontline' documentary, *New York Times* editor Bill Keller exclaimed: 'I wake up every day grateful for the Sulzberger family' (Talbot, 2007). This kind of family ownership model has become the primary guarantee of journalistic excellence in the United States. With the Bancroft family's sale of the *Wall Street Journal* to Murdoch's News Corporation in 2007, today only the Grahams at the *Washington Post* and the Sulzbergers at the *New York Times* retain majority control of their newspapers. But is it wise to place so much responsibility on the shoulders of a few supposedly indispensable individuals? As the time of writing, as the *New York Times'* balance sheet continues in freefall, Mexican multi-billionaire Carlos Slim Helú moved to increase his stake in the company to 20 per cent of the common stock, making him the single largest shareholder other than the Sulzberger family. We should not assume that the Sulzbergers will – assuming that they even can – forever and always hold the newspaper in trust.

The good news is that alternatives to commercial ownership are being publicly discussed as never before. In the same PBS documentary that quoted Keller's appreciation of the Sulzbergers, (then) *Los Angeles Times* editor Dean Bacquet expressed his enthusiasm for non-profit ownership models (such as the Poynter Institute's ownership of the *St. Petersburg* (Florida) *Times*, which would be similar to the Scott Trust's ownership of the *Guardian*). And in a recent op/ed essay published by the *New York Times*, two Yale investment officers made the case for tax policies that would allow endowments similar to those used by universities, to underwrite quality journalism (Swensen and Schmidt, 2009). In the letters to the editor responding to this article, one writer argued that this proposal didn't go far enough, that what is really needed is the kind of 'public media' represented by the BBC.

What about the BBC? No doubt there has been some erosion in its quality over the past decade, as Lee-Wright suggests (Chapter 4). But truth be told, the BBC and its long, distinguished record of doing 'substantive justice to the main social and political issues of the day' (Blumler and Gurevitch, 2001: 392), embodies an 'inconvenient truth' that many American journalists would prefer to ignore. In the United States, a BBC-style solution has long been precluded by an absolutist (or what might be better termed 'fundamentalist') interpretation of the First Amendment. For the absolutists, when the First Amendment says 'Congress shall make no law restricting freedom of speech, or of the press ...', it means literally 'no law'. Scepticism toward the state remains the dominant view among US journalists, even those otherwise critical of the current state of affairs (Nordenson, 2007), and thus it is difficult to imagine US journalists embracing either an expansion in public television or the kind of solution developed recently in France, in which the state will provide all 18-year-olds with a free subscription to the newspaper of their choice (Pfanner, 2009; Leparmentier and Ternisien, 2009). Still, in the light of the global financial crisis and the resulting changed zeitgeist, government-led reforms, even in the United States, are not inconceivable. Increasingly, the argument is being heard that the US government has and continues to play a positive role in supporting the media (Cook, 1999; Starr, 2004). Legal scholar C. Edwin Baker (2002), for example, makes the persuasive case that states must intervene where advertising-dominated markets fail, such as in supporting reporting on controversial or complex social problems, or news about the poor and the working class – in short, all forms of journalism either offensive or not of interest to advertisers and the high disposable income audiences they seek to reach, yet nevertheless crucial to the functioning of a democratic society.

What's clear is that simply tinkering with the 'old' business model will not provide a complete solution. A few elite media organizations with extremely loyal audiences, such as the *Wall Street Journal* or the *New York Times*, may be able to successfully charge readers for access to content, thus overcoming the weaknesses of the advertising model on the internet.[8] But this solution, if it is one, will only be available to a few. It's also clear, as shown by Curran and Witschge's case study of *openDemocracy* (Chapter 6), that relying on the benevolence of foundations and other wealthy benefactors is not a reliable, long-term guarantor of journalistic autonomy. No single solution will suffice. We thus need to think of autonomy in the plural rather than the singular. Contra Bourdieu, the state is not necessarily allied with the market at the heteronomous pole of the field; it may be a crucial support for journalistic autonomy. Each form of autonomy has its limits directly related to the way in which it is secured. But in a system with multiple types of ownership and funding – private, government (with guarantees of independence from direct partisan control), non-profit, journalist-owned (as at *Le Monde*), etc. – there is a greater likelihood of ensuring that no powerful actors or public problems will be able to elude critical journalistic attention.

In all of this discussion, we need to keep in mind that 'quality' journalism as represented by the BBC or *Le Monde* or the *Frankfurter Allgemeine Zeitung* is only part of the full democratic equation. The question of journalistic autonomy seems most urgent in relation to the press's 'watchdog' role as envisioned by democratic elitist theory. However, a little less autonomy might be just fine when it comes to making room for greater deliberation and pluralism. Scholars and intellectuals can and are increasingly playing a role in expanding reasoned deliberation on the web. Likewise, a range of social movement groups, blogs, and partisan media are expanding pluralism. To the extent that journalistic-produced news content is increasingly homogenized across media outlets (see also Boczkowski and Santos, 2007), links to such outside sources (even if they themselves, of course, are often commenting on mainstream news) can provide some limited means of escaping from the echo chamber.

In his classic essay, 'Rethinking Media and Democracy', James Curran (2000) presents a public sphere 'wheel' composed of a public television sector in the centre, surrounded by four spokes – a private enterprise sector, a professional sector under the control of journalists, a civic sector that social organizations including political parties support, and a closely related sector of ideologically or culturally marginal media that operate in the market with partial subsidies from the state. In this working model of 'complex democracy' (Baker, 2002), each sector would help promote certain kinds of discourses and voices necessary for democratic self-deliberation. As part of this mix, I would just add, we also shouldn't discount the positive democratic role that is often performed by so-called 'entertainment media' – television talk shows and dramas, music, and films – in placing various social problems on the public agenda (Delli Carpini and Williams, 2001). In this context, it is tempting even to think that we could do without journalism altogether, and distance ourselves from the 'values' guiding mainstream journalism, as that doctor blogger did so memorably in his interview with Nick Couldry (Chapter 8): '"Values" … You have to be joking. Have you ever read the *Daily Mail*?'

But if *New Media, Old News* has shown us anything, it is that the practices of smaller scale media and NGOs often tend to parallel those of the leading mainstream media – even on the internet! If indeed, as Fenton (Chapter 9) persuasively demonstrates, NGOs engage in 'news cloning', that is, 'giv[e] journalists what they want – ready made copy that fits pre-established news agendas', then it is crucially important 'what' precisely journalists want.

In sum, the challenge for the future is threefold: first, to maintain and even strengthen the autonomy of core mainstream media, whether public or private; second, to maintain and expand diversity at the margins (using the state to promote speech that is under-produced by the market, when necessary); and most of all, third, to figure out ways to connect the two. In many ways, the internet makes it easier to do this than before, but it won't just happen 'naturally'. As Freedman insists in Chapter 2, the problem of journalism is not one of audiences or advertising, it is one of underinvestment. Certainly, this is true. I would just add that when it comes to deliberative and pluralist democratic goals, an open mind may be just as important as money. Journalists will need to embrace these purposes as their own, and even loosen their monopoly on the public sphere in order to make more room for other professionals and citizen publics to contribute. There are encouraging signs that at least some of the most respected news media organizations are moving in this direction. In the age of the internet, the challenge will be to bring together both private and public economic and cultural capital so that journalism can fully assume its democratic responsibilities.

Endnotes

1. Matthew Powers, an NYU Ph.D student, provided research assistance for this chapter.
2. Newspaper readership figures are derived from WAN (World Association of Newspapers, 2007: i, 2, 27–29), Hallin and Mancini (2004: 23), and Kuhn (1995: 28).
3. Net profit margins were obtained from Hoover's annual income statements for each of the aforementioned companies, which are publicly available at www.Hoovers.com. Historical company share prices were obtained from historical price charts available on finance.yahoo.com.
4. Elitist democracy, the term also used by Baker (2002) corresponds to Ferree et al.'s (2002) 'representative liberal' model. 'Deliberative' corresponds to Baker's 'republican' and Ferree et al.'s 'discursive' model, both of which are closely aligned with Habermas. My 'pluralist' model brings together Baker's 'interest group pluralist' with Ferree et al.'s 'participatory liberal' and 'constructionist' models, the latter based in the feminist critique of Habermas; while there are some differences among these models, all basically stress broad inclusion and acceptance of diverse discursive styles (not just rational argumentation).

5. There are some exceptions to this tendency, such as the new non-profit online investigative reporting website Politico.com, headed by a former *Wall Street Journal* editor and generously funded by savings-and-loan billionaires Herb and Marion Sandler (Hirschman, 2008).

6. Sadly No! self-reports a focus on 'finding embarrassing slips or untrue statements by conservatives and linking to a refutation' and a 'daily traffic of between 7,000 and 15,000 visits'. Blogrunner uses an automated algorithm 'based on links from blogs or other websites', but 'editors can add items to the list if they find something interesting' and likewise they can 'take off items' (Hansell, 2007). *The Washington Post*, long considered an innovator in online journalism, has a 'Who's Blogging' link attached to individual articles, but the *Post*'s website does not put blogs and other external media links front and centre in the way that Times Extra does.

7. I have cited here only a few examples of 'best practices'. Perhaps most media come nowhere near this level of democratic performance, but of course this has long been the case (at least in the US). Even if we can only say that the best are using the internet to get even better, this still represents some measure of progress.

8. In an online chat with readers (http://www.nytimes.com/2009/01/30/business/media/02askthetimes.html?_r=1&hp=&pagewanted=all, accessed 3 February, 2009), executive editor Bill Keller said that a 'lively, deadly serious discussion continues within *The Times* about ways to get consumers to pay for what we make', including a subscription model, a micro-payment model (similar to Apple's iTunes), and new reading devices such as the Kindle.

References

Accardo, A. (ed.) (1998) *Journalistes précaires*. Bordeaux: Editions Le Mascaret.

Adams, P. (2007) *Altantic Reverberations: French Representations of an American Presidential Election*. Aldershot, UK: Ashgate.

Agence France Presse (2008) 'Los Angeles Times to Axe 250 jobs' (3 July).

Advertising Association/WARC (2008) *The Advertising Statistics Yearbook 2008*. London: AA/WARC.

Aitkenhead, D. (2006) 'Hot gossip', *Guardian* Weekend section, 6 May.

Ala-Fossi, M. (2008) 'Newspapers', in L. Kung, R. Picard, and R. Towse (eds.), *The Internet and the Mass Media*. London: Sage. pp. 149–54.

Alavi, N. (2007) 'Iran's circle of power', openDemocracy (23 October). Available at: http://www.opendemocracy.net/article/democracy_power/irans_circle_of_power

Albrow, M., Anheier, H., Glasius, M., Price, M.E. and Kaldor, M. (2008) *Global Civil Society 2007/08: Communicative Power and Democracy*. London: Sage.

Allan, S. (2006) *Online News: Journalism and the Internet*. Maidenhead: Open University Press.

Allan, S., Adam, B. and Carter, C. (eds) (2000) *Environmental Risks and the Media*. London: Routledge.

Altheide, D.L. and Snow, R.P. (1979) *Media Logic*. Beverly Hills, CA: Sage.

Anderson, A. (1997) *Media, Culture and the Environment*. London: UCL Press.

Anderson, A. (2004) 'Environmental activism and news media', in S. Cottle (ed.), *News, Public Relations and Power*. London: Sage. pp. 117–33.

Appadurai, A. (1991) 'Global ethnoscapes: notes and queries for a transnational anthropology', in R. G. Fox (ed.), *Recapturing Anthropology: Working in the Present*. Santa Fe, NM: School of American Research Press. pp. 191–210.

Atton, C. (2004) *An Alternative Internet*. Edinburgh: Edinburgh University Press.

Attwood, B. (2008) 'National Papers are Stealing Our Show', *Press Gazette*, London, 1 August.

Baird, N. (2001) 'On Street Safari', openDemocracy, 29 November. http://www.opendemocracy.net/ecology-climate_change_debate/article_461.jsp

Baker, C.E. (2002) *Media, Markets, and Democracy*. Cambridge, UK: Cambridge University Press.

Barnhurst, K.G. and Nerone, J. (2001) *The Form of News: A History*. New York: The Guilford Press.

BBC (2008) 'Analysis: Responsible Journalism', Transmitted on Radio 4, 3 July.

BBC Trust (2008) *Impartiality Report: BBC Network News and Current Affairs Coverage of the Four UK Nations*. London: BBC Trust.

Beckett, C. (2008) *SuperMedia: Saving Journalism So It Can Save the World*. Oxford: Wiley-Blackwell.

Behabib, S. (1992) 'Models of public space: Hannah Arendt, the liberal tradition and Jürgen Habermas', in C. Calhoun (ed.), *Habermas and the Public Sphere.* Cambridge, MA: MIT Press. pp. 73–98.

Benkler, Y. (2006) *The Wealth of Networks: How Social Production Transforms Markets and Freedom.* Yale: Yale University Press.

Bennett, W.L. (2005) 'Social movements beyond borders: understanding two eras of transnational activism', in D. della Porta and S. Tarrow (eds.), *Transnational Protest and Global Activism.* Lanham: Rowman and Littlefield. pp. 203–27.

Bensinger, G. (2009) 'Los Angeles Times to cut 300 jobs, 70 in newsroom.' Bloomberg.com (30 January).

Benson, R. (2006) 'News media as a "Journalistic Field": what Bourdieu adds to New Institutionalism, and vice versa.' *Political Communication,* 23, 2: 187–202.

Berners-Lee, T. (2000) *Weaving the Web.* London: Orion.

Bernstein, C. and Woodward, B. (1974) *All The President's Men.* New York: Simon and Schuster.

Blondheim, M. (1994) *News over the Wires: The Telegraph and the Flow of Public Information in America, 1844–1897.* Cambridge, MA: Harvard University Press.

Blumler, J.G. (1990) 'Elections, the media and the modern publicity process', in M. Ferguson (ed.), *Public Communication: The New Imperatives.* London: Sage. pp. 101–13.

Blumler, J.G. and Gurevitch, M. (2001) '"Americanization" reconsidered: UK–US campaign communication comparisons across time', in W.L. Bennett and R.M. Entman (eds), *Mediated Politics.* Cambridge: Cambridge University Press. pp. 380–403.

Boczkowski, Pablo (2004) *Digitizing the News.* New Baskerville: MIT Press.

Boczkowski, P. and Santos, M. de (2007) 'When more media equals less news: patterns of content homogenization in Argentina's leading print and online newspapers', *Political Communication,* 24 (2): 167–80.

Bohman, J. (2004) 'Expanding dialogue: the internet, the public sphere and prospects for transnational democracy', *Sociological Review,* 131–55.

Bolter, J. and Grusin, R. (2000) *Remediation.* Cambridge, Mass.: MIT Press.

Bonfadelli, H. (2002) 'The internet and knowledge gaps: a theoretical and empirical investigation', *European Journal of Communication,* 17 (1): 65–84.

Boorstin, D. (1962) *The Image.* London: Weidenfeld and Nicolson.

Born, G. (2004) *Uncertain Vision: Birt, Dyke & the Reinvention of the BBC.* London: Secker & Warburg.

Bourdieu, P. (1993) *The Field of Cultural Production.* Cambridge: Polity.

Bourdieu, P. (1998) *On Television and Journalism.* London: Pluto Press.

Bourdieu, P. (2005) 'The political field, the social science field and the journalistic field', in R. Benson and E. Neveu (eds) (2005) *Bourdieu and the Journalistic Field.* Cambridge: Polity. pp. 29–47.

Boyd-Barrett, O. (1998) 'Global News Agencies', in O. Boyd Barrett and T. Rantanen (eds.), *The Globalisation of News.* London: Sage.

Brandenberg, H. (2006) 'Pathologies of the virtual public sphere', in S. Oates, D. Owen and R. Gibson (eds.) (2006) *The Internet and Politics: Citizens, Voters and Activists.* London: Routledge. pp. 207–22.

Briggs, A. (1985) *The BBC – The First Fifty Years*. Oxford: Oxford University Press.

Brookes, R., Lewis, J. and Wahl-Jorgensen, K. (2004) 'The media representation of public opinion: British television news coverage of the 2001 General Election', *Media, Culture and Society*, 26 (1): 63–80.

Buffett, W. (2007) Letter to Shareholders of Berkshire Hathaway Inc., 28 February. Available at http://www.berkshirehathaway.com/letters/2006ltr.pdf

Burns, T. (1997) *The BBC: Public Institution and Private World*. London: Macmillan.

Burton, C. and Drake, A. (2004) *Hitting the Headlines in Europe: A Country-by-Country Guide to Effective Media Relations*. London: Kogan Page.

Cable Authority (1990) *Annual Report and Accounts*. London: Cable Authority.

Calhoun, C. (1988) 'Populist politics, communications media and large-scale societal integration', *Sociological Theory*, vol. 6: 219–41.

Calhoun, C. (ed.) (1992) 'Introduction', in *Habermas and the Public Sphere*. Cambridge, Mass.: MIT Press.

Calhoun, C. (2004) 'Information technology and the international public sphere', in D. Schuler and P. Day (eds.), *Shaping the Network Society: The New Role of Civil Society in Cyberspace*. Cambridge, MA: MIT Press. pp. 229–51.

Carey, J. (1986) 'The dark continent of American journalism', in R. Manoff and M. Schudson (eds.), *Reading the News*. London: Pantheon.

Carrier, J. and Miller, D. (1998) *Virtualism: A New Political Economy*. Oxford: Berg.

Cassidy, J. (2003) *Dot.Con*. London: Penguin Books.

Castells, M. (2002) *The Internet Galaxy*. Oxford: Oxford University Press.

Castells, M. (2008) 'Public sphere: global civil society, communication networks, and global governance', *The Annals of the American Academy of Political and Social Science*, 616 (1): 78–93.

Chadwick, A. (2006) *Internet Politics: States, Citizens and New Communication Technologies*. Oxford: Oxford University Press.

Christians, C., Ferré, J. and Fackler, M. (1993) *Good News: Social Ethics and the Press*. New York: Longman.

CNA (Canadian Newspaper Association) (2007) '2007 Daily Newspaper Paid Circulation Data', http://www.cna-acj.ca/en/aboutnewspapers/circulation. Accessed 17 January 2009.

Cohen, E. (2002) 'Online journalism as market-driven journalism', *Journal of Broadcasting and Electronic Media*, 46 (4): 532–48.

Coleman, S. (2004) 'Connecting parliament to the public via the internet: two case studies of online consultations', *Information, Communication & Society*, 7 (1): 1–22.

Colombo, F. (ed.) (2004) *TV and Interactivity in Europe*. Milan: Vita and Pensiero.

Cook, T. (1999) *Governing with the News*. Chicago: University of Chicago Press.

Corner, J. and Pels, D. (2003) *Media and the Restyling of Politics*. London: Sage.

Cottle, S. (2003) 'Introduction', in S. Cottle (ed.), *News, Public Relations and Power*. London: Sage. pp. 3–24.

Couldry, N. (2006) *Listening Beyond the Echoes: Media, Ethics and Agency in an Uncertain World*. Boulder, CO: Paradigm Books.

Couldry, N. (2008) 'Media ethics: towards a framework for media producers and media consumers', in S. Ward and S. Wasserman (eds.), *Media Ethics Without Borders*. Cape Town: Heinemann.

Couldry, N., Livingstone, S.M., and Markham, T. (2007) *Media Consumption and Public Engagement: Beyond the Presumption of Attention*. Basingstoke: Palgrave Macmillan.

Coyer, K., Dowmunt, T. and Fountain, A. (2007) *The Alternative Media Handbook*. London: Routledge.

Crouch, C. (2004) *Post-Democracy*. Cambridge: Polity.

Crouse, T. (1973) *The Boys on the Bus*. New York: Random House.

Curran, J. (2000) 'Rethinking Media and Democracy', in J. Curran and M. Gurevitch (eds.), *Mass Media and Society*, 3rd edn. London: Arnold. pp. 120–54.

Curran, J. (2002) *Media and Power*. London: Routledge.

Curran, J. and Seaton, J. (2009) *Power without Responsibility*, 7th edn. Abingdon: Routledge.

Curran, J., Gaber, I. and Petley, J. (2005) *Culture Wars*. Edinburgh: Edinburgh University Press.

Curran, J., Iyengar, S., Lund, A.B. and Salovaara-Moring, I. (2009) 'Media System, public knowledge and democracy: a comparative study', *European Journal of Communication*, 24 (1) (expected date of publication: March 2009).

Dahlberg, L. (2005) 'The corporate colonization of online attention and the marginalization of critical communication', *Journal of Communication Inquiry*, 29 (2): 160–80.

Dahlberg, L. (2007) 'Rethinking the fragmentation of the cyberpublic: from consensus to contestation' in *New Media and Society*, 9 (5): 827–47.

Dahlgren, P. (2005) 'The internet, public spheres, and political communication: dispersion and deliberation', *Political Communication*, 22 (2): 147–62.

Daily Mail and General Trust (DMGT) (2008) *Annual Review 2007*. London: DMGT.

Dalton, R. (2004) *Democratic Challenges, Democratic Choices: The Erosion of Political Support in Advanced Industrial Democracies*. Oxford: Oxford University Press.

Davies, N. (2008) *Flat Earth News*. London: Chatto & Windus.

Davis, A. (2002) *Public Relations Democracy: Public Relations, Politics and the Mass Media in Britain*. Manchester: Manchester University Press.

Davis, A. (2004) 'Public relations and news sources', in S. Cottle (ed.), *News, Public Relations and Power*. London: Sage. pp. 927–43.

Davis, A. (2007) 'Comparing the influences and uses of new and old news media inside the parliamentary public sphere.' Paper presented at the Futures of the News symposium, Goldsmiths, University of London.

Davis, A. (2007) *The Mediation of Power: A Critical Introduction*. London: Routledge.

Davis, R. (2005) *Politics Online: Blogs, Chatrooms, and Discussion Groups in American Democracy*. Routledge: New York.

Davis, R. and Owen, D. (1998) *New Media and American Politics*. Oxford: Oxford University Press.

Dayan, D. (2007) 'On morality, distance and the other: Roger Silverstone's *Media and Morality*', *International Journal of Communication*, vol. 1, 113–22. Available at http://ijoc.org/ojs/index.php/ijoc/article/view/114/53

Deacon, D. (1996) 'The voluntary sector in a changing communications environment: a case study of non-official news sources', *European Journal of Communications*, 11 (2): 173–99.

Deacon, D. (2004) 'Non-governmental organizations and the media', in S. Cottle (ed.), *News, Public Relations and Power*. London: Sage. pp. 99–117.

Dean, J., Anderson, J.W. and Lovinck, G. (eds.) (2006) *Reformatting Politics: Information Technology and Global Civil Society*. London: Routledge.

DeChaine, D.R. (2002) 'Humanitarian space and the social imaginary: Médecins Sans Frontières/Doctors Without Borders and the rhetoric of global community', *Journal of Communication Inquiry*, 26 (4): 354–69.

Delli Carpini, M.S. and Williams, B.A. (2001) 'Let us infotain you: politics in the new media environment', in W.L. Bennett and R.M. Entman (eds.), *Mediated Politics: 'Communication in the Future of Democracy*. Cambridge: Cambridge University Press. pp. 160–81.

Department for Culture, Media and Sport (DCMS) (2003) *Privacy and Media Intrusion*. The Government's response to the Fifth Report of the Culture, Media and Sport Select Committee on 'Privacy and Media Intrusion'. Cm 5985. Norwich: TSO.

Deuze, M. (1999) 'Journalism and the web: an analysis of skills and standards in an online environment', *Gazette*, 61 (5): 373–90.

Deuze, M. (2003) 'The web and its journalisms: considering the consequences of different types of newsmedia online', *New Media and Society*, 5 (2): 203–30.

Deuze, M. (2007) *Media Work*. Cambridge, UK: Polity Press.

Dikötter, E. (2002) 'Bring out the beast: body hair in China', openDemocracy (4 December). http://www.opendemocracy.net/arts-china/article_811.jsp

Domingo, D. (2008) 'Participatory journalism practices in the media and beyond', *Journalism Practice*, 2 (3): 326–42.

Downing, J. (2001) *Radical Media: Rebellious Communication and Social Movements*. Thousand Oaks, Calif.: London: Sage Publications.

Dryzak, J. (2002) *Deliberative Democracy and Beyond: Liberals, Critics, Contestations*. Oxford: Oxford University Press.

Dutton, W. and Blumler, J. (1988) 'The faltering development of cable television in Britain', *International Political Science Review*, 9 (4): 279–303.

Economist (2006) 'More media, less news', *Economist.com*, 24 August. Available at http://www.economist.com/business/displaystory.cfm?story_id=7827135

Edelman, M. (1964) *The Symbolic Uses of Politics*. Urbana: University of Illinois Press.

Efficient Frontier (2008) 'UK search engine performance report released', press release, 15 May. Available at http://blog.efrontier.com/insights/

Epstein, E. (2005) *The Big Picture*. New York: Random House.

Fawcett Society (2005) Press release: 'Record number of women MPs'. http://www.fawcettsociety.org.uk/documents/Women_MPs_May05.pdf (last accessed October 2008).

Fenton, B. (2008) 'Bad ad news ripples across sector', *Financial Times*, 1 July.

Fenton, N., Bryman, A., Deacon, D. and Birmingham, P. (1998) *Mediating Social Science*. London: Sage.

Fenton, N. (2007) 'Bridging the mythical divide: political economy and cultural studies approaches to the media', in Eoin Devereux (2007) (ed.), *Issues and Key Debates in Media Studies*. London: Sage. pp. 7–31.

Fenton, N. (2008a) 'Mediating solidarity', *Global Media and Communication*, 4 (1): 37–57.

Fenton, N. (2008b) 'Mediating hope: new media, politics and resistance', *International Journal of Cultural Studies*, 11 (2): 230–48.

Ferree, M.M., Gamson, W.A., Gerhard, J. and Rucht, D. (2002) *Shaping Abortion Discourse: Democracy and the Public Sphere in Germany and the United States*. Cambridge: Cambridge University Press.

Fishman, M. (1980) *Manufacturing News*. Austin: University of Texas.

Foucault, M. (1984) in Rabinow, P. (ed.) (1994) *Ethics: The Essential Works of Michel Foucault, Volume 1*. Harmondsworth: Penguin. pp. 281–303.

Fountain, N. (1988) *Underground: The London Alternative Press 1966–74*. London: Routledge.

Franklin, B. (1997) *Newzak and News Media*. London: Arnold.

Franklin, B. (2005) 'McJournalism: the local press and the McDonaldization thesis', in S. Allan (ed.), *Journalism: Critical Issues*. Maidenhead: Open University Press. pp. 137–50.

Fraser, N. (1992) 'Restructuring the public sphere: A consideration of actually existing democracy', in C. Calhoun (ed.), *Habermas and the Public Sphere*, Cambridge, MA.: MIT Press. pp. 109–42.

Fraser, N. (1997) 'Rethinking the public sphere: a contribution to the critique of actually existing democracy', in C. Calhoun, *Habermas and The Public Sphere*. MA.: MIT Press.

Fraser, N. (2007) 'Transnationalizing the public sphere: on the legitimacy and efficacy of public opinion in a post-Westphalian world', *Theory, Culture and Society*, 24 (4): 7–30.

Frost, C. (2004) 'The Press Complaints Commission: a study of ten years of adjudications on press complaints', *Journalism Studies*, 5 (1): 101–14.

Galperin, H. (2004) *New Television, Old Politics*. Cambridge: Cambridge University Press.

Gandy, O. (1982) *Beyond Agenda Setting: Information Subsidies and Public Policy*. NJ: Ablex Publishing Corporation.

Gans, H.J. (1979) *Deciding What's News: A Study of CBS Evening News, NBC Nightly News, Newsweek and Time*. New York: Pantheon.

Garnham, N. (2007) 'Habermas and the public sphere', *Global Media and Communication*, 3 (2): 201–14.

Garrison, B. (2000) 'Diffusion of a new technology: on-line research in newspaper newsrooms', *Convergence: The Journal of Research into New Media Technologies*, 6 (1): 84–105.

Garrison, B. (2001) 'Diffusion of online information technologies in newspaper newsrooms', *Journalism*, 2 (2): 221–39.

Garrison, B. (2003) 'How newspaper reporters use the web to gather news', *Newspaper Research Journal*, 24 (3): 62–75.

Gaskin, K., Vlaeminke, M. and Fenton, N. (1996) *Young People's Attitudes to the Voluntary Sector*. London: National Council for Voluntary Organizations.

Gentzkow, M. (2007) 'Valuing new goods in a model with complementarity: online newspapers', *The American Economic Review*, 97 (3): 713–44.

Gibson, O. (2007) 'Code breaker', *Media Guardian*. 29 January.

Gillmor, D. (2004) *We the Media: Grassroots Journalism by the People, for the People*. Sebastopol: O'Reilly Media.

Gitlin, T. (2001) 'Is this our fate?', openDemocracy (11 September 2001). http://www.opendemocracy.net/conflict-us911/article_213.jsp

Goldberg, D., Prosser, T. and Verhulst, S. (1998) 'Introduction' in D. Goldberg et al. (eds.), *Regulating the Media*. Clarendon Press.

Golding, P. and Elliott, P. (1979) *Making The News.* London: Longman.

Goodwin, P. (1998) *Television Under the Tories*. London: British Film Institute.

Graham, J. (2008) 'Huffington's vision prospers on blog', *USA Today*, 25 September. Available at http://www.usatoday.com/tech/webguide/2007-09-25huffington_n.htm?loc=interstitialskip.

GroupM (2008) *This Year, Next Year: UK Media and Marketing Forecasts*. London: GroupM.

Gulati, G. (2004) 'Members of Congress and presentation of self on the World Wide Web', *Harvard Journal of Press/Politics*, 9 (1): 22–40.

Gunter, B. (2003) *News and the Net*. London, New Jersey: Lawrence Erlbaum.

Habermas, J. (1989) *The Structural Transformation of the Public Sphere: An Inquiry into a Category of Bourgeois Society*. Cambridge: Polity.

Habermas, J. (1996) *Between Facts and Norms*. Cambridge: Polity.

Hachten, W.A. (2005) *The Troubles of Journalism: A Critical Look at What's Right and Wrong with the Press*. 3rd edn. London: Lawrence Erlbaum.

Hafez, K. (2007) *The Myth of Media Globalization*. Cambridge: Polity.

Hall, S., Critcher, C., Jefferson, T., Clarke, J. and Roberts, B. (1978) *Policing the Crisis.* London: Macmillan.

Hallin, D. (1989) *The 'Uncensored War'*. Berkeley: University of California Press.

Hallin, D. (1994) *We Keep America on Top of The World: Television, Journalism and the Public Sphere*. New York: Routledge.

Hallin, D. and Mancini, P. (2004) *Comparing Media Systems: Three Models of Media and Politics*. Cambridge: Cambridge University Press.

Hansell, S. (2007) 'The Robot in the Newsroom', *New York Times,* Bits, 1 November. http://bits.blogs.nytimes.com/2007/11/01/the-robot-in-the-newsroom

Hargreaves, I. (2003) *Journalism: Truth or Dare*. Oxford: Oxford University Press.

Hay, C. (2007) *Why We Hate Politics*. Cambridge: Polity.

Held, D. (2004) *The Global Covenant*. Cambridge: Polity.

Held, D., McGrew, A., Goldblatt, D. and Perraton, J. (1999) *Global Transformations*. Cambridge: Polity.

Hemmingway, E. (2008) *Into the Newsroom*. Abingdon: Routledge.

Hendy, D. (2007) *Life on Air: A History of Radio Four*. Oxford: Oxford University Press.

Herbert and Thurman (2007) 'Paid content strategies for news websites', *Journalism Practice*, 1 (2): 208–26.

Herman, E. and McChesney, R. (1997) *The Global Media: The New Missionaries of Global Capitalism*. London: Cassell.

Hill, K. and Hughes, J. (1998) *Cyberpolitics: Citizen Activism in the Age of the Internet*. Oxford: Rowman & Littlefield.

Hirschman, D.S. (2008) 'So what do you do, Paul Steiger, editor-in-chief, ProPublica?', Media Bistro. http://www.mediabistro.com/articles/cache/a10060.asp (February 13), accessed 19 December, 2008.

Hirst, P. and D. Held (2002) 'Globalisation: the argument of our time', openDemocracy. http://www.opendemocracy.net/globalization-institutions_government/article_637.jsp

HMSO (2000) *A New Future for Communications*. London: Stationery Office.

HoC (July 2005) *Twenty-Seventh Annual Report – Financial Year 2005/2006*. London, House of Commons Commission.

Hoge, J. (1997) 'Foreign news: who gives a damn?', *Columbia Journalism Review.*

Horton, D. and Wohl, R. (1993) 'Mass communication and para-social interaction', in J. Corner and J. Hawthorn (eds.), *Communication Studies: An Introductory Reader,* 4th edn. pp. 156–64.

House of Lords Select Committee on Communications (2008a) *The Ownership of the News*. Vol I: Report. Norwich: The Stationery Office Limited.

House of Lords Select Committee on Communications (2008b) *The Ownership of the News*. Vol II: Evidence. Norwich: The Stationery Office Limited.

Horwitz, R. (1989) *The Irony of Regulatory Reform*. New York: Oxford University Press.

Hunt, Lord (1982) *Report of the Inquiry into Cable Expansion and Broadcasting Policy*. London: Home Office, HMSO.

Hutchins Commission (1947) *A Free and Responsible Press*. Chicago: Chicago University Press.

IFJ (International Federation of Journalists) (2006) *The Changing Nature of Work: A Global Survey and Case Study of Atypical Work in the Media Industry*. Research report. http://www.ifj.org/pdfs/ILOReport070606.pdf

Information Technology Advisory Panel (ITAP) (1982) *Cable Systems*. London: Cabinet Office, HMSO.

Internet Advertising Bureau (IAB) (2008) *Fact Sheet: Online Adspend – 2007*. Available at http://www.iabuk.net

iProspect (April 2008) *iProspect Blended Search Results Study*. Available at: http://www.iprospect.com/about/researchstudy_2008_blendedsearchresults.htm (last accessed October 2008).

Jackson, N. and Lilleker, D. (2004) 'Just public relations or an attempt at interaction?: British MPs in the press, on the web and "in your face"', *European Journal of Communication*, 19 (4): 507–33.

Jansen, B. and Spink, A. (2005) 'An analysis of Web searching by European AlltheWeb.com users', *Information Processing Management*, 41 (2): 361–81.

Jansen, B. and Spink, A. (2006) 'How are we searching the world wide web? A comparison of nine search engine transaction logs', *Information Processing and Management*, 42 (1): 248–63.

Jarvis, J. (2008) 'Forget shorthand: a cameraphone is the new tool of the journalist's trade', *The Guardian* media section, 11 February.

Jensen, J. (2006) 'The Minnesota E-Democracy Project: mobilising the mobilised?', in S. Oates, D. Owen, and R. Gibson (eds.) *The Internet and Politics: Citizens, Voters and Activists*. London: Routledge. pp. 39–58.

Kahn, R. and Kellner, D. (2004) 'New media and internet activism: from the "Battle of Seattle" to blogging', *New Media & Society*, 6 (1): 87–95.

Kahn, R. and Kellner, D. (2005) 'Globalisation, technopolitics and radical democracy', in L. Dahlberg and E. Siapera (2007) *Radical Democracy and the Internet: Interrogating Theory and Practice*. London: Palgrave Macmillan. pp. 17–37.

Kamouchi, Misaki (2004) 'Sakura', openDemocracy (29 July) http://www.opendemocracy.net/arts/article_2123.jsp

Kant, I. (1983) 'Perpetual peace', in *Perpetual Peace and Other Essays*. Indiana: Hackett Publishing. pp. 106–41. (Originally published 1795).

Keen, A. (2007) *The Cult of the Amateur: How Today's Internet Is Killing Our Culture and Assaulting Our Economy*. London: Nicholas Brealey.

Khan, F. (2004) 'Getting real about globalisation in Bangladesh', openDemocracy (14 April). http://www.opendemocracy.net/globalization-trade_economy_justice/article_1851.jsp

Klein, N. (2000) *No Logo*. New York: Flamingo.

Klinenberg, Eric (2005) 'Convergence: news production in a digital age', *The Annals of the American Academy of Political and Social Science*, 597: 48–64.

Knapp, J. and Saxon-Harrold, S. (1989) *The British Voluntary Sector*, Discussion Paper 645. Personal Social Services Unit, University of Kent, Canterbury.

Koopmans, R. (2004) 'Movements and media: selection processes and evolutionary dynamics in the public sphere', *Theory and Society*, 33 (3): 367–91.

Kress, G. (2003) *Literacy in the New Media Age*. London and New York: Routledge.

Kuhn, R. (1995) *The Media in France*. London: Routledge.

Kung, L. Picard, R. and Towse, R. (2008) 'Conclusions', in L. Kung, R. Picard and R. Towse (eds.), *The Internet and the Mass Media*. London: Sage. pp. 170–77.

Kushova, Alma (2004) 'Besa', openDemocracy (21 July) http://www.opendemocracy.net/arts/article_2114.jsp

Lance Bennett, W. (2003) 'Lifestyle politics and citizen consumers: identity, community and political action in late modern society', in J. Corner and D. Pels (2003) *Media and the Restyling of Politics*. London: Sage. pp. 137–50.

Lee, C., Chan, J., Pan, Z. and So, C. (2005) 'National prisms of a global "media event"', in J. Curran and M. Gurevitch (eds.), *Mass Media and Society*. 4th edn. London: Hodder Arnold.

Leigh, D. (2007) 'Are Reporters Doomed?' the *Guardian* media section, 12 November.

Leparmentier, A. and Ternisien, X. (2009) 'L'Etat débloque 600 millions d'euros pour soutenir la presse', *Le Monde*, 23 January.

Lewis, J., Williams, A., Franklyn, B., Thomas, J. and Mosdell, N. (in press) *The Quality and Independence of British Journalism*. Cardiff University.

Lievrouw, L. and Livingstone, S. (2006) 'Introduction', in L. Lievrouw and S. Livingstone (eds.), *The Handbook of New Media*, 2nd edn. London, Sage. pp. 1–14.

Lippmann, W. (1997 (1922)) *Public Opinion*. New York: Free Press.

Livingston, S. and Bennett, L.W. (2003) 'Gatekeeping, indexing, and live-event news: is technology altering the construction of news?', *Political Communications*, 20 (4): 363–80.

Livingstone, S. (2005) 'Critical debates in internet studies: reflections on an emerging field', in J. Curran and M. Gurevitch (eds.), *Mass Media and Society*, 4th edn. London: Hodder Arnold.

Loader, B. (ed.) (2007) *Young Citizens in the Digital Age: Political Engagement, Young People and New Media*. London: Routledge.

Lovink, G. (2008) *Zero Comments: Blogging and Critical Internet Culture*. London: Routledge.

Lusoli, W., Ward, S. and Gibson, R. (2006) '(Re)Connecting politics? Parliament, the public and the internet', *Parliamentary Affairs*, 59 (1): 24–42.

Lyon, D. (1995) *The Electronic Eye: The Rise of the Surveillance Society*. London: Routledge.

MacGregor, B. (1997) *Live, Direct and Biased? Making Television News in the Satellite Age*. London: Arnold.

MacIntyre, A. (1981) *After Virtue*. London: Duckworth.

MacMillan, R. (2008) 'Bronstein: The future of news, and other buzzwords', Reuters blog, 29 March. Available at http://blogs.reuters.com/mediafile/2008/03/29/bronstein-the-future-of-news-and-other-buzzwords/

Maddox, B. (1972) *Beyond Babel*. New York: Simon and Schuster.

Manning, P. (1998) *Spinning for Labour: Trade Unions and the New Media Environment*. Aldershot: Avebury.

Manning, P. (2001) *News and News Sources: A Critical Introduction*. London: Sage.

Marr, Andrew (2004) *My Trade: A Short History of British Journalism*. London, Macmillan.

Marsh, K. (2008) 'Journogeek: old world meets new for the newshound of the future', *Press Gazette*, 24 June. p. 33.

Martin, J. (1978) *The Wired Society*. Englewood Cliffs, NJ: Prentice-Hall.

Mautner, G. (2005) 'Time to get wired: using Web-based corpora in critical discourse analysis', *Discourse and Society*, 16 (6): 809–28.

Mayo, E. and Steinberg, T. (2007) 'The Power of Information', available at: www.tinyurl.com/yps9sn. Last accessed August 2007.

McChesney, R. (2005) *Rich Media, Poor Democracy: Communication Politics in Dubious Times*. University of Illinois Press: United States.

McChesney, R.W. (2008) *The Political Economy of Media: Enduring Issues, Emerging Dilemmas*. New York: Monthly Review.

McCollam, D. (2008) 'Sulzberger at the barricades: can Arthur Sulzberger Jr. transform The New York Times for the digital age?', *Columbia Journalism Review* (July/August): 24–31.

McCoy, M.E. (2001) 'Dark alliance: news repair and institutional authority in the age of the internet', *Journal of Communication*, 51 (1): 164–93.

McGirk, J. (2006) 'Thailand's king and that democracy jazz', openDemocracy (11 June). Available at: http://www.opendemocracy.net/democracy-protest/thailand_king_3633.jsp

McKercher, C. (2002) *Newsworkers Unite: Labor, Convergence and North American Newspapers*. Lanham, MD: Rowman and Littlefield.

McNair, B. (1999) *News and Journalism in the UK*. London: Routledge .

McNair, B. (2000) *Journalism and Democracy: An Evaluation of the Public Sphere*. London: Routledge.

McRobbie, A. (1994) *Postmodernism and Popular Culture*. London: Routledge.

Médecins Sans Frontières (2000) *Médecins Sans Frontières/Doctors Without Borders Information*. New York: Doctors Without Borders USA.

Merrill Lynch (2007) *Daily Mail and General Trust PLC: More than a Newspaper*. 13 November. London: Merrill Lynch.

Messner, M. and Distaso, M.W. (2008) 'The Source Cycle', *Journalism Studies*, 9 (3): 44–6.

Meyer, C. (2006) 'We know better than the courts', *British Journalism Review*, 17 (3): 27–32.

Meyer, P. (2004) *The Vanishing Newspaper: Saving Journalism in the Information Age*. Columbia: University of Missouri Press.

Miller, D. and Dinan, W. (2007) *A Century of Spin*. London: Pluto Press.

Miller, D. and Slater, D. (2000) *The Internet: An Ethnographic Approach*. Oxford: Berg.

Miller, D. and Williams, K. (1993) 'Negotiating HIV/AIDS information: agendas, media strategies and the news', in J. Eldridge (ed.), *Getting the Message: News, Truth and Power*. London: Routledge. pp. 126–42.

Miller, L.C. (1998) *Power Journalism: Computer Assisted Reporting*. Fort Worth, TX: Harcourt Brace.

Moorehead, C. (2003) 'Burundi: A Life in Fear', openDemocracy (5 October). http://www.opendemocracy.net/people-migrationeurope/article_1524.jsp

Mosco, V. (2005) *The Digital Sublime*. Cambridge, Mass.: MIT Press.

Murray, R. (1989) 'Benetton Britain', in S. Hall and M. Jacques (eds.), *New Times*. London: Lawrence and Wishart.

National Union of Journalists (NUJ) (2007) *Sharing the Future: Commission on Multi-Media Working*. London: NUJ.

Negroponte, N. (1995) *Being Digital*. London: Hodder and Stoughton.

New Media Age (2008) 'NMA Effectiveness Awards 2008, Winner: Sky News', Available at http://www.nmaawards.co.uk/Winners2008.aspx?key=&CatID=1e4bd4db-730c-48f3-9f1e-15bff96a76df

Newspaper Association of America (NAA) (2008) *Advertising Expenditures*. Available at http://www.naa.org/TrendsandNumbers/Advertising-Expenditures.aspx

New York Times (2007) *Audit Bureau of Circulation Readership Report*.

Nordenson, B. (2007) 'The Uncle Sam solution: can the government help the press? should it?', *Columbia Journalism Review* (September/October).

Norris, P. (2000) *A Virtuous Circle: Political Communications in Postindustrial Societies*. Cambridge: Cambridge University Press.

Norris, P. (2001) *Digital Divide: Civic Engagement, Information Poverty and the Internet Worldwide*. Cambridge: Cambridge University Press.

Norris, P. (2002) *Democratic Phoenix: Reinventing Political Activism*. Cambridge: Cambridge University Press.

Norton, P. (2007) 'The House of Commons', in B. Jones, D. Kavanagh, M. Moran, P. Norton, *Politics UK*. 6th edn. Harlow, Essex: Pearson.

O'Neill, O. (2002) *A Question of Trust*. Cambridge: Cambridge University Press.

Oates, S., Owen, D. and Gibson, R. (eds.) (2006) *The Internet and Politics: Citizens, Voters and Activists*. London: Routledge.

Ofcom (2004a) *The Communications Market 2004 – Television, Appendix: The Public's View Survey Results*. London: Ofcom. http://www.ofcom.org.uk/research/cm/cmpdf/cmr04_print/tele_apndx.pdf). Accessed 21 November, 2008.

Ofcom (2004b) 'Ofcom establishes one-stop-shop for all advertising regulation through transfer of responsibility to the ASA', news release, 1 November. Available at http://www.ofcom.org.uk/media/news/2004/11/nr_20041101

Ofcom (2006a) *Digital Local Options for the Future of Local Video Content and Interactive Services*. http://www.ofcom.org.uk/tv/psb-review/digital-local.pdf. (Accessed 12 August, 2008.)

Ofcom (2006b) *Digital Local Options for the Future of Local Video Content and Interactive Services*, Annex A. Available at http://www.ofcom.org.uk/tv/psb_review/digital_local.pdf (Accessed 12 August, 2008.)

Ofcom (2007a) *The Communications Market 2007*. London: Ofcom. Available at: http://www.ofcom.org.uk/research/cm/cmr07/tv/tv.pdf. (Accessed 21 November, 2008.)

Ofcom (2007b) *New News, Future News: The Challenges for Television News after Digital Switch-over*. London: Ofcom.

Ofcom (2007c) *New News, Future News*. London: Ofcom.

Office of Communications (Ofcom) (2007b) *Annexes to New News, Future News: Research and Evidence Base*. London: Ofcom.

Ofcom (2008a) *The Communications Market 2008*. London, Ofcom. Available at: http://www.ofcom.org.uk/research/cm/cmr08/tv/tv.pdf. (Accessed 21 November, 2008.)

Ofcom (2008b) *Ofcom's Second Public Service Broadcasting Review. Phase One: The Digital Opportunity*. London: Ofcom.

Olsen, S. (2008) 'News Corp. COO: "scarcity" key to online advertising', *News.com*, 22 July. Available at http://news.cnet.com/8301-1023_3-9997124-93.html

Orwell, G. (1949) *Nineteen Eighty-Four*. London: Secker & Warburg.

Ossman, S. (2002) 'Hair goes global: the view from the salons of Casablanca, Cairo and Paris', openDemocracy (19 December). http://www.opendemocracy.net/arts-hair/article_857.jsp

Page, B. (1996) *Who Deliberates? Mass Media in Modern Democracy*. Chicago: University of Chicago Press.

Panitch, L., and Leys, C. (1999) *Socialist Register 1999: Global Capitalism Versus Democracy*. Rendlesham: Merlin Press.

Papacharissi, Z. (2002) 'The virtual sphere: The internet as a public sphere', *New Media & Society*, 4 (1): 9–27.

Park, A. (2004) *British Social Attitudes: The 21st Report*. London: Sage.

Park, D. (2004) 'Blogging with authority: strategic positioning in politically oriented Weblogs.' Paper presented to ICA Conference, New Orleans, 23–27 May.

Paterson, C. (2003) 'Prospects for a democratic information society: the news agency stranglehold on global political discourse', paper presented to the New Media, Technology and Everyday Life in Europe Conference, London.

Paterson, C. (2005) 'News agency dominance in international news on the internet', in D. Skinner, J. Compton and M. Gasher (eds.), *Converging Media, Diverging Politics: A Political Economy of News in the United States and Canada*. Lexington: Rowman and Littlefield. pp. 145–64.

Paterson, C. (2006) 'News agency dominance in international news on the internet', Centre for International Communications Research, Papers in International and Global Communication, 01/06.

Paupst, J. (2000) 'A meditation on evil', *Maclean's*, 1 July, 54–6.

Pavlik, J. V. (2001) *Journalism and New Media*. CA: Columbia University Press.

PEJ (Project For Excellence in Journalism) (2008) *The State of the News Media 2008*. Executive summary. Available at http://www.stateofthenewsmedia. org/2008/chapter%20pdfs/PEJ2008-Overview.pdf? cat=9&media=1

Pfanner, E. (2009) 'France Expands Its Financial Support for Newspapers', *The New York Times*, 24 January: B2.

Picard, R. (2002) *The Economics and Financing of Media Companies*. New York: Fordham University Press.

Picard, R. (2006) *Journalism, Value Creation and the Future of News Organizations*. Joan Shorenstein Center on the Press, Politics and Public Policy. Available at http://www.hks.harvard.edu/presspol/research_publications/ papers/research_papers/R27.pdf

Pinker, R. (2004) *NUJ Conference Report*. Available at http://www.nuj.org.uk/ inner.php?docid=872 (accessed 31 October 2007).

Piore, M. and Sabel, C. (1984) *The Second Industrial Divide*. New York: Basic Books.

Polat, R. (2005) 'The internet and political participation', *European Journal of Communication*, 20 (4): 435–59.

Ponsford, D. (2004) 'Express staff call in PCC over anti-gypsy articles', *Press Gazette*, 30 January. Available at http://www.pressgazette.co.uk/ story.asp?sectioncode= 1&storycode=24921 (accessed 4 August 2008).

Pospisil, M. (2001) 'Holidays at home: the Czech enthusiasm for weekend cottages and allotments', openDemocracy (12 December). http://www.opendemocracy. net/node/440

Power, M. (1997) *The Audit Society*. Oxford: Oxford University Press.

Press Complaints Commission (PCC) (2008) *Editors' Code of Practice*. Available at http://www.pcc.org.uk/cop/practice.html

Preston, P. (2001) 'It's a bit of a bodge, but the PCC is the best we've got', *Guardian*, 3 September.

Private Eye (2008) 'Street of Shame', *Private Eye*, 7 July.

Putnam, R. (2000) *Bowling Alone: The Collapse and Revival of American Community*. New York: Simon and Schuster.

Quandt, T. (2008) '(No) news on the World Wide Web?', *Journalism Studies*, 9 (5): 717–38.

Quandt, T., Loffelholz, M., Weaver, D., Hanitzsch, T. and Aitmeppen, K. (2006) 'American and German online journalists at the beginning of the 21st century: a bi-national survey', *Journalism Studies*, 7 (2): 171–86.

Quinn, S. (2002) *Knowledge Management in the Digital Newsroom*. St. Louis, MO: Focal Press.

Rash, W. (1997) *Politics on the Net: Wiring the Political Process*. New York: WH Freeman and Co.

Ray, R. (2009) 'Globe and Mail offering severance packages, layoffs likely', Canadian Journalism Project website (January 9). http://www.j-ource.ca/english_new/detail.php?id=3196. Accessed 17 January, 2009.

Reddick, R. and King, E. (1997) *The Online Journalist: Using the Internet and other Electronic Resources*. Fortworth, TX: Harcourt Brace.

Reich, Z. (2008) 'How citizens create news stories: the "news access" problem reversed', *British Journalism Review*.

Rheingold, H. (1993) *The Virtual Community: Homesteading on the Electronic Frontier*. Reading, Mass: Addison-Wesley.

Rheingold, H. (2002) *Smart Mobs: The Next Social Revolution*. Cambridge, MA: Perseus Publishing.

Richieri, G. (1982) *L'Universo Telematico*. Bari: De Donato.

Richieri, G. (2004) 'The history of interactive TV', in F. Colombo (ed.), *TV and Interactivity in Europe*. Milan: Vita and Pensiero.

Ricoeur, P. (2007) *Reflections on the Just*. Chicago: University of Chicago Press.

Riddell, M. (2003) 'Media mediator', *MediaGuardian.co.uk*, 3 March. Available at http://media.guardian.co.uk/presspublishing/story/0,7495,906146,00.html

Ritzer, G. (1998) *The McDonaldization Thesis*. London: Sage.

Ritzer, G. (2004) *The McDonaldization of Society*. Thousand Oaks: Pine Forge Press.

Rivas-Rodriguez, M. (2003) *Brown Eyes of the Web: Unique Perspectives of an Alternative US Latino Online Newspaper*. London: Routledge.

Robins, S. (2003) 'The East is offering its riches to Britainnia', openDemocracy (22 January). http://www.opendemocracy.net/node/916

Robinson, S. (2007) '"Someone's gotta be in control here": the institutionalization of online news and the creation of a shared journalistic authority', *Journalism Practice*, 1 (3): 305–21.

Rogers, P. (2006) 'The countdown to war', openDemocracy (5 April). http://www.opendemocracy.net/conflict/countdown_3426.jsp

Rorty, R. (2004) 'Americas dreaming', openDemocracy (30 August). http://www.opendemocracy.net/democracyletterstoamericans/article_2067.jsp

Rosen, J. (1999) *What are Journalists For?* New Haven, CT: Yale University Press.

Rosenberg, S. (2007) 'The blog haters have barely any idea of what they are raging against', the *Guardian*, 28 August.

Rushdie, S. (2005) 'Defend the right to be offended', openDemocracy (7 February). http://www.opendemocracy.net/faith-europe_islam/article_2331.jsp

Saba, J. (2005) 'Dispelling the myth of readership decline', *Editor & Publisher*, 28 November.

Salter, L. (2005) 'Colonization tendencies in the development of the world wide web', *New Media & Society*, 7 (3): 291–309.

Schlesinger, P. (1978) *Putting 'Reality' Together*. London: Constable.

Schlesinger, P. (1987) *Putting 'Reality' Together: BBC News*, 2nd edn. London: Methuen.

Schlesinger, P. (1990) 'Rethinking the sociology of journalism: source strategies and the limits of media-centrism', in M. Ferguson (ed.), *Public Communication: The New Imperative*. London: Sage. pp. 61–83.

Schlesinger, P. and Tumber, H. (1994) *Reporting Crime: The Media Politics of Criminal Justice*. Oxford: Clarendon.

Schudson, M. (1978) *Discovering the News*. New York: Basic Books.

Schudson, M. (2008) *Why Democracies Need an Unlovable Press*. Cambridge, UK: Polity Press.

Schultz, T. (1999) 'Interactive options in online journalism: a content analysis of 100 U.S. newspapers', *Journal of Computer-Mediated Communication*, 5 (1). Available at: http://jcmc.indiana.edu/vol5/issue1/schultz.html (last accessed October 2008).

Scott, B. (2005). 'A contemporary history of digital journalism', *Television & New Media*, 6 (1): 84–126.

Seelye, K. (2007) 'Drop in ad revenue raises tough question for newspapers', *New York Times*, 26 March. Available at http://www.nytimes.com/2007/03/26/business/media/26paper.html

Sennett, R. (2006) *The Culture of the New Capitalism*. New Haven: Yale University Press.

Seymour-Ure, C. (1991) *The British Press and Broadcasting Since 1945*. Oxford: Blackwell.

Shirky, C. (2008) *Here Comes Everybody*. London: Allen Lane.

Siklos, R. (2007) 'Newspapers down but definitely not out', *Fortune*, 23 October. Available at http://money.cnn.com/2007/10/22/magazines/fortune/siklos_newspapers.fortune/index.htm

Silverstone, R. (1988) 'Television myth and culture', in J. Carey (ed.) (1988) *Media Myths and Narratives: Television and the Press, Sage Reviews of Communications Research*, vol. 15, pp. 20–37.

Silverstone, R. (2006) *Media and Morality: On the Rise of the Mediapolis*. Cambridge: Polity.

Silvia, T. (ed.) (2001) *Global News: Perspectives on the Information Age*. Iowa: Iowa State University Press.

Singer, J. (1997) 'Still guarding the gate? the newspaper journalists role in an on-line world', *Convergence: The International Journal of Research into New Media Technologies*, 3 (1): 72–89.

Singer, J. (1998) 'Online Journalists: Foundation for Research into their Changing Roles', *Journal of Computer Mediated Communication*, 4 (1), available at http://www.asusc.org/jcmc/vol4/issue1/singer.html

Singer, J. (2001) 'The metro wide web: changes in newspapers' gatekeeping role online', *Journalism and Mass Communication Quarterly*, 78 (1): 65–80.

Singer, J. (2003). 'Who are these guys? The online challenge to the notion of journalistic professionalism', *Journalism: Theory, Practice and Criticism*, 4 (2): 139–68.

Sklair, L. (2002) *Globalization*. 3rd edn. Oxford: Oxford University Press.

Smith, R.L. (1972) *The Wired Nation*. New York: Harper Colophon Books.

Sparks, C. (2000) 'From dead trees to live wires: the internet's challenge to the traditional newspaper', in J. Curran and M. Gurevitch (eds.), *Mass Media and Society*. 3rd edn. London: Arnold. pp. 268–92.

Sparrow, B.H. (1999) *Uncertain Guardians: The News Media as a Political Institution*. Baltimore MD: John Hopkins University Press.

Sriramesh, K. and Verčič, D. (2003) *The Global Public Relations Handbook: Theory, Research, and Practice*. London: Lawrence Erlbaum.

Stabe, M. (2008) 'Spackman: journalism and search optimisation are "completely interwoven" at Times Online', *Press Gazette*, 7 May. Available at http://www.pressgazette.co.uk/story.asp?storyCode=41073&sectioncode=1

Starr, Paul. (2004) *The Creation of the Media: Political Origins of Modern Communications*. New York: Basic Books.

Stelter, B. (2009) 'Can the go-to site get you to stay?', *The New York Times*, 18 January, p. B-1, 2.

Stiglitz, J. (2002) *Globalization and Its Discontents*. London: Penguin.

Stratton, J. (1997) 'Cyberspace and the globalisation of culture', in D. Porter (ed.), *Internet Culture*. New York: Routledge.

Strauss, K. (2006) 'Gender inequality, risk and European pensions: working papers in employment, work and finance', available at: http://www.geog.ox.ac.uk/research/transformations/wpapers/wpg06-13.html (last accessed November 2008).

Sunstein, C. (2001) *Republic.Com*. Princeton, NJ: Princeton University Press.

Sweeney, M. (2008) 'Internet ad spending will overtake television in 2009', *Media Guardian*, 19 May.

Swensen, D. and Schmidt, M. (2009) 'News You Can Endow', *The New York Times*, 28 January: A31.

Talbot, S. (producer) (2007) 'News war, part 3: what's happening to the news', PBS Frontline Documentary, transcript posted 13 February, 2007, available at http://www.pbs.org/wgbh/pages/frontline/newswar/etc/script3.html

Thompson, J. (1995) *The Media and Modernity: A Social Theory of the Media*. Cambridge: Polity.

Thompson, J. (2000) *Political Scandal*. Cambridge: Polity Press.

Thurman, N. and Hermida, A. (2008) 'Gotcha: how newsroom norms are shaping participatory journalism online', in G. Monaghan and S. Tunney (eds.), *Web Journalism: A New Form of Citizenship*. Eastbourne: Sussex Academic Press.

Tiffen, R. (1989) *News and Power*. Sydney: Allen and Unwin.

Tifft, S.E. and Jones, S.E. (1999) *The Trust: The Private and Powerful Family Behind The New York Times*. Boston: Back Bay Books.

Tomlinson, J. (1999) *Globalization and Culture*. Cambridge: Polity Press.

Trinity Mirror (2008) *Annual Report & Accounts 2007*. London: Trinity Mirror.

Trippi, J. (2004) *The Revolution Will Not be Televised: Democracy, the Internet and the Overthrow of Everything*. New York: Regan Books.

Tsaliki, L. (2002) 'Online forums and the enlargement of the public space: Research findings from a european project', *The Public*, 9: 95–112.

Tuchman, G. (1972) 'Objectivity as a strategic ritual: an examination of newsmen's notion of objectivity', *American Journal of Sociology*, 77 (4): 660–79.

Tunstall, J. (1996) *Newspaper Power: The National Press in Britain*. Oxford: Oxford University Press.

Tunstall, J. (2008) *The Media were American: U.S. Mass Media in Decline*. New York: Oxford University Press.

Ugarteche, O. (2007) 'Transnationalizing the public sphere: a critique of Fraser', *Theory, Culture and Society*, 24 (4), 65–9.

UNESCO (n.d.) Newspaper statistics, UNESCO's Institute for Statistics. Available at http://stats.uis.unesco.org/unesco/TableViewer/tableView.aspx?ReportId=398

United Nations Development Programme (2003) 'Patterns of global inequality', in D. Held and A. McGrew (eds.), *The Global Transformations Reader*, 2nd edn. Cambridge: Polity.

United Nations (2006) *World Economic and Social Survey 2006: Diverging Growth and Development*. Available at http://www.un.org/esa/policy/wess/wess2006files/wess2006.pdf (last accessed November 2008).

Van Dijk, J. (2005) *The Deepening Divide*. Thousands Oaks, CAL: Sage.

van Duyn, A. (2007) 'Rise in online advertising at US papers', *Financial Times*, 28 May.

Volkmer, I. (2003) 'The Global Network Society and the Global Public Sphere', *Development*, 46 (1): 9–16.

WAN (World Association of Newspapers) (2007) *World Press Trends*. Paris: World Association of Newspapers and ZenithOptimedia.

Ward, S. (2005) 'Philosophical foundations for global journalism ethics', *Journal of Mass Media Ethics*, 20 (1): 3–21.

Waters, R. (2008) 'Online ad group adds to sector's worries', *FT.com*, 17 July. Available at http://www.ft.com/cms/s/0/1efc8894-543a-11dd-aa78000077b07658.html

Webb, P. and Farrell, D. (1999) 'Party members and ideological change', in G. Evans and P. Norris (eds.), *Critical Elections: British Parties and Voters in Long-Term Perspective*. London, Sage. pp. 44–63.

Weber, M. (1948) *From Max Weber: Essays in Sociology*, H. Gerth and C. Wright Mills (eds.). London, Routledge.

Weber, S. (2004) *The Success of Open Source*. Cambridge, Mass. London: Harvard University Press.

Wernick, A. (1991) *Promotional Culture – Advertising, Ideology and Symbolic Expression*. London: Sage.

Westerdal, J. (2007) 'Top 30 most popular online newspapers', http://blog.domaintools.com/2007/04/top-30-most-popular-online-newspapers/. Accessed 21 January 2009.

Williams, A. and Franklin, B. (2007) *Turning Around the Tanker: Implementing Trinity Mirror's Online Strategy*. Cardiff University. Available at http://image.guardian.co.uk/sysfiles/Media/documents/2007/03/13/Cardiff.Trinity.pdf

Williams, B. (2002) *Truth and Truthfulness: An Essay in Genealogy*. Princeton: Princeton University Press.

Williams, R. (2003 (1974)) *Television, Technology, and Cultural Form*. London: Routledge Classics.

Winston, B. (1995) 'How are media born and developed?', in Downing, J. et al. (eds.), *Questioning the Media: A Critical Introduction*. Thousand Oaks: Sage.

Winston, B. (1998) *Media Technology and Society: A History From the Telegraph to the Internet*. Abingdon: Routledge.

Witschge, T. and Nygren, G. (forthcoming) 'Journalism: a profession under pressure?', *Journal of Media Business Studies* (expected publication date: spring 2009).

Wolff, M. (2007) 'Is this the end of news?', *Vanity Fair*, October. Available at http://www.vanityfair.com/politics/features/2007/10/wolff200710

Wouters, P., Hellsten, I. and Leydesdorff, L. (2004) 'Internet time and the reliability of search engines', *First Monday*, 9 (10). Available at: http://www.uic.edu/htbin/cgiwrap/bin/ojs/index.php/fm/article/view/1177/1097 (last accessed October 2008).

Zimmerman, A., Koopmans, R. and Schlecht, T. (2004) *Political Communication on the Internet*. Part 2: Link structure among political actors in Europe. For 5th Framework Programme of the European Commission. Available at: http://europub.wzb.eu/Data/reports/WP4/D4-7%20WP%204.2%20Integrated%20Report.pdf (last accessed October 2008).

Index

Advertising, revenues of, 15, 23, 37–39, 43, 55, 59, 91, 128, 130, 147, 188, 189, 190, 192, 195, 197, 199
Advertising Association, The, 38
Agenda Setting, 88, 142, 190
Alternative Media, 12, 139, 144, 162, 165, 166, 171, 179–181, 182, 183, 185, 187, 188
Audiences, 9, 10, 35, 37, 39, 43–44, 59, 72, 106, 122, 128, 189–190
  citizens as, 123
  of websites, 140, 147, 188, 189
  responsibility of, 66

BBC, The, 40, 43, 60, 62, 71–86, 90, 96, 162, 167, 171, 173–177, 183–186, 190, 196, 193, 198
  licence fee, 72, 73, 85
  – Radio 4, 162
  – Trust, 74, 86
  – World News, 117
Baker, Kenneth, 20, 28, 29, 32
Barnhurst, Kevin, 192
Beckett, Charlie, 36, 84, 93
Bell, Emily, 27
Benkler, Yokai, 165
Blair, Tony, 28–29
Blogging, 10, 138, 140–151, 187
  bloggers, 10, 12, 15, 46–47, 96, 123, 150–151, 165, 194, 198
  blogs, 93, 140–151, 159, 165, 194, 198
Blumler, Jay, 166
Boczkowski, Pablo, 5, 176, 177, 184, 198
Bourdieu, Pierre, 55, 56, 89–96, 139, 148, 198
Branding, 44–45, 101, 166
BSkyB, 40, 73
Buffett, Warren, 36

Cable television, 19–21, 25, 27, 31–32
Carey, James, 11
Castells, Manuel, 108, 177
Celebrity, 141, 142, 145, 146, 150, 158–159
Censorship, 55
Civil Society, 14, 102, 104, 107, 111, 113, 123, 150, 154, 155, 195
CNN, 117, 190
Community, 143, 149
Community television, 21–24, 32
  funding of, 23
Consumption (see also Audiences), 73, 124, 189, 195
Convergence, 44, 104

Cultural Studies, 5
Cultures of production, 112–115
Current TV, 171–172, 180

Daily Express, The, 58
Daily Mail, The, 96, 143, 157, 171
Daily Mail and General Trust (DMGT), 39, 40, 42, 44, 45, 47, 49
Daily Mirror, The, 29, 171
Daily Telegraph, The, 59, 96, 149, 152, 171
Davies, Nick, 7, 41, 48, 62, 83, 92, 129, 134, 153
Deacon, David, 156, 168
Dean, Jodi, 154
Dechaine, D. R., 155–156
Democracy news journalism, 3, 4, 5, 9, 10, 16, 39, 50, 51, 54, 57, 63, 75, 78, 79, 84, 99, 139, 141, 151, 187, 192–195, 198
  deliberative, 123, 193, 199
  direct, 123
  elitist, 193, 195
  internet and, 6, 7, 46, 88, 163
  lack of, 95, 104, 107
  pluralist, 194, 198, 199
Department for Culture, Media and Sport (DCMS), 63, 65
Deregulation, 19, 32–33
Dot Com, 24–25, 28, 29, 32

Economist, The, 20, 24, 29, 45, 117
Elliott, Philip, 100
Email, 94, 128, 130, 132, 134, 161, 164, 165, 183

Financial Times, The 20, 24, 44, 45
Foucault, Michel, 54
Franklin, Bob, 37, 128, 129, 134
Fraser, Nancy, 102, 117, 122, 123

Gandy, Oscar, 168
Gans, Herbert, 88
Giddens, Anthony, 177
Gillmor, Dan, 139
Gitlin, Todd, 105, 117
Globalization, 6, 12, 102, 124, 155
Golding, Peter, 100
Google, 41, 45, 46, 59, 76, 95, 97, 98, 142, 147, 149, 171–172, 180, 182–185
Gray, Steven, 29
Greenpeace, 88
Guardian, The, 22, 23, 27, 29, 38, 40, 41, 43, 46, 49, 62, 76, 90, 162, 171, 196

Habermas, Jurgen, 4, 87, 123, 199
Hall, Stuart, 88, 138
Hallin, Dan, 87, 189

Hargreaves, Ian, 6, 7
Hemmingway, Emma, 82
Hoge, J., 10
House of Lords Select Committee, 37, 41, 45, 46, 48, 49, 50
Hutchins Commission, 19
Hutton Inquiry, The, 80

Independent, The, 21, 22, 23, 24, 55, 157, 171
  on Sunday, 24
Indymedia, 171–172, 180
Interactive Television, 21–22, 26, 28, 30–33
Internet, 27, 28, 144, 166
  as archive, 7, 14, 178, 185, 188
  as information resource, 97, 98, 127, 129, 131, 134
  interactivity of, 6, 7, 10, 76–78, 103, 112, 115, 128, 163–166, 171, 180, 182–184, 194
  in newsrooms, 6, 191
  multiplicity, 7, 8, 9, 10, 163, 171, 179–182
  polycentrality, 7,8
  regulation of, 66,
  space of, 7,15, 156, 159, 161, 171, 173, 175, 192
  speed of, 6, 7–8, 79, 129, 130, 141, 171, 173, 175, 192
  (see also New Technology)
Independent Television News (ITN), 72, 75, 76, 80

Journalism, 53, 96, 97, 126
  and politics, 121–137
  as entertainment driven, 3
  as public good, 3
  citizen, 5, 10, 12, 14, 50, 85, 110, 123, 178, 184
  codes of, 51, 57, 63, 64
  ethics of, 15, 51, 53, 54, 56, 58, 60
  impact of new technology on, 4, 72, 93, 94, 112, 121–125, 129, 130, 131, 134, 136
  impartiality of, 8
  investigative, 41
  objectivity of, 8
  serious, 3
  values of, 143, 154
  (see also News)
Journalists, 12, 55, 56, 57, 60
  accountability of, 61, 62, 79
  as gatekeepers, 88
  as self-regulating, 63–66
  autonomy of, 8, 14, 54, 55–57, 59, 60, 63, 89, 90–93, 100, 113, 114, 196, 197, 198

Journalists *cont.*
  foreign correspondents, 41,
    177, 188
  freelance, 12
  insecurity of, 8, 55, 56, 57, 71,
    81, 90, 100, 129, 160,
    188, 191, 192
  investment in, 50
  multi-skilling of, 8, 81,
    130, 192
  pack behaviour of, 95, 135
  pressures on, 7, 8, 80, 96–97,
    100, 129, 130, 134, 154,
    160, 161, 164, 188, 193
  training of, 83
  trust of, 60, 63
  working environment of, 3, 51,
    54, 56, 61–65, 91, 160, 166

Klein, Naomi, 153

Le Monde, 194, 197, 198
Lewis, Justin, 94, 95
Lippman, Walter, 193
Lovinck, Geert, 151

MacGregor, Brent, 84
MacIntyre, Alisdair, 53
Maddox, Brenda, 26
Manning, Paul, 88, 95
Marsh, Kevin, 62
Methodology, 11–13
Meyer, Phillip, 36
McChesney, Robert, 104,
  125, 179
McNair, Brian, 8, 123
Murdoch, Rupert, 40,
  191, 196

National Union of Journalists
  (NUJ), 41–42, 49, 50, 58
Negroponte, Nicholas, 29,
  122–123
Neo-liberalism, 7, 12, 13, 32
Nerone, John, 192
New Media (see New
  Technology)
New Media Age, 43
New Social Movements, 102,
  155, 165
New Technology
  accessibility of, 6, 14, 104,
    108, 116, 153, 163,
    179, 188
  as democratizing, 6, 19, 122–
    123, 133, 136, 137, 179,
    182, 184
  as participatory, 6, 7, 10, 165,
    171, 182–184, 185
  enhancing plurality, 6
  for cost-cutting, 72, 125,
    129, 134
  investment in, 166
  pressures of, 90, 76–77,
    128, 130
  reporting of, 19–33
  weakening communication,
    84, 86, 89, 132, 137
  (see also Internet)
New York Times, 19, 189, 190,
  196, 197

News
  accuracy of, 53, 61, 96
  agendas, 154, 158
  aggregators, 46, 50
  as a business, 13, 14, 35–50,
    128, 188, 197, 192
  as watchdog, 3, 134, 198
  cannibalization of, 47, 49, 95,
    97, 99, 101, 134, 136,
    192
  cloning of, 154, 156–161,
    166, 198
  competition, 37, 90, 91, 96,
    128, 191
  (de)regulation of, 5, 6, 14, 19,
    32–33, 39, 50, 51, 63
  diversity of, 9, 53, 66, 107
  economics of, 5, 9, 13, 35–50,
    55, 59, 90, 109, 112, 114,
    116, 123, 128
  fragmentation of, 9, 151,
    189–190
  funding of (see also
    advertising), 5, 35–50,
    117, 123, 129, 146, 147
  futures of, 50, 62
  gathering, 8
  homogeneity of, 9, 10, 15, 91,
    101, 173–179, 184,
    188, 198
  international, 175
  local, 145, 147, 149
  marketization of, 6, 9, 55, 91,
    121, 125, 128, 130, 134,
    151, 158
  online, 8, 61, 77, 90, 95, 96,
    99–101, 104, 105, 128–
    129, 138, 171–186, 188,
    197
  ownership of, 11, 13, 179,
    181, 191, 196, 197
  production, 124, 134, 139,
    164, 171, 182–184, 185
  rationalization of, 121, 125,
    134, 191
  regional, 37, 41, 44, 48, 82,
    83, 92
  television, 103
  truth of, 57, 58, 60, 79, 87
  values, 10, 154
  (see also Journalism)
News agencies, 7, 12, 41, 61, 62,
  94, 95, 102, 134, 192
News of the World, 64
Newspapers, 47, 48, 55, 59, 91,
  188, 189
Newspaper Association of
  America (NAA), 38
News sources, 5, 8, 12, 25,
  87–101, 135, 141, 144, 145,
  148–149, 151, 176, 180
NGOs as, 5, 12, 15, 153, 154, 160
NGOs, 95, 111, 117, 147, 148,
  150, 153–168, 187, 198

O'Neil, Onora, 60, 63
Ofcom, 4, 7, 9, 16, 20, 22, 23, 37, 49,
  65, 66, 73, 74, 79, 86, 103,
  104, 122, 123, 177, 181, 184
openDemocracy, 104–118,
  171–172, 180

Project for Excellence in
  Journalism (PEJ), 39, 44,
  174, 191
Paterson, Chris, 9,
Picard, Robert, 48, 50
Political economy, 5
Preston, Peter, 65
Press Association, 62, 157,
  167, 175,
Press Complaints Commission
  (PCC), 57, 58, 60, 63, 64, 66
Private Eye, 59
Public Relations, 93, 94, 95, 111,
  134, 188
  of NGOs, 153, 156, 159,
    161, 166
Public Sphere, 4, 36, 87, 102,
  104, 117, 155, 166, 177,
  182, 193, 198, 199
Public service media, 32, 197
Putnam, Robert, 121, 123, 159

Reuters, 175
Rheingold, Howard, 8, 153, 179
Rosen, Jay, 187
Rushbridger, Alan, 38, 41, 46,
  49, 62

Schiller, Herbert, 44
Schlesinger, Phillip, 88, 94, 134,
  138, 158
Schoendorf, Joel, 24,
Search engines, 9, 181 (see also
  Google and Yahoo)
Sennett, Richard, 121,
  124–125, 137
Shirky, Clay, 84
Silverstone, Roger, 54, 58, 67,
  87, 187
Sky News, 76, 77, 96, 176
Social Networking Sites, 9, 12,
  15, 40, 75, 79, 98, 99, 100,
  171–173, 184, 185
Sparks, Colin, 39, 43
Sunday Mirror, The, 24
Sunday Telegraph, The, 20
Sunday Times, The, 21, 22,
  24, 29, 30
Sunstein, C., 9

Thatcher, Margaret, 32
The Times, 20, 21, 23, 28, 29,
  30, 41, 59, 149, 162,
  171, 194
Times Educational
  Supplement, 20
Tsaliki, L., 165
Tumber, Howard, 87
Trinity Mirror, 47

User Generated Content (UGC),
  10, 78, 83, 84, 86, 93, 139,
  183, 184

Williams, Bernard, 53
Wire Services, 175 (see also
  Press Association, Reuters)
Wolff, Michael, 35–36

Yahoo, 46, 142, 171–173, 180